The Diaries of
Betty Cora Johnson
1885 - 1886 - 1887 - 1888 - 1898

And the Diary of
Lewis Hamilton Titchenal
1887
And Other Historical Documents

Compiled by Vera Zachow

ElderBerry Books
CMP Publishing Group, LLC

For historical accuracy all spelling, capitalization and punctuation have been kept in their original form as written in the diaries and letters.

All family tree information was taken from family bibles and personal family histories and may not be the same as in other records.

Photos and documents contained herein are from the Titchenal Family archives carefully preserved through all generations.

"Stevens Pass, Gateway to Seattle, The Story of Railroading and Recreation in the North Cascades," Copyright ©1995 JoAnn Roe, ISBN 0-87004-428-1(alk.paper), Caxton Press, 312 Main Street, Caldwell, Id 83605.
Excerpts reprinted with permission.

"History of Wenatchee, The Apple Capital of the World," by John A. Gellatly. Published 1963 Wenatchee, Washington. LC Call No.: F899.W46G44. Control No. 3135741. Dewey No. 917.97/59
Excerpts reprinted with permission.

Newspaper articles from Wenatchee Daily World, Cashmere Valley Record, Restitution Herald, and the Waterville Empire Express have been printed here with permission.

"A History of Central Washington," compiled by Lindley M. Hull in 1929 is reproduced here, in part. Only those files originally provided to L. M. Hull by Mary and Cora Titchenal were used.

All inquires should be addressed to:
ElderBerry Books/CMPPG, LLC
27657 Highway 97
Okanogan, WA 98840
Email: cmppg@www.cmppg.com
Website: www.cmppg.com
       Or
Vera Zachow email: zachow7@msn.com

ISBN13: 978-1-937162-02-3

Library of Congress Control Number: 2011944808

Introduction

As I was growing up, holidays would find us enjoying a wonderful dinner at the home of our grandparents, Ray and Eunice Titchenal on their ranch nine miles north of Leavenworth, Washington. Grandma always made her delicious homemade rolls, home canned green beans and homemade dill pickles to go along with the turkey dinner, to be followed by her famous homemade pies. It was the most satisfying experience to be surrounded by our loving family. Dinner was followed by us gathering around Grandpa as he told us stories of his childhood. He would roll his own cigarette as he told of his older sister, Bessie and him hitching up the team of horses and driving them to the river to fill up two fifty-two gallon oak barrels with water and bringing the water back to their home. They would pull the water sled up to the kitchen door, their mother, Cora, would dip up a bucket of water and carry it into the house. After telling us different stories, Grandpa Ray would take out the red velvet, padded photo album and show us pictures of his grandparents, David Jackson and Mary Titchenal, his mother and father, Cora and Lewis Titchenal and photos of Lewis's brothers, Norman, Nim and John and sisters Phebe and Nancy.

It is my desire to share those photos, stories, diaries, letters and newspaper articles with all the members of my family and anyone interested in the development of our beautiful Washington State.

On April 2, 1879 Alice Johnson married James Hays in Bates County, Missouri. The next day they headed west, taking the Southern Pacific train to San Francisco. They took a steamboat to Portland, then came by boat to The Dalles, Oregon, arriving there the night the town burned. They bought a team and wagon to continue their trip to the Palouse country. James and Alice homesteaded on Hangman Creek near Waverly, Washington Territory, thirty-five miles southeast of where the city of Spokane is now located.

Alice's mother, Nancy Adaline Johnson, passed away on July 13, 1879, her father, William Rodney Johnson, several years earlier on May 4, 1872 so Alice asked her younger sister, Betty Cora Johnson, called Cora, to come live with them. Cora traveled across the plains in a covered wagon in 1880 with her older brother John Martin, his wife Eliza and their children, Buford, called Bud, who was five years old, three year old Jesse May, called Jet, and Elizabeth Maude, called Maude, who was eighteen months old at the time. Cora's brothers, Jesse, five years older than Cora and Joe, two years younger traveled with them as well. Their brothers William Henry and Moses Gilmore came west in 1882. The 1880 trip from Bates County, Missouri to Washington Territory took one hundred days. Cora was fourteen years old at the time. Cora was my great-grandmother.

David Jackson and Mary Moore Titchenal left Bates county Missouri heading for Washington Territory on April 1, 1882. With them were their children, Lewis, 22, Norman, 19, Nimrod, 17, Nancy, 12, John, 10 and Phebe, who was 7 years old at the time. Lewis was my great-grandfather.

This is their story. I want them to tell it in their own words through the diaries, letters, and speeches they gave about their life's journey.

For historical accuracy of the diaries, all spelling, capitalization and punctuation have been kept in their original form.

James Hays and Alice Johnson married and started to Washington the next day.

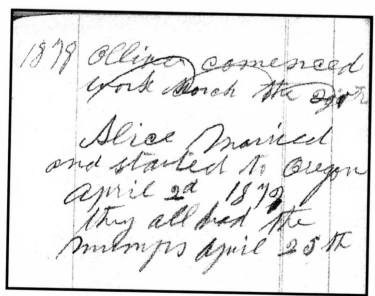

Cora's diary entry when her sister Alice began her trip west.

Cora's Letter

An account Cora wrote some fifteen years after coming to Washington Territory was kept in a dresser for seventy years before it inspired the first book about our history, writes Gilla Jacobson Bachellerie, Cora's great granddaughter. Gilla was referring to the book "The Tree of Thee and Me," written by Gilla's mother and father, Lois and Chet Jacobson.

That account is the letter Cora wrote for her descendants to describe her trip west.

A Letter to My Descendents

"In speaking of the pioneer days, we must remember that someday, we know not how soon, our lives may be snuffed out and there will be nothing left for the coming generations to know how their ancestors lived before the days of the automobiles and electricity. Hence, it seems to me that we should leave something in history relating some of our past experiences, together with dates of events that may otherwise be forgotten. So, lest we forget, for the benefit of our children and grandchildren, I will add a chapter in the history of the Pioneer Days of Washington.

"I was born in Saline County Missouri, August 16, 1865, (the same year the Civil War closed). I moved with my parent to Bates County, Missouri in 1870.

"My father died in May, 1872, so I was almost too young when he died to realize what it meant to have a father. I was next to the youngest of seven children, five brothers and one sister who was ten years older than I. She married April 2, 1879 and my mother died in July the same year. My oldest brother and his family moved into our house and lived with us until the following spring.

"My sister and her husband, Mr. and Mrs. James Hays, started west the next day after they were married. After mother's death and our home was broken up, my sister wanted me to live with her, so they wrote for us to come west.

"The personal property had all been sold at public sale and our home was rented. You can not imagine, nor can I describe, the feeling I had when the time came for us to leave our lovely home, and I was homesick many times, but have never been back to see it since. My two brothers, Henry and Gilmore, did not come west until several years later.

"There were no railroads to the Pacific Coast at that time, except to San Francisco, and the drive across the plains with a team seemed like quite an undertaking. However, it was decided that we would do it, and on April 15, 1880, we started from Bates County, Missouri. My oldest brother, John Johnson, with his wife and three children, brother Jesse, five years older than I and Joe, two years younger, with two covered wagons and five horses set out to make the trip. Our journey across the plains was not marred with any serious accidents, and we had no trouble with the Indians. A friend, Mr. Cobb, and his family came all the way with us. Others joined us in Kansas, and there were eight wagons altogether until we got to Baker City, Oregon, where four of them stopped and the men went to work.

"The most exciting time was when we came to the rivers on this side of the Rocky Mountains, as it was in June and the melted snow and rains had made the streams very high. In some places there were toll bridges, but when we reached the Bernt River there were no bridges and the water was too high to ford, so we had to make camp until the men could build rafts out of logs and take the wagons off and float them over one at a time, then swim the horses over. All was finally landed on the west shore and we proceeded on our journey without further difficulties until we reached the Boise Valley where our horses got poisoned from eating poisoned herb. None of them died, but we had to camp until they were able to travel.

"We landed in Boise on July 3rd and stayed over the 4th. There we saw the first irrigation ditches and the city certainly looked beautiful to us. The cherries and berries were ripe and the roses in bloom. It surely seemed like we had found a Garden of Eden after traveling for so long in the barren regions.

"I drove the team a good share of the way and we were just 100 days on the road and camped out every night.

"My sister and her husband had located on a homestead where Spokane is now, though there was no city or railroad there at the time. We landed at their log cabin on the 23rd of July, and you may be sure I was glad to reach our destination. I made my home with them for a few years and attended school in the first schoolhouse that was built in the Waverly district. My brother-in-law hauled all of his supplies from Walla Walla, a distance of about 175 miles.

"After the Northern Pacific Railroad was built in 1882, I attended school at the Cheney Academy, which afterwards burned down, and the Normal School buildings now occupy the grounds."

John Martin and his wife Eliza,.
Cora's older brother and his wife brought Cora with them when they came west in
the wagon along with their three children, Buford Capenter (Bud), Jessie May (Jet),
Elizabeth Maud (Maud). Children born in Washington Ter. were:
Edward Beattie Moses (Ed), James Gilmore (Gib), John William (Bill).

Quote from Cora's letter: "My oldest brother, John Johnson, with his wife and three children, brother Jesse, five years older than I and Joe, two years younger, with two covered wagons and five horses set out to make the trip."

William Rodney Johnson and Nancy Adaline Beattie Johnson

Johnson Family Tree

William Rodney Johnson
  born August 18, 1824
  d May 4, 1872
  Married January 1, 1851

Nancy Adaline Beattie
  born February 16, 1834
  d July 13, 1879

Their Children

John Martin
  born November 16, 1851
  d February 7, 1929
William Henry
  born July 7, 1853
  d May 31, 1929
Sarah Alice
  born July 29, 1855
  d September 20, 1941
Moses Gilmore
  born January 17, 1857
  d March 2, 1927

Jesse Cole
  born July 30, 1860
  d November 4, 1889
Virginia Lee
  born November 20, 1862
  d July 12, 1863
Betty Cora
  born August 15, 1865
  d May 15, 1942
Joseph Rodney
  born September 25, 1867
  d November 19,1922

9

TEACHERS' CERTIFICATE.

Spokan Falls, W. T. *Nov 7* 188*3*

I HEREBY CERTIFY that *Cora Johnson*
is of good moral character, and that *she* has passed an examination in the following branches, with the following result, and is entitled to a *third* grade certificate good for *one* years:

ORTHOGRAPHY	92	ARITHMETIC	60
READING	77	ENGLISH GRAMMAR	68
WRITING	75	PHYSIOLOGY	69
CONSTITUTION OF U. S.	62	THEORY AND PRACTICE	65
GEOGRAPHY	98	HISTORY OF THE U. S.	48

J. R. Welsh Examiner.

T. J. Warren
County Superintendent.

Cora Johnson's Teaching Certificate
November 7, 1883

April 2nd 1879 Diary Page

"April the 2nd 1879 Gilmore, Cora, Willy and Jody has the mumps. Jonny and Jepy commenced planting corn."

Gilmore - Moses Gilmore	Jody - Joseph Rodney
Corah - Betty Cora	Jonny - John Martin
Willy - William Henry	Jepy - Jesse Cole

The family presumes "Jody" [Jodie] is the family nickname for Joseph Rodney. Jody is mentioned often in Cora's diary

Cora and Alice Johnson

Cora Johnson's Story
This diary presented to Cora Johnson by: a friend,
June 20 A.D. 1885

May 26, 1885 Tuesday
I was teaching school at Waverly. Jesse started to Badger Mountain with the Titchenal boys to look at the country.

June 24, 1885 Wednesday
Came home from school, found L. [Lewis] here. He caught Leslie's pony and we went over to Mr. Hays', had a pleasant visit and returned by moonlight.

June 26, 1885 Friday
Walked from Mr. Davis' to school; came down to town at noon after Frisk. Mr. E. Gimble and Davis H. went to play ball with us. They got 15 tallies and we only 3. I went and helped Alice after school.

June 27, 1885 Saturday
I ironed in the A.M. Went to Mr. Hays' in P.M. and G Took me and Edna to Mr. Cobb's. Stayed over night. Had a pleasant visit.

June 28, 1885 Sunday
Went to Rockford to see Johnny's folks. It was a warm day to be with 14

children in a little house. They gave me a table. We started for home about 6 P.M. Jessie and Maudie came with us to Mr. Hays.

June 29, 1885 Monday
I came from Mr. H's to school. Mr. Eastman called in the P.M. Mr. and Mrs. Merriman came late and stayed over night. Had a pleasant visit with them. They were returning from camp-meeting.

June 30, 1885 Tuesday
Mrs. and Mr. M. started for Cheney. I came home from school and went to Mr. Roberts' to sew. Johnny's folks and Jesse and Lewis and Nim came. Just 20 of us together.

Lewis Hamilton Titchenal

July 1, 1885 Wednesday
Johnny's folks started for Walla Walla. I took a big cry and went to school. Felt bad all day. Sewed after school. Lewis heard me cry in my sleep that night.

July 2, 1885 Thursday
Jesse and E. [Emma] visited my school in the P.M. and went over to Mr. Hays' stayed until Sun. I sewed after school. Ada S. returned from Oregon. Jeff came to take me to Mr. T. to sing but did not feel well enough to go.

July 3, 1885 Friday
After breakfast baked a cake and Minnie and Sorenzo came before school time. Ada S. came home with me from school. Ada S. came home with me from school. I ironed and got supper for Jeff, Ada, L. and J. Was nearly sick, too.

July 4, 1885 Saturday

After doing up all the work finished my dress and S. took me to the celebration, Eat dinner with Mr. Thayer's, had a pleasant time in the P.M. eat ice cream and strawberries with Jeff. Came home and went to the "fireworks" in the evening.

July 5, 1885 Sunday

I was nearly sick but had to get dinner for 6 boys. Went to S. S. [Sunday School] in P.M. with S. eat ice cream and cake and went walking in evening down to picnic ground. Ada and J. R. went with us.

July 6, 1885 Monday

Lewis called to say "good bye" on his way to Spokane. After school, Jeff called. I got supper and cleaned up the kitchen. Mr. D. sent us some strawberries, they were fine.

Betty Cora Johnson

July 7, 1885 Tuesday

Cleaned up after breakfast and went to school.

July 9, 1885 Thursday

A rainy morning. I went home with the Tryon girls from school. Had a pleasant visit and much sport playing croquet.

July 10, 1885 Friday

Played croquet until school time. Went to Mr. Hays' after school and got a check from Mr. Dalton. Came home and went with Louis to sing at Mr. Thayer's.

July 11, 1885 Saturday

Louis carried water for me to wash. I finished washing by noon, got dinner and baked cookies and moped. Emma went to Uncle Jack's after currents. Jesse and Louis made the fence. Jodie went back to J.H.

July 12, 1885 Sunday

Cleaned up the house and studied my S. S. [Sunday School] lesson
with Louis. Went to S. S. and went to Mr. Sander's and spent a very
pleasant evening. Came home and drank lemonade and eat cake till
bed-time.

July 13, 1885 Monday

A warm day. I went to school.

July 14, 1885 Tuesday

Went to school. 'Twas very windy and cold all day. In the evening made
pies and got supper. Had a good visit with Nim while the rest of the
folks were catching chickens.

July 15, 1885 Wednesday

After school went over to Alice's and did some sewing for her. Jim and
Gilmore were gone to Spokane.

July 16, 1885 Thursday

Helped Alice until school time: came down to the P.O. at noon: went to
Mr. Huffman's and stayed over night.

July 17, 1885 Friday

Frisk come near throwing me while going to school. Emma and Lewis
came to the school house. E. took Frisk and went to Mr. Richardson's.
I walked home got supper, made light bread and said good night by
the water bucket.

July 18, 1885 Saturday

Helped get breakfast and clean up; wrote and received a letter from Ren;
ironed; mended my clothes. Mr. Mc G. called in P. M. Mr. Gimble
called in evening. We enjoyed some music.

July 19, 1885 Sunday

Got breakfast; went to S. S. at Rattler with Louis; .. .. .. Waverly in P. M.
Also to preaching. Louis said something in the eve that made feel bad
and I went to bed & had a big cry.

July 20. 1885 Monday

Helped do up the work before I went to school: Had a hard time to catch
Frisk but Nim finally caught him; went by the store got a net picket
rope; Jeff went to the schoolhouse with me. Mrs. Ella Gimble was
here when I came from school.

July 21, 1885 Tuesday
Helped with the work; Went to school, came home Fannie H – taking
her music lesson. Old lady Gimble called. Gilmore & Louis came
after we had gone to bed.

July 22, 1885 Wednesday
Minnie & Fannie came by & went to school with me. Went prayer
meeting with Nim. Had a good meeting.

July 23, 1885 Thursday
My school closed & we all had a splendid time but parted in tears. We
enjoyed a fine dinner which our friends brought with them. I rode
home with Mr. Roberts' folks & had a big cry to end the day with.

July 24, 1885 Friday
I washed all day. Emma helped me until noon, then she had to give
music lesson. Ada Sanders called. Nim helped me wash my carpet.

July 25, 1885 Saturday
I ironed until 6 P.M. then mopped the floor. Mrs. Anderson called in the
morning & paid me for the children tuition.

July 26, 1885 Sunday
I got up & got breakfast & partly cleaned up the house, then went to
Liberty with Jeff, Jodie & Ada; came back to Mr. S. for dinner: went
to S.S. at Waverly and had a splendid visit with Jeff after Sunday
School.

July 27, 1885 Monday
Helped do up the work & made pies. Mr. Dashiell called and brought
me some plums. In the P.M. went to Mr. Hays to do some sewing.

July 28, 1885 Tuesday
Went to Mr. Richardson's with Alice: learned to weave hair: sewed some
and came home in the eve via: of Mr. Sanders. Ada was quite sick.

July 29, 1885 Wednesday
Wend & stayed with Ada all day made a night dress for her. Dr. came in
eve and I went to Mr. Hays met Louis and Joe coming to Waverly.

July 30, 1885 Thursday
Sewed for Alice until evening then helped her gather berries. Mr.
McGhee was there for supper.

July 31, 1885 Friday
Sewed all day for Alice. Came home in evening, found no one here
except Nim so I went to Mr. R- and stayed over night.

Nimrod Titchenal

August 1, 1885 Saturday
Came home & eat breakfast alone: washed the windows and mopped
    the floor. Louis & Sink came. Jesse & Emma came from Mr. Smiths
    about noon. In the eve Emma & I went in Hangman bathing:
    enjoyed it, too.

Jesse Cole Johnson   Emma Griggs Johnson

August 2, 1885 Sunday
I got up, got breakfast & cleaned up the house and went to Alpha to
    church with Alice & Gilmore; I united with the church & was
    baptized. In evening went to see Ada S. she was better.

August 3, 1885 Monday
I churned & put the butter away & washed. Emma went to stay with
Ada. In the evening I enjoyed a visit with Nim on the porch & he
told me a good deal about himself. I stayed overnight with Anna.

August 4, 1885 Tuesday
Came home & got breakfast for Nim and myself. I wrote a letter to L.
and ironed. Was here alone all day until evening. Jodie & Nim came.
Jesse & Louis came from Spokane late. Gilmore sent Emma & I a
new dress.

August 5, 1885 Wednesday
Finished ironing and mended my clothes: had a good visit with Louis.
Jeff called in P.M. Made pie plant jelly. Mrs. Thrall called. Went to
prayer-meeting with Louis. Had a good meeting.

August 6, 1885 Thursday
Sewed, in the fore-noon. Jodie hauled wood for Jesse. In P.M. went to
Mr. Yount's after currants: found Sadie alone & asleep. Stopped at
Mr. Hays' a few minutes and came home & got supper for Louis & I.

August 7, 1885 Friday
Made my jelly and pie plant butter. Got dinner for Louis. Went to Mrs.
Davis' in P.M. to get my new dress cut. Stopped to see Ada as I came
home: she was better. Came home, got supper and made light bread.
Anna stayed over night with me.

August 8, 1885 Saturday
Mopped the floors & did my baking: got dinner and went to Mrs. Davis'
in P.M. Came back and stopped & stayed with Ada that night. Emma
came home nearly sick. She rode Frisk.

August 9, 1885 Sunday
Joe Kelso was there & wached me get breakfast. I cleaned up the house
for Ada. Louis brought my pony to me. Lorenzo came home with
me. We went to S.S. then to Mr. Sanders: then went riding and had a
great visit

August 10, 1885 Monday
Helped Emma with the work: went to the store & then to Mr. Sanders.
Got dinner & sewed in the afternoon. I got supper & cleaned up the
things. Frank Dashiell was there to supper & dinner.

August 11, 1885 Tuesday
I got breakfast & dinner & washed until 4 o'clock. Then mopped the

floor. Ed. Gimble called while I was mopping and warned me not to work <u>too</u> hard.

August 12, 1885 Wednesday

I ironed & done the cooking: went to Mrs. Davis' in the PM to get my new dress cut. Went home about dark & found Em. sick & the harvest hands to be there next day.

August 13, 1885 Thursday

I got up & got breakfast for Lewis & myself: then churned & baked bread & got dinner for the header crew. Mr. Davis called in the P.M. to see about my organ. I wrote to Kate Plaster & got Supper & prepared things for breakfast & went to bed at 11 o'clock.

August 14, 1885 Friday

Emma helped me get breakfast & dinner. Mrs. Connolly called in the after-noon. I sewed some & took a big cry & went to the store: came back & got supper & cleaned up.

August 15, 1885 Saturday

I helped do up the morning work & went to Alice's after some vinegar: Came back & went to Mrs. Davise's, back home & milked & lined Jodie's hat.

August 16, 1885 Sunday

I got breakfast and cleaned up the house: went with Lewis to meeting and then we all went to Mr. Hays' to eat my birthday dinner. All had a nice time and returned home via Mr. Sander's to take Ada home. We drank lemonade, had a pleasant chat, and so ended my natal day.

August 22, 1885 Saturday

Day Grant B. was buried.

August 23, 1885 Sunday

I got breakfast and cleaned up. It rained all morning and was cold. I went to S. S. with Lewis. Not many there. Brother Moore preached and called a few minutes in the evening.

August 24, 1885 Monday

Helped do up the work, wrote a letter to Lewis and one to Mont., Ward & Co., went to the store and back and got ready and went to Alice's to help her while the men were away with the header.

August 25, 1885 Tuesday

I helped Alice with the work then Emma came and we worked on Jodie's quilt, till time to do up the chores.

August 26, 1885 Wednesday
I sewed a while, then worked on the quilt till dinner. In the PM I went to
Mrs. Davis' to get some things for Alice. Emma and Ada finished the
quilt. I was nearly sick.

August 27, 1885 Thursday
I helped with the work and cooked some fruit over to keep it from
spoiling. We sewed the rest of the day. Mr. Bragg came in the evening
and brought us some melons. He was drunk.

August 28, 1885 Friday
I made melon preserves for Alice. In the afternoon we made peach
preserves and pickles. I wrote to Mrs. Merriman and after supper
milked 3 cows.

August 29, 1885 Saturday
Alice and I worked hard to get dinner for Mr. Bragg's harvesters, then
they did not come. Emma came over and we sewed in the P.M.

August 30, 1885 Sunday
I walked about a mile after the cows, milked them and helped Alice clean
up the house. Jodie came and we went to S. S. Then we all went to
Mr. Sanders'. Had much fun eating melons.

August 31, 1885 Monday
I helped get breakfast and did some baking for the harvesters. After
dinner I sewed some, then got supper.

Hays and Thayer with their header crew

September 1, 1885 Tuesday
I helped cook for the hands until after dinner. Then I went home and
wrote two letters. Lewis came while I was there and went back with
me as far as the school house.

September 2, 1885 Wednesday

We cooked for the harvest hands and sewed in the afternoon.

September 3, 1885 Thursday

I helped get breakfast and dinner. After dinner I went with Edna and
May out to the field. I helped Gilmore unload his wagon and then
helped Frank stack till they finished. We then eat some melons and I
sewed till dark.

September 4, 1885 Friday

Alice and I helped Jim and G. start their cattle off and then we cleaned
up the kitchen and went to bed. After dinner we sewed some. Mr.
Dow came to see me about school and stayed overnight.

September 5, 1885 Saturday

I helped Alice till noon, then went home and fixed my clothes and went
to Mr. Cobb's and stayed overnight: Had a pleasant visit.

September 6, 1885 Sunday

Came home Sunday morning and in the afternoon went to Sunday
School with Lewis. Mr. White preached after S. S. and came home
with us. I had the headache and stayed on the porch with Lewis until
dark.

September 7, 1885 Monday

Was busy with little jobs and settled up with Jesse. In the afternoon went
to Mr. Davis' to get my dress and to Mr. Smith's and Mr. Brittendall's
to get my school money.

September 8, 1885 Tuesday

Packed a box of my things to send to Cheney with Jesse. Went to Mr.
Yeargen's to Mr. D. Huffman's. In the P.M. E. and I went to Mr.
Thayer's and had a pleasant visit. Mr. F. went with me to Mr. Robert's
and then back to Mr. T's for supper. We had melons, too.

September 9, 1885 Wednesday

Fixed some of my clothes and polished my hat. Went to the P.O. and
then to Mr. I. N. Huffmans. It was very windy and had been raining.
Frisk came near throwing me. Back home and then to Mr. Hays'.
Came home and found Minnie and Fannie there; we had a pleasant
time together.

September 10, 1885 Thursday

I washed all day. Jim came and brought Edna. Alice sent me some
tomatoes to make preserves. Emma went to Mr. Rothgeb's and Jesse

to Mr. Sanders to help thrash. Lewis came in evening. Anna stayed overnight with me.

September 11, 1885 Friday
I made my preserves and ironed til 7 o'clock. Jodie was there to dinner. Mr. Drashiell came and brought me some melons. Nim and Jodie were there to supper. After supper Emma and Lewis came. Lewis got hurt and said he would take me to Cheney.

September 12, 1885 Saturday
I packed my things to go to Cheney to school. We ate dinner and started about noon and it was pouring down rain. Got to Cheney about 8 o'clock and was very tired and wet. Got supper at the bakery and stayed at the C. hotel overnight. A day long to be remembered.

September 13, 1885 Sunday
Took breakfast at the hotel and came up to Mrs. M.'s. Lewis brought the things up and unloaded the wagon: We eat a melon and had a little chat. Lewis went home and I went to Mrs. M's.

September 14, 1885 Monday
Started to school and everything went nicely. After school I unpacked some of my things and went down town in the evening. Did some trading for Alice.

September 15, 1885 Tuesday
Wrote a letter to Alice. Went down town before school and bought some things for myself and Mrs. M. Went to P.O. after school, also to Kaminsky's and got me a pair of new shoes. Studied in the eve and stayed at Mrs. M's over night.

September 16, 1885 Wednesday
Eat breakfast with Mrs. M. Went down town trading before school. After school I commenced to make my carpet. Went to the P.O. and studied in the evening. (Put my stove up.)

September 17, 1885 Thursday
Came home from Mrs. M.'s and eat breakfast. Went to school and came home and finished making my carpet; wrote a letter to L. and went to the P.O.

September 18, 1885 Friday
Went to school, came back and wrote a letter to Lewis and went to the P.O. Varnished my table and went to stay at Mrs. M.'s overnight. Mr. and Mrs. Range were there. Mr. Hoyt called. Edith took a big cry.

September 19, 1885 Saturday
Worked hard cleaning the house and getting things straight. L. came
about 5 o'clock. We went to the Oaks house to supper and back by
the millinery store. I got a new hat.

September 20, 1885 Sunday
Enjoyed a <u>nice</u> visit. L. went to the hotel for dinner, then for a drive to
Medical Lake and back. Went to the Temperance meeting in the eve,
came home and had lunch at 10.

September 21, 1885 Monday
Studied a while before school: came home at recess in P.M. Rena and
Louisa called. I went downtown to do some trading: came back and
wrote to Emma. Went to the P.O. with Edith and back to Mrs. M.'s
and studied.

September 22, 1885 Tuesday
Did my work up and went to school: came home and fixed my old hat
over and sewed some. Jodie came. Edith came by for me to go to hear
lecture on "Africa".

September 23, 1885 Wednesday
I got breakfast for Jodie and myself, then went downtown to do some
trading for Alice. Came back and went to school: went home with
the headache but did some writing and went to the lecture at night
with Edith.

September 24, 1885 Thursday
Got breakfast and cleaned things up and studied some before school. I
was just commencing supper when Jodie and Eliza Thayer came. They
stayed overnight and Jodie carried water for me to wash with. Had a
pleasant visit with them.

September 25, 1885 Friday
Got breakfast, went to school and left Eliza here. She went to Spokane
on the train. After school sewed some on Mrs. Todd's machine. Went
downtown to the lecture and back to Mrs. M.'s.

September 26, 1885 Saturday
I washed and mopped, made light-bread, cooked a squash and cooked
my tomato pickles over to keep them from spoiling. Expected Jodie
but he but he didn't come. I stayed alone.

September 27, 1885 Sunday
Edith came over and awoke me. In the morning I went to church alone.

In the afternoon went to S. S. alone and came home and wrote a letter and went to the P.O. Went to church in the evening with Edith and Louisa. Came home and stayed all alone.

September 28, 1885 Monday
Mrs. McNeilly called before school time. It was a rainy day. After school I did some writing and went to Mrs. M.'s a few minutes. Then studied a while and went to the theater in the evening.

September 29, 1885 Tuesday
Jodie came and awoke me: he talked a few minutes and went back to Hangman. I went down town at noon and met Mr. Power and he invited me to dine with him. We enjoyed a nice dinner. Went to the P.O. in the eve and studied till bedtime and went to stay overnight with Mrs. M.

September 30, 1885 Wednesday
Came home, got breakfast and cleaned things up and went to school. After school I wrote to Minnie and Fannie and to Alice. Gilmore and Jodie came and G. eat supper with me, then they went downtown and I went to stay with Mrs. Merriman.

October 1, 1885 Thursday
Just as I was ready to eat breakfast, Gilmore and Jodie came with a load of wood. I went to P.O. before school: After school wrote a letter and went to P.O. then examined papers and studied.

October 2, 1885 Friday
I made yeast and was busy until school time. Came home and wrote letter, went to Mrs. Hall's, to the P.O. then back and ate supper, made light bread and wrote a letter.

October 3, 1885 Saturday
I did some baking for Mrs. Merriman and some for myself. Mr. McNeilly called. I ironed until 8 P.M. and was sewing when I heard a gentle wrap on the door. Had a short visit with L. then stayed alone overnight.

October 4, 1885 Sunday
After I had the work done and was dressed in my best, L. came and we went for a stroll, then to the hotel to dine. After dinner we had a visit with Miss Gibson. Went to church in eve and had a great visit all day.

October 5, 1885 Monday
Jodie and Nim came before I got up. I got breakfast for them and J.

stayed to attend school. Nim went back to Waverly. After school I enjoyed a horseback ride on Frisk, came back, got supper and studied until 10 o'clock.

October 6, 1885 Tuesday

Jesse came before we had breakfast. We studied awhile before school. I had the headache all day. In the eve, we went down to town. I went home via Mrs. Hall's. Mrs. Lockhart called. After supper we studied and I examined papers till bedtime. Good night.

October 7, 1885 Wednesday

I made light bread in the morning. After school Mrs. M stopped and we had a chat about school. J. and I went to the P. O., then studied till bedtime.

Moses Gilmore Johnson

October 9, 1885 Friday

Gilmore and Jesse came and brought Jodie's trunk. Gilmore took breakfast and dinner with us and then started on his trip to the Big B. J. and I went downtown after school. Mrs. Hall called a few min. then I went to church to practice and when I came back J. was gone with the key so I went to the Academy and Mrs. M. and I found ourselves locked in and we climbed out at a window. Lewis came and stayed overnight.

October 10, 1885 Saturday

I got breakfast for us three, washed, mopped, fixed the straw ticks, made cookies and light-bread. Monroe called in the morning. Edith called in the P.M. I went to bed late and was tired.

October 11, 1885 Sunday

I got up late. We went to church in the morning and to Sunday school in the P.M. I went walking with Edith and Ida, then home and studied until time to go to the concert. It was splendid and the house was crowded.

October 12, 1885 Monday

I put things "to right" and went to school but felt bad all day. In the evening we went downtown to do some trading. After supper I made yeast and we studied. I went to Mrs. M.'s staid with her. (every night).

October 13, 1885 Tuesday

I made light bread and when we came home at noon my yeast was running over the table and floor. After school I baked my bread and read and studied until bedtime.

October 14, 1885 Wednesday

Jodie went to Mrs. M.'s and awoke me. I did the work up and went to school. Came home and went to Mrs. Sessions to look at the goods, came back and made out an order for goods to Ehrich Bros, studied and went to bed at home.

October 15, 1885 Thursday

Went downtown to mail my letter and was tardy to school. After school we went downtown to do some trading. Saw Mr. Hayes. Alice sent us some things and I went to Mr. Covington's to get some bottles for her. We met Mrs. Connolly in the store.

October 16, 1885 Friday

After school we were just starting down town when we saw Lewis coming. He brought my organ and some vegetables for us. Rena came in the eve. And we all had a pleasant visit.

October 17, 1885 Saturday

Lewis stayed and he and Jodie hauled wood. I went down to do some shopping in the morning. Came back and did some baking for Mrs. M. After dinner I ironed some and in the evening enjoyed a visit with Lewis and practiced some.

October 18, 1885 Sunday

I got breakfast and cleaned up the house. Rena and Monroe came and stayed a little while. Lewis started home after dinner. We went to S.S. I taught a class and came home feeling bad. We then studied some and went to church in the evening.

October 19, 1885 Monday
I did the work up and went to school: felt bad all day. I practiced my
music some and studied.

October 20, 1885 Tuesday
I came home from school sick and before noon Jodie went down and got
some medicine for me; then I got better and went to the church to
practice for the temperance meeting and wrote a letter.

October 21, 1885 Wednesday
I felt better and studied some before school. I got along nicely all day.
After school I had my hair shingled and went to Mr. Session's on
an errand. In the evening I studied and went to Mrs. M.'s to stay
overnight with her.

October 22, 1885 Thursday
I went to school and all had remarks to make about my hair. After school
we went to the church to practice. Lewis came in the evening and
went over to Mrs. M.'s with me.

October 23, 1885 Friday
Went to school, came home and practiced, then went down town with
Mrs. M. Came back, got ready and went to the church festival: had a
very pleasant time and came home at 9:15 P.M.

October 24, 1885 Saturday
I washed, did some baking for Mrs. M, went to the church to practice:
came back and put my clothes away, mopped and ironed some. Mrs.
Andrus called. I made yeast, mended our clothes and went to stay
with Mrs. M.

October 25, 1885 Sunday
A rainy day. When I came over, Jodie had breakfast ready. I did not feel
well enough to go to church but went to S.S. and to the temperance
meeting in the eve. And everything went off nicely.

October 26, 1885 Monday
Went to school. In the evening went to pay Mr. Percival for rent, met Mr.
Dixon and he came home with me and stayed a few minutes. After
supper we studied.

October 27, 1885 Tuesday
Things went along well at school: I practiced at noon: after school I wrote
a letter: Rena was here: after supper we went downtown, came home
and studied. I examined papers, and cried after I went to bed.

October 28, 1885 Wednesday
Jodie came over to wake me: we had chicken for breakfast. A rainy day and we girls had fun at school. Jodie and I went to P.O. and studied.

October 29, 1885 Thursday
Went to school. Jodie went with me to the store and P.O. Mrs. M. came by for me to go to hear Mrs. Dunaway but I stayed at home and studied.

October 30, 1885 Friday
Nothing unusual until after school. I took my music lesson and after supper I prepared some tomatoes for preserves and made light bread for Mrs. M. and went to stay with her over night.

October 31, 1885 Saturday
I went down town in the morning and came back and did some baking for Mrs. M. and myself: went to take dinner with Mrs. M. Made some preserves and pickles and in the eve we enjoyed a pleasant call at Mrs. Hall's with R. and Mr. P.

November 1, 1885 Sunday
J. and I went to the M. E. church. Mr. Inkster's folks called: we went to S.S.. I practiced some and wrote a letter. Went to Mrs. M.'s a few minutes and to church in the evening. Finished my letter at 10:00 P.M.

November 2, 1885 Monday
A rainy day. We went to school. In the evening we went to the store and saw Mr. Kennell and he told us of our new nephew. After supper I examined papers until I could hardly see, then went to Mrs. Merriman's and to bed.

November 3, 1885 Tuesday
After school I went to Mrs. Hall's to get her to fix my dress. We went to prayer meeting in the evening and met Mr. Stroud there. Had a good meeting. Came home and studied.

November 4, 1885 Wednesday
I came over in the rain and awoke Jodie: practiced some and took my music lesson after school. I examined papers and baked bread. Went to stay with Mrs. Merriman.

November 5, 1885 Thursday
First snow. I got up and found things white with snow and it snowed till noon. I practiced some and wrote a letter and studied. Heard bad

news from home about Alice and cried myself to sleep at night.

November 6, 1885 Friday
Snowed again but after noon was sunshine. Jodie and I went down town, came back and called at Mr. Imkster's. Mrs. M. stopped and left the papers but said that I needn't stay the nights.

November 7, 1885 Saturday
Rained all day. I varnished my chairs and done some baking for Mrs. M. and some for myself: Ironed and sewed some on Mrs. Todd's machine.

November 8, 1885 Sunday
I went to hear Father Ells preach: it was communion day: went to S. S. alone, came back and practiced some. Nim was here and we all went to church in the evening. After church we had a lunch and enjoyed a nice visit.

November 9, 1885 Monday
Nim stayed until school time. After school I went to Mrs. Hall's to see about my dress; came back and wrote to Alice and examined papers until I was so sleepy I could hardly see.

November 10, 1885 Tuesday
After school we went down town. Maude was here to supper. I examined two sets of papers and wrote a letter.

November 11, 1885 Wednesday
I came away from school and went to mail my letter but went back and studied like a good girl. After school I took my music lesson and after supper we went to the P.O. and printing office. Mr. Hoyt called. We studied til 10:00

November 12, 1885 Thursday
Went to school and had my lessons well. Practiced at noon while Joe got dinner. After school went to Mrs. Hall's, examined papers and studied until late.

November 13, 1885 Friday
After school we recited our normal lessons. Joe and I went down town. I mixed my light-bread.

November 14, 1885 Saturday
I washed a three week washing and did some baking. Jodie mopped the kitchen for me. I sewed on my dress. Lewis came in the evening and stayed over night. We enjoyed a little chat.

November 15, 1885 Sunday
We did not go to church, but went to S.S. Joe ate his dinner before we went and Lewis and I ate after we came back and we had a splendid visit, but perhaps the last one for some time.

November 16, 1885 Monday
I bade Lewis a long farewell and went to school. We were dismissed at 2:30. I went to Mrs. Hall's to sew and in the evening went to Mrs. Andrus' to a S.S. teachers' meeting.

November 17, 1885 Tuesday
I practiced my music before school. After school I went to Mrs. Hall's and finished my dress. In the evening we went to the young folk's prayer meeting. Mr. Walters from Colfax delivered an address.

November 18, 1885 Wednesday
I made light bread. After school I took my music lesson. Mr. Spedgerwood's came and Mrs. and Mrs. Todd and I went over a few minutes. I did some writing for Mrs. M.

November 19, 1885 Thursday
After school I practiced my music some. Lizzie O'Donnell called. I went to Mr. Ledgerwood's a little while.

November 20, 1885 Friday
I wrote to Alice. Things went along nicely at school. I stayed to recite our normal lesson. After supper Jodie and I went down town to do a little trading.

November 21, 1885 Saturday
I cleaned the house and made preserves. Mr. Dow called. I copied a piece for him. Did a lot of baking for Mrs. M. and myself, then ironed and finished some sewing. Took my bath. Went to bed at 10:45 very tired.

November 22, 1885 Sunday
I went with Mr. and Mrs. M. to the Lance school house to hear preaching but there was none. Nim was here when I came back. Lewis and Norman came, then Jesse and Emma. We went to church and all had a pleasant time together til 11 o'clock.

November 23, 1885 Monday
I got breakfast and dinner for the folks, then they started on their trip for Badger. I felt very sad all day. Nim stayed till late. Mr. and Mrs. Anderson called in the evening. Had a nice visit, but enjoyed a cry after I went to bed.

November 24, 1885 Tuesday

I went to school but did not feel very well. After school we stayed to practice for the exhibition, then I came home and washed some. Mrs. Lockhart called to see Jodie about practicing a song.

November 25, 1885 Wednesday

A rainy morning. After school I took my music lesson. After supper we went down town to find a way of going to Waverly but came back discouraged.

November 26, 1885 – Thanksgiving Thursday

Jodie got Mr. McNeilly's buggy and team. I went to Mrs. Tucker's to practice my piece. We started for Waverly around noon. The roads were so muddy that it was dark when we got there. We surprised the folks but they seemed glad to see us. Alice was quite sick.

November 27, 1885 Friday

Jodie went for the doctor. And she got better. In the evening we took Edna and May and went to Mr. Thayer's. We enjoyed a nice visit.

November 28, 1885 Saturday

After a late breakfast, we went back to Jim's. On our way back we called at Mr. McGee's and went to Jesse's house for some things. I waited on Alice and helped her what I could.

November 29, 1885 Sunday

We started for Cheney and stopped at Mr. Sanders'. Ada came with us to Mr. Davis' and I stayed there till Jodie took her home. We reached the city just as the first church bell was ringing, tired and cold.

November 30, 1885 Monday

I went to school and after school we practiced our pieces. I came home by Mr. Ledgerwood's. Mrs. L. and Mary went with us to hear Miss White lecture on Temperance. It was good.

December 1, 1885 Tuesday

In the evening Jeff called: we went to Mrs. Merriman's and then to the lecture but I had to go to Mrs. Tucker's at 8 o'clock to practice my piece.

December 2, 1885 Wednesday

I did not go to school in the afternoon: we went to the Oaks house to practice. I did not take my music lesson. Mrs. Lockhart forgot me.

December 3, 1885 Thursday

I went to school. After school I learned painting from "The celebrated

Mr. Bemis." After supper I did some sewing and went to Mr. Inkster's for some yeast.

December 4, 1885 Friday
We went to school but were dismissed to practice our piece. At 10 o'clock we went to the Oaks' house. In the evening Jeff and Ada came and went to the exhibition with us. It was good. Ada stayed over night with me.

December 5, 1885 Saturday
Jeff came before we had breakfast. I went with him and Ada to Mrs. M.'s. I felt bad all day but washed our flannel clothes and did some baking for Mrs. M. In the evening went down town with Ada and to Mrs. Ledgerwood's. Fay came home.

December 6, 1885 Sunday
I did not feel very well. We went to church in the morning, also in the evening. Ada went with us. Did not go to S.S. Fay, Mary and Ada called. Had a pleasant time.

December 7, 1885 Monday
I went to school in the morning but was sick all day: did not go in the afternoon. In the evening went to the P.O. and to see Mrs. Dorne about the "paint."

December 8, 1885 Tuesday
I did not feel well and did not get up until 8 o'clock but went to school and felt better. Fay called in the eve. I went to the P.O. with Ada.

December 9, 1885 Wednesday
I felt better and went to school. I took my music lesson and after supper we studied until late bedtime.

December 10, 1885 Thursday
Ada came by and we went to school together. After school we went to the P. O. I saw Mrs. L. a few minutes and in the evening wrote a letter and Ada and Maude called.

Cheney, Dec. 11th 1885

Dear Friend Lewis:

I received your welcome letter last night and was glad to learn you had arrived safe, but know your trip was pleasant (?) in so much rain. I often thought of you wondering if the weather was as disagreeable where you was as it was here. I hope the skies will be clear when I move out there or any place else. But don't know when that will be.

I know the folks were glad to welcome you home and were disappointed because Nim did not go: he stayed here until after nine o'clock that night and did not seem very anxious to get back to Waverly. We did not see him when we were out there. We enjoyed our visit and surprised all the folks. It rained the day we went out but we did not get wet because we were in Mr. McNeilly's top buggy. What do you think of that? He said we could use his buggy & team when ever we wanted to without any cost. Who would not be a friend of the bachelors?

I found everyone enjoying very good health except Mrs. Hays; she is no better and I fear will not be well for a long time if ever. I think our little nephew is, or will be very good looking after I take some shoe polish & black his hair.

It made me feel lonesome to go back to Jesse's place, but I had no desire to stay. Every thing seemed very quiet but some were excited about the R.R. I saw Frank but not to speak to him. I hope the R.R will pass through there if it will add any to his happiness. Mr. McGhee has 24 scholars. They have adjourned to S.S. until next spring. I heard they were going to start their literary society next week, also that they were going to have a Christmas tree there.

We have only one week of school then two weeks vacation. We will have a good time then, and all of us children will hang up our stockings for Santa Clause to fill. If I get mine full I will have enough to divide with you. (if you want me to)

December 12, 1885 Saturday
I washed, did some baking and cleaned the house; in the evening Fay called, Ada came over and went down town. I had my hair cut again, we had some fun, too.

December 13, 1885 Sunday
I went to church in the morning and to S.S. in the P.M. Then to the P.O. and got a letter and while I was reading it Mr. Eastman came and I slipped in the kitchen but Nim and Ada came and I went in and we had a pleasant chat.

December 14, 1885 Monday
We had late breakfast. Nim started to Waverly when we went to school. After school I went down town with Mrs. Tucker to select Mr. Dow's Christmas present. We chose a nice book.

December 15, 1885 Tuesday
I was late to school on account of my work. After school I did some

baking and cleaned things in the kitchen. Went down town with Ada and examined papers for Mrs. Merriman.

December 16, 1885 Wednesday
I wrote a letter in the morning. After school I took my music lesson. After supper I studied and examined papers.

December 17, 1885 Thursday
Rena brought me a note at noon. After school I went down town. In the evening we went to Mrs. Ledgerwood's and enjoyed a pleasant visit but I got my ear hurt. Mr. L was at home. We had popcorn.

December 18, 1885 Friday
A rainy day. I went to school. In the evening Mr. Thayer called. I went with Mr. Power to a church social at Mrs. Martin's, had a pleasant time.

December 19, 1885 Saturday
A bright _warm_ day. I washed some and did some baking, cleaned the kitchen; in the evening I ironed. Ada was here most all evening. Louise Tucker called a few minutes.

Memoranda
Arrived in Cheney Sept. 12 to attend school. I then had $52.25. I rented Mr. Felch's house at the rate of $5.00 per month. After the first 2 months we get the house for $4.50. Commenced buying milk Sept. 19th at 6 cts per qt. Commenced taking music lessons from Mrs. Lockhart, Oct. 30th. Only take one lesson a week. Dec. 3, I paid four dollars for learning to "paint", $2.00 for enamel and 80 cents for ornaments. Commenced to examine school papers for Mrs. Merriman the second term on Dec. 15, 1885

Receipt for Diaries

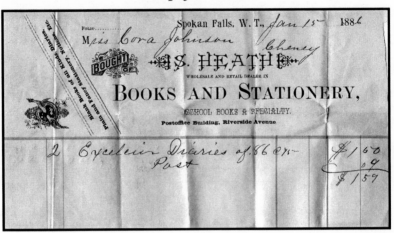

An invitation sent to Cora

> Gilla provided the following information. This letter was folded diagonally several times into a diamond shape and fitted into a small 3 x 5 envelope addressed to "Miss Johnson, Waverly, Wash. Ter."

Spaugh, W. T. July 25th 1881
  Miss Johnson

My friend

*Will you kindly grant me the
pleasure of your company to the
party, to be given here Friday (29th) evening.
I most sincerely hope that our
short acquaintence will not
influence you toward declining.*

*Respectfully
yours
Charles A Hinchcliff*

Valentine Received by Cora

To Miss Johnson
Feb. 12, 1881.

Near me in the hour of night
Comes a spirit-bird that sings,
Haunting all the world around,
With the beauty of her wings.
Sweet warbler, when in the distance you go winging,
Over a whitish homely tree,
Pause and read the name of her of whom you're singing,
And to her, bear this now for me.
To you whose name the spirit-bird,
Gladly reads upon the tree;
Come now, take up your escritoire
And send a kind word to me.
Tell me that you do forgive & freely forget
That I was so cross, so unkind;
Then in the future I'll not foregret
That I was once your valentine.
Composed for the occasion, & Extempore.

Cora Johnson's Story
1886 Diary

Presented to Miss Cora Johnson by a Friend, February 28, 1886

January 13, 1886 Wednesday
I finished my letter, went to the P. O. and was late to school. After school I went to Mrs. Hall's and she told me of her trouble. I brought Mrs. Lockhart's bird home with me.

January 14, 1886 Thursday
Mr. Cobleigh visited our school. We had much fun reciting our normal lessons to Mrs. Tucker. After supper I wrote a letter and went to the P.O. with Ada, then to church.

January 15, 1886 Friday
I ironed some, took Mrs. Todd's iron home and went to school. In the evening studied until late on U.S. History preparing for the teachers' examination.

January 28, 1886 Thursday
I went to school as usual. In the evening wrote a letter. Mr. Thayer called and told us that Alice's baby was very sick.

January 29, 1886 Friday
After school we recited our normal lessons. Mrs. Lockhart called and took her bird home with her. I went to the P.O. was nearly sick all day. I wrote a letter and went to bed.

January 30, 1886 Saturday
I cleaned the house and ironed. I felt bad all day. Mrs. Merriman called in the evening. Jodie stayed down town until late. It was a nice warm day and the snow was melting.

January 31, 1886 Sunday
Mary Ledgerwood came by and we went to the Baptist church. Fay called. Jodie and I went to S.S. Nim came. Albert Plaster called. Ada S. had a great time with her teeth and sent for me. I stayed until 9 P.M.

February 1, 1886 Monday
Nim took breakfast and dinner with us. After school we remained a while and Mr. Dow asked us for advice in regard to whispering in school.

February 2, 1886 Tuesday

I ironed some, took Mrs. Todd's iron home and went to school. After school I went to see Ada a few minutes. Snowing and cold. Fay called. I studied until <u>late</u> in the evening.

February 3, 1886 Wednesday

After school I went to the P.O. After supper I studied some. Jeff came and gave me some of the Waverly news.

February 4, 1886 Thursday

I was late to school and things went wrong all day. I whispered and had to stay after school. I went to the P.O. and Fay walked back home with me and stayed a while. In the evening Mary called.

February 5, 1886 Friday

I went to school as usual and enjoyed the day some better than the one before it. We spelled down and then recited our normal lesson.

February 6, 1886 Saturday

I done a large washing besides my baking and other work but Jodie helped me most of the day.

February 7, 1886 Sunday

Jodie and I went to church in the morning and to S.S. in the afternoon. I was not well and did not go to church in the evening.

February 10, 1886 Wednesday

I was nearly sick but attended the examination. Ab. Robinson walked down to the P.O. with me: I got a letter and walked home very tired.

February 11, 1886 Thursday

I got through with my examination at 2 o'clock and went home discouraged. Ab. Robinson, Fay and Katie called. We had a pleasant time. Ab. stayed till <u>late</u> and Katie stayed over night.

February 12, 1886 Friday

I went to school. Fay took Kate home. Ab and Mrs. Strong visited the academy and Ab went home with us from school.

February 13, 1886 Saturday

I did not feel very well but had plenty to do to keep me busy all day. Joe was cutting wood for Mrs. Merriman and could not help me much.

February 14, 1886 Sunday

I went to church and S.S. as usual. In the evening Albert Plaster, Mr. Eastman and Fay called. I went to church with Albert. I received two valentines.

February 15, 1886 Monday
I went to school. Nothing very important occurred.

February 16, 1886 Tuesday
After school I wrote a letter. In the evening Albert Plaster came and told me about school. We went to the Young People's meeting.

February 17, 1886 Wednesday
After school Jodie and I went to Mrs. Ledgerwood's. Mary was washing and Mrs. L. was making fried cakes but Fay entertained us and we had a pleasant time.

February 18, 1886 Thursday
In the evening Jodie and I went to the lecture.. Rev. Strong , of Walla Walla, Mr. Hill, of Sprague, lectured on "local opton." It was very good.   R.L.I. T.B.H.

February 19, 1886 Friday
I did not go to school in the afternoon. Mrs. Ledgerwood called. Albert Plaster came and took me to the entertainment given by Mrs. Bane. Albert stayed until late and we had quite a "conflab."

February 20, 1886 Saturday
A beautiful day. I washed some and scrubbed the kitchen. I went over and helped Ada awhile to get ready for the party. In the evening Mary and I went to the party at Mrs. M.'s and had a nice time. Several there.

February 21, 1886 Sunday
I went to Mrs. Merriman's after my dishes. Ada and Leebeaure went to Spokane. I went to the train with them: did not go to church but went to S.S. with Mary. Went to church in the evening with Fay. Mr. Westfall preached.

February 22, 1886 Monday
As it is "Birthington's washday" we had no school in the P.M. I wrote a letter and went over to help Mrs. M. do some writing. The other girls played ball. Ada came back with the blues.

February 23, 1886 Tuesday
Went to school. It was a windy day. In the evening, I wrote a letter. Mary L came by and we went to the Young people's meeting. Rhoda's cat followed her to church and made us laugh. Mrs. M. led the meeting.

February 26, 1886 Friday
I was at Cheney but did not go to school.

FEBRUARY,   SUNDAY 21.   1886.

I went to Mrs. Merriman's
after my dishes.
Ada & Lebeaure went to Spo
kane. I went to the train
with then; did not go to chu
but went to S. S. with Mary.
went to church with in evenin
with Fay. Mr. Westfall preached?

MONDAY 22.

As it is "Birthington's washday" we had no school in the
p.m. I wrote a letter and
went over to help Mrs. M.
do some writing.
The other girls played ball
Ada came back with the blue

TUESDAY 23.

Went to school. It was
a windy day.
In the evening I wrote
a letter. Mary L— came
by & we went to the Young
people's meeting.
Rhoda's cat followed
her to church & made us
laugh. Mrs. M— led the meeting

*Cora's dishes and utensils traveled west in the covered wagon with her
They had passed to her from her parents and grandparents.*

V. R. Zachow

Note with plate:
Cora Johnson left Bates County Missouri in the covered wagon
with her brothers in 1880.

History of the plate
1. Great Grandmother Johnson
2. Grandma Betty Cora Johnson Titchenal
3. Father Charles A. Titchenal
4. Daughter Maebelle Rose
5. Son Frank Lewis Titchenal

These spoons that traveled across the plains with Cora still remain
in the family.

February 27, 1886 Saturday
Jodie and I went to Spokane Falls on the cars. Met L. at the depot and
went to the resterant for dinner. In the P.M. I did some trading and L.
and I went out for a pleasant drive.

40

February 28, 1886 Sunday

We went to the resterent for breakfast. L. and I went to church then took a stroll down by the river, called on Sarah, went back to Cheney on the train and went to church in the evening. I gave A. P. the "G.B."

March 1, 1886 Monday

I was called up at 5 o'clock by the cry of fire. We went down and saw the Oakes house burn. I went with L. to the train. After dinner I went to help Mrs. Hall and we all went with Mr. Power to supper. He spent the evening with me.

March 2, 1886 Tuesday

I went to Mrs. Hall's and Rena off on the train. They went to Mims'. Mrs. Ledgerwood called before dinner. In the afternoon I commenced to pack my things, getting ready to go to Badger.

March 3, 1886 Wednesday

Jodie and I went to Mrs. Hall's to get the things she had given me. Jodie went to school, I washed till noon. After noon Ethel and Edith called. I visited the school a while and Mary L. went with me to the P.O.

March 4, 1886 Thursday

I went to Waverly with Mr. J. Huffman, took Alice's bird to her, found them as well as usual and glad to see me. Mrs. Peace was there. Jodie stayed in Cheney until school closed.

March 5, 1886 Friday

Gilmore brought my organ. I did some sewing. Lorenzo came about sundown and we all went to the literary in the evening. We went in the wagon. I was the "judge".

March 6, 1886 Saturday

I made my first "mother-hubbard" dress. L. went to Mr. Thayer's but came back in the evening and we went to church. Mr. Jackson was there to supper.

March 7, 1886 Sunday

We went to the quarterly meeting at Waverly. Mr. and Mrs. Hoagland, Eliza, Minnie and L. came home with us. We all went to church that night and after church we enjoyed a nice chat at Alice's. L. stayed over night.

March 8, 1886 Monday

At Alice's. Sewed most all day. L. went after his pony and after Mr. Hays' trees.

March 9, 1886 Tuesday

I sewed on my dress. Jeff came and we had quite a chat. L. came back and started for Spokane that afternoon. In the evening I practiced some.

March 10, 1886 Wednesday

I sewed until noon. In the afternoon went to the P.O. and to Mr. Dawson's to see about getting the school. back to Alice's again.

March 11, 1886 Thursday

In the morning ironed some. In the afternoon Edna and I went with Gilmore to Mr. Roonta's and came back by Mr. McPeak's to see about the Spring Valley School. Didn't get it.

March 12, 1886 Friday

I sewed for Alice. We all went to the literary except Alice and Mr. Lumus. Among the exercises of the evening was "The Frog Hollow Lyceum".

March 13, 1886 Saturday

I finished my dress and helped Alice. It was a very disagreeable day, windy and snowed some.

March 14, 1886 Sunday

Another disagreeable day. I wrote a letter to Willie and in the afternoon I went to Mr. Thayer's and stayed over night. I had a very pleasant time. Gilmore started to Snake River.

March 15, 1886 Monday

I went with Mr. Thayer to Cheney. It was a cold, windy day. We got to Cheney about 5 o'clock. I found that Jodie had kept house nicely but was glad to see me. Mary L. went with us to hear Mr. Dean preach that night.

March 16, 1886 Tuesday

Jodie went home with Mr. Thayer and left me alone. I sent some of my things to Alice. I took dinner at Mrs. Merriman's. I went to church with Mary L. and stayed that night.

March 17, 1886 Wednesday

I packed some of my things in the morning and in the afternoon Mr. Eastman called. Before he left Ada Covington and Ada Sanders came. Lorenzo came on the train and we went to the hotel to supper and from there to church.

March 18, 1886 Thursday

L. came and brought me a telegram from Jesse at Ritzville waiting for me. We were in a little trouble for a little while but had a good visit and he left on the train at 1 o'clock. Jodie came and went back after my saddle and clothes that I left at Alice's. Remember <u>our</u> picnic at the train. I stayed with Mary over night.

March 19, 1886 Friday

I packed my things and took my departure at 4 o'clock P.M. for Ritzville; Jodie came with my saddle a little before train time. I had a pleasant time on the train and formed the acquaintance of Mr. Rob. I found Jesse waiting and stayed at a Dutch hotel that night.

March 20, 1886 Saturday

About 7 o'clock we started from Ritzville for Badger Mountain. Mr. Dennison traveled with us two days. The wind was very disagreeable and we traveled over prairie. We stayed in a bachelor's house that night.

March 21, 1886 Sunday

We started early and traveled over a rocky road until noon. It began to rain on us and we stopped at Mr. Richardson's over night. They are very pleasant people and did not charge us anything. 7 of us slept in one room.

March 22, 1886 Monday

Still cloudy and rained on us again in the afternoon. We traveled over a sage brush country all day and stayed at Mr. Gandy's – a bachelor – that night. I slept in the wagon and Jesse slept in the house.

March 23, 1886 Tuesday

We started next morning at sunrise. Mr. Stephens ate dinner with us. The wind was blowing a gale and we were in a snow-storm about two hours, finally found our way to Mr. Titchenal's. All were glad to see us and we soon enjoyed a good supper. Had nothing warm to eat since Sun. morning.

March 24, 1886 Wednesday

I felt very tired and stayed at Mr. T.'s til about 4 o'clock when Jesse and I came over to his place. Emma soon came home from school but acted very indifferent. Things soon went on all right.

March 25, 1886 Thursday

There was no school on account of the teacher's examination. Mr. Payne was here in the morning. Lewis and Nannie came by going to the P.O. I straightened my things around some and was writing a letter when they came back. They did not stay long.

Mary Moore and David Jackson Titchenal
Parents of Lewis, Norman, Nimrod, Nancy, John and Phebe Titchenal

March 26, 1886 Friday
I went to school with Emma and took items, got acquainted with the
  scholars and the surroundings. Walked home and I wrote until
  supper. Lewis was here to supper and stayed awhile.

March 27, 1886 Saturday
I did not feel very well but Emma and I washed. Lewis was here to dinner
  and stayed until dark. I cleaned up the dishes and had a good visit
  with L.

March 28, 1886 Sunday
I studied my S.S. lesson awhile and then went out for a stroll, all alone.
  In the afternoon Lewis went with me to S.S. We walked and I went
  home with him and rode "Ginger" home.

March 29, 1886 Monday
I taught my first day of school at the Barbar Creek school house.
  Everything went off all right but I did not feel very well. After school
  I wrote a letter.

March 30, 1886 Tuesday
At school but did not feel well. I finished my letter at school. After
  school I went with Jesse to look at a claim; came back, got supper and
  cleaned up the dishes. Phebe came home with E.

March 31, 1886 Wednesday
Emma wanted my pony to ride to the P.O. so I walked to school. I was
  very tired after school, did some writing and got supper. Emma did
  not get back until late. I did not get any letter.

April 1, 1886 Thursday

At school things went along very well. It was a rainy morning.

April 2, 1886 Friday

Emma was sick. Mr. Will worked for Jesse. After school I went to Mr. Titchenal's to take "Ginger" home and to get the irons and some milk. Lewis came back with me and carried the irons for me.

April 3, 1886 Saturday

I finished a letter and ironed some. L. came by going to the P.O. and stayed until after dinner. I mended some of my clothes and walked to Mr. T.'s to take the irons home and get some milk. L. brought me a letter and spent the evening. "Beware of the stove-hook"

April 4, 1886 Sunday

I took a walk and picked some flowers. Emma and I read some and studied our S.S. lesson. L. and I walked to S.S. and had a pleasant talk afterwards. Emma and I sang some. L. stayed "until late".

April 5, 1886 Monday

A bright, warm day at school but things did not go to suit me. After school I did some writing and cried for the first time since I left Cheney.

April 6, 1886 Tuesday

Another nice day. Emma, Mrs. Hodges and Mr. Dayne visited my school in the P.M. I went back to Jesse's and finished my letter, then went to Mr. Titchenal's and stayed over night.

April 7, 1886 Wednesday

I enjoyed my visit at Mr. T.'s. Went to school and back to Jesse's. Mrs. Payne was there. Jesse had gone after some horses and did not get back til late. I wrote a letter to Katie.

April 8, 1886 Thursday

"Ginger" got away and I walked to school. Mr. Payne brought my mail to the school house. After school I was reading in the papers I had received when L. came and brought "Ginger". He stayed until late.

April 9, 1886 Friday

Mr. Will came and awoke us. A nice rain the night before. Jesse went after a horse and Emma and I stayed alone. I did some writing in the evening. After school I went by my claim and put a notice on.

April 10, 1886 Saturday

We slept until 7 o'clock. Lewis and Mr. Payne came by going to the P.O.

Emma and I carried water, washed and mopped. She shingled my hair. I mended my dress.

April 11, 1886 Sunday
Mr. Payne and Mr. Wall called. Emma and I sang and studied our S.S. lesson. Lewis and Norman called and we all went to S.S. and sang awhile afterwards. L. and I enjoyed a nice visit. I wore my "mother-hubbard".

April 12, 1886 Monday
A rainy morning. L. came over before I went to school. Mr. Green called at the school house to announce Mr. Wixon's funeral. Lewis visited my school and fixed the window: he came back by Jesse's and stayed awhile.

Cora's Teaching Contract
This agreeement made and entered into this 12th day of April 1886, between Cora Johnson, party of the first part, and Common School Directors of School District #6 of Douglas County, Washington Ter., between Cora and J. C. Johnson and D. J. Titchenal to teach school.

April 13, 1886 Tuesday
Ginger got away so I walked to school and Jesse brought him at recess. Emma went to the funeral. I got supper and L. was there and we had a short chat in the moonlight.

April 14, 1886 Wednesday
I helped Emma some and went to school. After school E. and I went to Mr. Payne's calling. Had a very pleasant time. Norman brought me a letter and was there to supper. I felt bad and gave vent to <u>tears</u>.

April 15, 1886 Thursday
A rainy morning. Jesse and Emma started to Waverly. I went to school but felt a little lonesome. After school I came by Jesse's and then to Mr. Titchenal's. The men folk were on the mountain.

April 16, 1886 Friday
It snowed and rained all the morning. Phebe and I rode Ginger to school. I only had four scholars. It was a lonesome day for me. I was staying at Mr. Titchenal's.

April 17, 1886 Saturday
I went over to Jesse's to do some writing. Nannie came by and we went to the Badger P.O. my first trip there. Came back by Jesse's and got my valise. I was tired. Got two letters.

April 18, 1886 Sunday

I read some and studied my S.S. lesson. In the afternoon we all went
to S.S. It snowed on us while we were going and rained on us going
back. Only a few there. I felt bad for a while but was comforted.
G.N.K.

April 19, 1886 Monday

Phebe rode to school with me. Everything went along nicely. After school
I ironed some. We were all bad children and laughed at the supper
table. L. and I had a little chat.

April 20, 1886 Tuesday

I went to school as usual. After school I wrote two letters. It was a cold,
windy day. I went to bed at 10:30.

April 21, 1886 Wednesday

Lewis was hauling posts and mailed my letters. After school I went by
Jesse's to get my writing material, and got back to Mr. Titchenal's just
at supper time.

April 22, 1886 Thursday

A nice warm day. At school during noon I took a strole and gathered
some flowers. I punished the children for laughing. L. brought me
two letters and a paper.

April 23, 1886 Friday

Was at school but was nearly sick with a cold. After school I went to stay
with Mrs. Hodges over night and milked the cow for her. I was a little
lonesome.

April 24, 1886 Saturday

I went to Jesse's and came back to Mr. Hodges and wrote a letter. In the
afternoon Lewis came by and we went to see Miss Brown, returned to
Mr. T.'s at 8 o'clock. I ironed the boys sirts after supper.

April 25, 1886 Sunday

At Mr. Titchenal's. I did not feel well but went to S.S. in the afternoon.
L. and I had quite a chat and I came back to stay with Mrs. Hodge.

April 26, 1886 Monday

A very windy day. I wrote a letter to Alice and went to school. My cold
made me feel bad. I wrote another letter.

April 27, 1886 Tuesday

Mrs. Hodge went to visit Mrs. Titchenal. I came down at noon, ate my
dinner alone and finished my letter. Norman came by the school

house going to the P.O. and took my letters.

April 28, 1886 Wednesday

I studied my S.S. lesson until school time. After school came back to Mrs. Hodge's and wrote a letter to Gilmore and read some.

April 29, 1886 Thursday

I went to school as usual. After school I came back to Mr. Titchenal's. Mr. Payne came to the school house and brought me a letter. Lewis came from the P.O. and brought me two more letters.

April 30, 1886 Friday

After school I did some sewing.

May 1, 1886 Saturday

A cold, windy day. I did not feel very well: finished my sewing and wrote a letter. After Lewis came back from the school meeting we went over to Jesse's place after my trunk.

Cora's trunk traveled west on the covered wagon and remains in the family today.

May 2, 1886 Sunday

Very dusty. I studied my S.S. lesson and walked to S.S. Nannie and Phebe went to the Methodist S.S. L. and I had quite a pleasant chat. I formed the acquaintance of Mr. Mitchell, Mr. Ward and Mr. Rowell.

May 3, 1886 Monday

I patched my dress and went to school. After school I commenced to write a letter but L. came from the trial and we talked until supper. After supper I washed the dishes. Two strangers stayed here over night.

May 4, 1886 Tuesday
I washed the dishes and went to school. I only had five pupils and felt a
little discouraged. After school I finished my letter. G.N.H.

May 5, 1886 Wednesday
I went to school with a headache. John Payne brought me a letter that
Mr. Wills brought from Emma. He rode Frisk. In the evening some
Indians were here.

May 6, 1886 Thursday
John Titchenal fell in the branch and we had much fun at his expense.
Coming home from school we met Mr. Will and with Frisk and
brought him home: he ran away with John. L. came from the P.O.
and brought me two letters.

May 7, 1886 Friday
A rainy morning. I rode Frisk to school and he ran away with me. School
seemed a little dull. In the evening I wrote a letter.

May 8, 1886 Saturday
A nice day but windy. Nannie and I washed and ironed and did not get
through until late. I did some sewing. Some Indians were here.

May 9, 1886 Sunday
We went to the lake to S.S. They made use of me as teacher and as
chorister. Came back "home" for dinner. Mrs. T. had the headache.
Mr. Ballard was here. We went to S.S. in the P.M. at Badger Creek
school house.

May 10, 1886 Monday
I went to school but did not feel very well. I had eight scholars. After
school I wrote a letter. In the evening L. and I had a little chat. I had
the blues and gave vent to tear after all others were asleep.

May 11, 1886 Tuesday
I was nearly sick and did not get up until breakfast was nearly ready. I
felt better in the afternoon. Frisk ran away with me as we came from
school. Mr. Redfield stayed over night here.

May 12, 1886 Wednesday
A very windy day. Mr. Payne came by the school house at noon and
brought me three letters. I felt in better spirits then. Norman brought
me some papers and read until 11 o'clock.

May 13, 1886 Thursday
Something was said just as I started to school which set me to thinking.

The day seemed long. After school I tried to write some but my thoughts were scattered. L. and I had a long chat.

May 14, 1886 Friday
I went to school as usual but did not feel very well. After school I wrote a letter and had another visit with L. I tried to banish all unpleasant thoughts by reading.

May 15, 1886 Saturday
A cool windy day. I did not do much except to write five letters. In the evening Norman and I played ball with the rest of the children. L. mended my shoe.

May 16, 1886 Sunday
A warm day. We went to hear Mr. Corbaley preach, came back by S.S. got home at 6 P.M. hungry and tired after riding twenty miles without any dinner. In the evening L. and I took a stroll up by the garden

May 17, 1886 Monday
The warmest day we have had this season. I did not feel very well and went in the granary and rested awhile after school. Mr. Payne called. After supper I drew Lewis' picture.

May 18, 1886 Tuesday
Saw two snakes as we went to school. John killed one of them. Two Indians came to the school house at noon and I bought a buck-skin from them. In the evening I did some writing.

May 19, 1886 Wednesday
L. got hurt by a horse. Frisk's back was sore and I rode the white pony to school. John and I ran a race as we came home. Norman brought me a letter and I read it to L.

May 20, 1886 Thursday
I went to school as usual.

May 22, 1886 Saturday
A very pleasant day. My school closed. I shall ever remember our coming home, yet not with pleasure. I had a head-ache

May 23, 1886 Sunday
Nannie was away and Mrs. T. had the headache. I helped do up the work, then went for a little stroll, studied my S.S. and gathered flowers. We went to S.S. in the wagon: had a very good school.

May 24, 1886 Monday
We did not have to go to school but done a very big washing. I was tired and layed down to rest a while and went to sleep, and woke up sick, and nervous.

May 25, 1886 Tuesday
I did not feel very well and did not do much but write some letters. In the morning I went over to Jesse's place and found a mouse in the can of honey.

May 26, 1886 Wednesday
I was too near sick to do any thing but lounge around all day. I wrote two letters. A very warm day. The mercury stands at 90 in the shade.

May 27, 1886 Thursday
I ironed in the forenoon and mended my clothes in the afternoon. I felt very well until John brought me some letters and I could not help giving vent to tears after reading them.

May 28, 1886 Friday
Nannie went with me to see Miss. Harden. We started at 9 A.M. and returned at 4:30 P.M. I was tired and hungry besides having a severe headache but felt better in the evening.

May 29, 1886 Saturday
I made out my school report. Mr. James came after Mrs. T. and left Nannie and I kept house. I stemed some goose-berries and did some sewing and got supper.

May 30, 1886 Sunday
Nanny and Norman went to preaching. I cleaned up the house and read some. Mrs. T. came home just as we started to S.S. and she went with us; only a few there. R.T.G.N. K.- S.

May 31, 1886 Monday
We washed in the forenoon and in the afternoon I cut and fit Nannie's new dress, and sewed some on it. I shall remember my dream in the morning which was partially realized.

June 1, 1886 Tuesday
A very warm day. I sewed until I was tired and wrote a letter.

June 2, 1886 Wednesday
I wrote another letter and sewed until sundown. I sprinkled my clothes to iron, and then went to meet John as he came from the post office. I got a letter which caused me to shed me some big tears.

Nancy Moore Titchenal   *Nimrod David Titchenal*

John David Titchenal   *Norman Stanley Titchenal*
Lewis Titchenal brothers and sister

June 3, 1886 Thursday
I did my ironing and finished Nannie's dress before dinner. In the afternoon took a lesson in spelling from the "<u>sentinel</u>". <u>We</u> had lots of fun. I did some writing and read some.

June 4, 1886 Friday
The warmest day of the season. 95 in the shade. I turned the grindstone for L. to grind his ax. I did not do much but mend some of my clothes.

June 5, 1886 Saturday
Mrs. Corbally and Mary went to visit Mrs. Titchenal. I made Phebe's dress skirt. In the evening <u>we</u> hauled a load of posts, gathered some flowers and I wrote a letter.

June 6, 1886 Sunday

I read some and studied my S.S. lesson. Mrs. Hodges and her sister called. We had a very good S.S. and large attendance. Norman went to Okanogan and brought me a letter.

> The original Town of Okanogan was established near the present site of Douglas, but soon was abandoned due to lack of water.

Phebe and Nancy [Nannie] Titchenal, Sisters of Lewis

June 7, 1886 Monday

A cold day. I cut and fit Phebe's red dress and sewed some on it.

June 9, 1886 Wednesday

We caught Frisk and he bucked around with L. for awhile. We went after some sugar and I rode Frisk home. I wrote two letters and cut Lewis' hair. In the evening I read some of the Cheney news.

June 10, 1886 Thursday

Mr. Nash and several others were here. I finished Phebe's dress and read till I was sleepy. 'Twas a cold evening and we sat around the stove like it was winter weather.

June 11, 1886 Friday

I cut and almost made Phebe a gingham dress. L. hauled a load of lumber to build my house. I ate onions for dinner but did not enjoy it very much.

Waverly, W.T.   *July 11th 1886*

Dear Friend Lewis:

I believe we decided not to exchange letters during your absence but it pleases me to surprise people when I think the surprise will be an agreeable one which I feel sure will be the case with this.

Since writing to Gilmore this morning, I got to thinking about it and thought perhaps he would let you read, or tell you what was in my letter and you would feel better satisfied to receive one yourself. But will send it in the same envelope with his so that the people with prying eyes might be none the wiser; for you see it has been less than a week since I saw you but I wish it had been less than a day, don't you?

I had a very pleasant trip to Cheney. Went to Mr. Covington's and stayed until after supper then played a game of croquet with the girls and Mr. Thrall, who happened to be in town that night. I stayed over night with my friend Mrs. Todd. I did not see Mr. Hays to speak with him until next morning. We started home at 1 o'clock and got here at 8.

I was quite sick on the road for a while and was the next day, but am feeling better to day though was not able to go to Sunday School. Alice and Jim went horse back and left the children with me.

I feel a little lonesome & might wish you were here, but my wishes are like shadows: they lengthen as the sun declines and I am left alone to meditate. But think I have done real well. I have not cried since I saw you and find that I am better off when I can control myself and as I told you, will try to be as cheerful as possible under the circumstances.

Jesse was here when I got home but went away that night & have not seen him since. I have not done any work since I came home and don't expect to until I feel better.

You needn't be surprised to find me at Medical Lake when you come back for I am going if I have a chance.

This has been a very warm day and I have almost melted.

I suppose you are at home now but know you have had a very warm dusty trip. I fear Phebe will be sick & not want to come back any more.

The first thing Edna said was "Aunt Codie, why didn't Luce and Ebe come back." She often speakes of you. But I think oftener than I speak.

I hope Gilmore will like & get a place.

I shall not expect an answer to this but hope to see you soon.

Your true friend
Cora J.

I have not heard any more news yet. I will write to Nannie soon.

June 12, 1886 Saturday

The day of the S.S, picnic at Waverly. I finished Phebe's dress and did some other sewing and made out my school report. It was a very cold disagreeable day.

June 13, 1886 Sunday

A more pleasant day but very windy. L. and I went 10 miles to church and I went back home with the sick headache. Was not able to go to

S.S. L. was my Dr. I heard some unpleasant news about L. E. R.

June 14, 1886 Monday
I did not feel well and did not do much. I helped some with the washing
and cut out Mrs. Titchenal's black dress.

1886 - The first page of the following letter is missing.

*He said he was likely to be gone before then but did not say where he
was going but is going away to get work. I have had no chance to visit with
him any yet. Jesse & Mr. Norton are breaking this R.R. land east of Jim's
pasture. We came back that way yesterday evening & was near enough that
I spoke to Mr. Norton but he did not know me until we had nearly passed
him. They say he seems very well contented here.*

*Jesse & Emma stayed over night at Mr. Huffman's since they came I have
not been hardly any place yet; but am expecting Mr. Thrall this afternoon
and we are going to Mr. Thayer's for a "sing". I have not been any place on
horseback, except over to Mr. Younts, but will go that way this afternoon.*

*I am glad you were so successful in hauling, and if you think it best to
haul the lumber for Mr. Stephens, I wish you much success with it.*

*I hope Miss Titch. will be well enough pleased with the country to feel
that she is paid for the rough introduction she received in getting there.
But poor Mr. Ladd! I really feel sorry for him to think he was not more
successful in the Co. examination. But Lewis I am very thankful that I am
not in his office & I know you are too. I hope he will do his duty in other
respects better than Miss Brown did.*

*Lewis, I try real hard to keep in good spirits but feel almost discouraged
sometimes. I was weighed last Tuesday & only weigh 132 pounds: so you see
the way I am gaining. But you need not worry about me working too much
for I do not do hardly anything. I have not done one bit of washing and
only ironed four pieces since I left there & have sewed a very little. I received
a new book this week and spend a good deal of time in reading & writing
& sleeping! I generally go to sleep about ten o'clock and do not get up until
6 or 7 next morning – just when I feel like it, for nobody calls me. Now,
Lewis don't you think I will get lazy if I don't work any more than that? I
believe I had rather be lazy than not be able to work.*

*I have only been in the garden twice – once after flowers. The only
flowers I have gathered since I came down the coulee hill. We camped for
noon there one day and after dinner I walked a little ways before the wagon
came up with me and I gathered a nice little boquet and thought of the
times we had been along there together; so when the wagon caught up with*

me I laid down and went to sleep with flowers in my hand and dreamed of giving them to you; when I awoke the flowers were out of my hand but the thoughts of you were not out of my mind. That was the only time I slept any while we were traveling but it was not the only time I have dreamed of you. I dreamed one night of going with you to haul a load of lumber & that you had bad luck & I heard you swear so plain that you cannot imagion my feelings when I awoke. Oh! Lewis, I am so thankful it was only a dream & sincerely hope & pray it will never be true. I have so much confidence in you that I could scarcely believe my own ears if I should hear you swear & hope I will never have to believe any such thing. "Yield not to temptation for yielding is sin: each victory will help you; some other to win"

I had to chop my other letter off before I wanted to in order to mail it so you could get to-morrow but I think my letters have been long enough that you cannot complain, can you?

Be a good boy and I hope in next letter you can tell me when you are coming. I want you to come to the camp-meeting if you can, if not come soon as you can.

Your own true little girl
B.C.J.

July 16, 1886 Friday
A very warm day. The thermometer stood at 104 in the shade. I ironed until 1 o'clock. In the evening I wrote two letters.

July 17, 1886 Saturday
I had the headache all day but finished Alice's dress and went to Waverly to preaching with Mr. Hayes.

July 18, 1886 Sunday
I did not feel well enough to go to church, wrote a letter and read some. In the afternoon we all went to preaching in the hack. There was no one here except the home folks.

July 19, 1886 Monday
I felt too bad to do much. I read some and helped Alice about dinner; in the evening I sewed some and practiced awhile. Geo. Yount called.

July 20, 1886 Tuesday
I helped Alice about the work and we murdered bugs by burning the bedstead. In the P.M. we went to Mr. Thayer's after currents. Had a pleasant time and Mrs. Tyee came home with us.

July 21, 1886 Wednesday
I went to the pasture after a horse and went to the P.O. then to see Jesse

in Mr. Thayer's field. I helped with dinner and in the afternoon we made currant jelly and gooseberry preserves. I printed 5 pounds of butter.

July 22, 1886 Thursday
I had the headache all day but kept going. I put away 24 glasses of jelly and helped with the work; cut and made Edna a dress. Mrs. Tyree and Ollie were here.

July 23, 1886 Friday
Mrs. Braman was here to get berries. Ab. Robinson called in the evening. Six years ago today I first saw Hangman creek. One year ago my school closed at Waverly. Mark the changes since then.

July 24, 1886 Saturday
I helped Alice with the housework and did some baking. In the evening I took the hack and team and went after Eliza Thayer to work for Alice. Lewis and Nim came back to Waverly.

July 25, 1886 Sunday
I went with Mr. Thrall to the Rattler Run S.S. Bro. Moore came home with us. Lewis was here. In the afternoon we all went to S.S. and preaching at Waverly. In the evening we enjoyed some music. L. and I had a pleasant chat.

July 26, 1886 Monday
"A cool morning." Lewis and I picked raspberries until noon. Mrs. Tyree and Dollie came over to help with the berries. In the afternoon I cut the girl's aprons and sewed some. In the evening L. and I gathered berries until late.

July 27, 1886 Tuesday
I did not feel very well; but helped do up the work, mended L.'s gloves and cut Edna's hair. After dinner we went to school, called at Mr. Tyree's and Mr. Anderson's. I got a letter.

July 28, 1886 Wednesday
Nim came over and told me lots of news, and stayed until after dinner. The men were putting up hay. L. was gathering berries. I finished the girl's aprons and almost made May a dress.

July 29, 1886 Thursday
L. helped me wash. I sewed and practiced some in the afternoon. L. went home after supper and left me feeling bad. I had a big cry after I went to bed.

July 30, 1886 Friday
I was nearly sick. Mrs. Thayer and Mrs. Braman came after berries. Jesse
came over and eat his birthday dinner with us. L. came with him
and in the evening we gathered and L. went back to Waverly. Mr.
Richardson stayed over night here.

July 31, 1886 Saturday
I ironed and cleaned up the house. Mrs. Tyree and Dollie came after
berries. Lorenzo, Gilmore and Norman came. L. and I had a little
chat in the evening.

August 1, 1886 Sunday
L. and I did not have much time to chat until evening and then our visit
was not a very pleasant one but one that will ever be remembered. We
did not go to S.S. Jesse and Nim came over.

August 2, 1886 Monday
I gathered berries for two hours and came to the house with a head-ache.
In the afternoon I wrote two letters, rode Frisk to the P.O. and went
to see Mrs. Davies. Returned about dark.

August 3, 1886 Tuesday
I took Mr. Hay's hack and team and took Mrs. Thayer to Rockford
visiting. We had a pleasant time and I got home at sundown; found
Lewis here and in the evening we had a little visit.

August 4, 1886 Wednesday
I did not feel well but helped with the work and done a little sewing. In
the afternoon I did some writing and practiced some. Gathered some
raspberries for supper.

August 5, 1886 Thursday
Gilmore helped us and we put out a <u>big</u> washing. Mrs. Tyree called. I did
some writing and sprinkled the clothes to be ironed.

August 6, 1886 Friday
A very warm day. Mr. Hayes started his header. I ironed most all day. Ab.
Robinson called as he returned home from his school but "got left."

August 7, 1886 Saturday
I put things to right and cleaned up the house. In the afternoon Gilmore
went with me to the P.O. and Lewis came home with me. H. Hayes
called and gave us some apples.

August 8, 1886 Sunday
L. took Eliza, Alice, Edna, May and I to Rattler's Run to church. Also to

Waverly to S.S. in the afternoon. In the evening we enjoyed a little chat and a few raspberries.

August 9, 1886 Monday
As Eliza was not well I done up the work and kept house with Edna and Claude while Alice and Eliza went visiting. I cut out some sewing but did not sew very much. A lonesome day.

August 10, 1886 Tuesday
I picked raspberries until I had the headache. In the afternoon Lewis called and was nearly sick. I mended his gloves for him. And then sewed a little for myself. In the evening I milked three cows all alone.

August 11, 1886 Wednesday
I helped with the house work and sewed most all day – made little Jesse and Mamie each a white dress.

August 12, 1886 Thursday
Another wash day but I was not well enough to help much: it was very windy and the line broke and let the clothes in the dirt. Norman, Lewis and Jesse called. L. traded his mules off. In the evening we picked and ate some berries.

August 13, 1886 Friday
After helping with the other work I sprinkled the clothes and ironed the rest of the day. I was very tired. Gilmore came home late and brought me three letters which made me feel better but caused the tears to flow.

August 14, 1886 Saturday
I had a severe head ache and felt bad all day but Eliza was sick all week and I had to help with the work. I baked a big cake in the afternoon, went to see Mrs. Davis. Lorenzo came home with me and we found Jodie here. A pleasant surprise.

August 15, 1886 Sunday
I had a pleasant visit with Jodie and L. Lewis came and in the evening Thrall called. The boys went back to Kingston and took Jessie, Gilmore and Norman with them. Lewis and Nim stayed until the candle burned out.

The silver thimble Cora received on her 21st Birthday.
Held by Vera Zachow.

August 16, 1886 Monday

I am 21 years old today but ate my cake yesterday while the boys were
here to enjoy it with us. I didn't get any whipping but received a few
presents, a gold pen, a silver thimble, a mirror and cook book. I hope
to be happier when I am 42 than now. I went to the P.O. called at Mr.
Tryee's and Lewis came home with me. (lots of paint).

August 17, 1886 Tuesday

L. helped me milk the cows and put my pony on the grass. He stayed till
nearly noon. I cut out and basted some sewing. Mr. Richardson took
supper with us. After milking I went to water Frisk and he hurt me
and ran away from me.

August 18, 1886 Wednesday

The men-folks all being away during harvest I have to be milk-maid and
"chore boy" and what ever else I find to do.

August 20 1886 Friday

In the morning helped with the usual work. In the afternoon I harnessed
the team, took Edna and Mary with me in the hack and went to
Waverly. We called at Mr. Dashield's as we returned.

August 21, 1886 Saturday

After milking the cows I went to Mr. Dashield's after apples. On my
return found Ida here who told us of the death of Mrs. Davis' baby.
I made the shroud and did my Saturday's work, besides sweeping the
house all over and was very tired at night.

August 22, 1886 Sunday

I did not feel well all day. Mr. Thrall came and we went to the funeral on
horseback and from there to Spangle in the hack with Mr. Hays and
Eliza. After supper we enjoyed some singing.

August 23, 1886 Monday

Alice went to help Mrs. Davis and stayed over night. Eliza washed some.
I ripped and washed my worsted dress. Mr. Richardson called. In the

evening as I was watering Frisk Lewis came and helped me milk. After supper we had a chat which ended very unpleasantly.

August 24, 1886 Tuesday
I did not feel very well after spending a wakeful night but felt better after having a more pleasant talk with L. He went to see about the cattle, came back and stayed over night again. I did some sewing.

August 25, 1886 Wednesday
I commenced to make a dress for Edna and sewed most all day. In the evening L. went to the office and brought me some letters. After supper we went to the garden after melons.

August 26, 1886 Thursday
L. went to Cheney. I wrote three letters and in the afternoon went to Waverly after meat for the header crew. Came back, made a cake and went to Uncle Jack's after currents. They commenced heading here about 3 o'clock P.M.

August 27, 1886 Friday
I went to the field for corn and to the garden for melons. Then made some "moon-shine" to be eaten with Jim's birthday cake. L. came and brought my paintings. After dinner I sewed some. Ab. Robinson called.

August 28, 1886 Saturday
I did not get up until late; helped get dinner for the hands and in the afternoon finished Edna's dress and fixed the waist to my alpaca dress. Frisk got loose and I had quite a chase after him. Mr. Davis helped me catch him.

August 29, 1886 Sunday
I swept the rooms upstairs and front room, then studied my S.S. lesson and wrote a letter. L. came and we went to S.S. After returning we enjoyed eating melon until Mr. Dashiell came. L. stayed until 10.

August 30, 1886 Monday
They finished heading at Mr. Hay's. In the afternoon I harnessed the team and we all went to the field for a drive, then to the P.O., came back and got supper. I played and sang for the boys until I was tired and forgot to eat any supper.

August 31, 1886 Tuesday
After helping some with the work I got ready and went to Mrs. Davis' to get her to help me with my sewing. I stayed over night and had a nice visit, too.

September 1, 1886 Wednesday
I went to the store after some dress lining, then back to Mrs. Davis' and sewed on my green dress the rest of the day. We had fresh peaches for supper.

September 2, 1886 Thursday
At Mr. Davis' yet. Jeff called while we were eating breakfast. I sewed quite steady until 5 o'clock then saddled my cayuse and started for "Haysburg" via. of Waverly, but got no letters.

September 3, 1886 Friday
A <u>very</u> windy day. I finished my dress and in the evening took a walk with the children and took Frisk to water. Jeff called with his "dude" hat on.

Family with Thrashing Crew

September 4, 1886 Saturday
The house was almost full of dust after the hard wind. I swept and cleaned until I was tired. It was a cool day. As Alice and I were sitting by the fire sewing, something in the stove exploded and scared us.

September 5, 1886 Sunday
Mr. Cobb was here. I sang and played some. Jim did not go to S.S so I drove the team and we went in the hack. It rained on us as we came home. In the evening L. came and was nearly sick. I made him some pepper tea.

September 6, 1886 Monday

L. and I went after melons and picked goose-berries until noon. We rested a while then finished picking berries for this season and ate a melon, came to the house and helped Alice make some pickles.

September 7, 1886 Tuesday

Eliza was over at Layts so I helped Alice get breakfast and do the kitchen work. L. sat by the stove and shivered. In the afternoon we read some and I sewed on Mamie's dress but was quite sick for a while. L. went to Waverly.

September 8, 1886 Wednesday

I did not feel well enough to do much but sewed some and finished May's dress. In the afternoon did some writing. I went to bed early feeling very bad and cried myself to sleep.

September 9, 1886 Thursday

I felt some better and made me some under clothes but Alice did most of the machine work. In the evening wrote a letter and went with Alice and the children to get melons.

September 10,1886 Friday

After doing my part of the house work I drove the cows into the field and brought the horses to the barn. In the afternoon I helped Alice with some sewing. As I was bringing Frisk to water he threw me and made me lame.

September 11, 1886 Saturday

I did not feel well enough to do much. But sewed some and in the afternoon I rode Frisk and went to Mr. Thayers', stopped at town and got two letters so I came back feeling some better in body and in spirit.

September 12, 1886 Sunday

L. came before dinner and in the afternoon he drove the team and we went to S.S. in the hack. Came back got some tomatoes and melons. After supper we had music and quite a chat but parted in tears.

September 13, 1886 Monday

Mrs. Thayer came in her new hack, and spent the day with us. I felt very bad all day; had a severe head-ache and went to bed before dark but did not sleep very soon. I thought and cried until my head felt like it would pop open.

September 14, 1886 Tuesday

I did not get up till 9 o'clock but felt some better. I rote a letter to Emma and in the afternoon went to the "primary," cast my first vote, came back and helped get supper for the thrashing men.

October 20, 1886 Wednesday

We started about sun-up and nooned 6 miles from Okanogan. I rode with Gilmore till we got this side of the Lake then got on Frisk came on and overtook Nannie at Barber Creek at sundown, went on and found the folks glad to see us return.

October 21, 1886 Thursday

I felt very tired and had the headache all day. We stayed at Mr. Titchenal's until after dinner then went over to Jesse's place. The mice had been keeping house all summer and some got into the honey can. Phebe came with us.

October 22, 1886 Friday

At Jesse's place to keep house for him awhile. I spent most of the day cleaning and putting things to right but would have to work awhile and rest awhile. Phebe stayed until after dinner.

October 23, 1886 Saturday

Gilmore put up a shelf for me and I got things pretty well straightened. Phebe came over and brought us some milk and butter. In the evening I sewed some.

October 24. 1886 Sunday

Jesse and Gilmore went to hunt their horses and left me here alone until about noon. Lewis came back with them and after dinner we took a stroll and went up to the "old maid's" shanty and had a pleasant chat.

October 25, 1886 Monday

I rode Frisk and went with Jesse up to Nashland; we took dinner with Mrs. Jefferson, then went to Mrs. Nixon's and from there home about sundown. We met Mr. Peerpoint and had a very pleasant talk concerning politics.

October 26, 1886 Tuesday

I did not feel very well after my ride of about 25 miles and did not do any thing but the house work and wrote a letter. Jesse commenced plowing for me. Lewis was here to dinner and until dark.

October 27, 1886 Wednesday

I wrote another letter, made pies for dinner which cost a cat's life. Nannie came and stayed until next morning. After dinner I made yeast and baked lightbread. Jesse rode Frisk and went to the P.O. We had a little shower of rain in the morning.

October 28, 1886 Thursday
Mr. Wills called before I got the breakfast dishes washed. Gilmore helped wash until noon. Manford called and after dinner Gilmore went off with him. I finished my washing and was here alone until most dark.

October 29, 1886 Friday
I did not feel very well so Gilmore helped me mop. Lewis came and brought us some fresh pork and some butter. I made watermelon preserves and went home with Lewis after some milk and the irons.

October 30, 1886 Saturday
After cleaning the house I swept the door-yard and ironed before dinner. I mended the cloths and put them away, then baked my light-bread and after supper made Jesse a pair of socks. L. called as he came from the P.O. but no letter for me.

October 31, 1886 Sunday
We went to Mrs. Titchenal's and help eat her birthday dinner. Manford and Gip came about noon. Jesse went with Mr. T. and Norman after some venison. We had a pleasant visit and returned by moonlight. I rode Frisk and Jesse walked.

November 1, 1886 Monday
I worked in the yard a while then mended a rug. Mr. Hodges called. After dinner I mended Jesse's vest, made him a pair of mittens. I was here alone most all day and was a little lonesome. Lewis was here to supper.

November 2, 1886 Tuesday
ELECTION DAY! I went to a little log school house and cast my first vote. Jesse took me and Mr. and Mrs. Titchenal in the spring wagon.

November 3, 1886 Wednesday
After doing the usual work I sewed a while and was reading old letters when L. came by to go to the P.O. Gilmore came back from the Coulee about 3 P.M. Jesse hauled wood, Phebe was here. L. was here to supper but I got no letter. A very windy day.

November 4, 1886 Thursday
A nice sunny day. Gilmore and Jesse hauled wood. I washed, wrote a letter and took it over to Norman to mail at Spokane. I stayed until

after dinner at Mr. T.s', came home and found the cat's keeping house. I got supper and the boys came about sundown.

November 5, 1886 Friday
I papered, scrubbed the floor and ironed. The boys came with their wood about 4 o'clock, then I got supper: in the evening I mended the clothes and put them away.

November 6, 1886 Saturday
I swept the yard. Mr. Titchenal was here to dinner. L. called as he went to the mill. Mr. T. and Manford were here to supper and stayed until late. I did not feel very well.

November 7, 1886 Sunday
Jesse went to the coulee. Lewis and Nannie were here. Mr. Nash called. Gilmore went to the Lake and Manford came home. He brought me a letter which caused me to feel bad. L. Stayed over night.

November 8, 1886 Monday
L. stayed until nearly noon. I did some baking for the boys to go to Spokane. In the evening I wrote a letter to Alice. Was very tired.

CERTIFICATE OF ELECTION.

DOUGLAS COUNTY.

Territory of Washington, } ss.

COUNTY OF DOUGLAS.

To _L. Titchenal_

This Certifies, That at the general election held in Douglas County. Washington Territory, on the _second day of November A.D._ '86, you were duly elected _Constable of Bracken Precinct of said County in said Territory_ for the term of two years.

In Witness Whereof, I have hereunto set my hand and affixed my official seal, this _ninth_ day of _November A.D._ 188 6.

B. L. Martin

Auditor Douglas County.

November 9, 1886 Tuesday
I got up with a head-ache. The boys started about 10 o'clock. I washed and cleaned the house and went over to Mr. Titchenal's to stay while they were gone.

November 10, 1886 Wednesday

I came back over to Jesse's after some things and wrote a letter while
there. I went back to Mr. Titchenal's and sent my letter by Mr. Brown
– the mail carrier. He and Mr. Godlove ate dinner there.

November 19, 1886 Friday

I sewed some and dressed myself in a becoming costume very much to
the amusement of Mrs. T. and the girls. Nannie and Phebe went after
Gracie Hughes.

November 20, 1886 Saturday

I was suffering with a sore finger and could not do anything but read. I
took a stroll up the canyon alone and cut my name in a tree near the
wood road.

November 21, 1886 Sunday

Eight inches of snow had fallen the night before and it was a cold,
gloomy day. I spent a part of the day in reading. In the evening I got a
letter which made me feel some better.

November 22, 1886 Monday

I rode Frisk and took Gracie Hughs home, came back by Jesse's then
went on over to Mr. Titchenal's. It was a very cold day.

November 23, 1886 Tuesday

I read some and helped Mrs. Titchenal cut carpet rags.

November 24, 1886 Wednesday

I rode Frisk and went alone to the P.O. The mail was late so I stayed over
night with Mrs. Corbaley and had a very pleasant visit. A Chinook
wind took some of the snow off.

November 25, 1886 Thursday

A nice day. I went to the P.O. and got only one letter and came back to
Mrs. Titchenal's. They were washing. I got there at 11 o'clock.

November 26, 1886 Friday

My finger was so sore I could not do anything but watch Nannie make
hair flowers. Manford was there about half the day.

November 27, 1886 Saturday

My finger was better and I made two garments for the men folks and
read some.

November 28, 1886 Sunday

John could not find the horses so I walked over to Jesse's place and wrote
two letters.

December 3, 1886 Friday
I was very restless until Nannie, Phebe and I started for a ride. Nannie got hurt. After supper us girls listened until we heard the wagons, then went to meet the boys as they returned. I walked over to Jesse's about 8 o'clock.

December 4, 1886 Saturday
At Jesse's again. Jesse and Emma were nearly sick. I walked over to Mr. Titchenal's but rode back with L. as he brought my organ and we soon enjoyed some music. I got dinner and L. and Nannie stayed awhile.

December 5, 1886 Sunday
I had breakfast ready before Jesse and Emma got up. Manford called at the door. I had a severe headache all day and was taking a quiet stroll when L. came. Gilmore came from the coulee in the evening.

December 6, 1886 Monday
Gilmore packed his things and went to the coulee to remain a while. Emma and I did a big washing but it was not a very nice day to dry clothes. I did not feel very well and retired early.

December 7, 1886 Tuesday
We found the ground covered with snow but it was all gone before night. Emma and I papered the cabin. In the evening I did some writing.

December 8, 1886 Wednesday
I did not feel very well but got some sewing ready for the machine and got dinner. Emma and I had a real good visit and she told me lots of news about the Missourians.

December 9, 1886 Thursday
After helping with the work I took some sewing and walked over to Mrs. Titchenal's but only stayed a short time. Mr. and Mrs. Will spent the evening with us.

December 10, 1886 Friday
I did not do much of importance. In the evening Emma and I were talking of the past and I was crying bitterly when Jesse and Norman came. Norman spent the evening.

December 12, 1886 Sunday
I read some and was practicing when L. came. In the evening we enjoyed some music and L. and I also enjoyed a pleasant visit which afterwards caused some sorrow and much thinking.

December 13, 1886 Monday

A nice day. Jesse and Emma went to Okanogan and left me alone but
Phebe and Martha soon came and spent the day. I wrote a letter and
ripped up an old dress to make over. I read some after supper.

December 14, 1886 Tuesday

We all walked over to Mr. T.'s. Jesse went to the coulee. Emma and I
spent the day there. L. and Phebe came home with us. Phebe stayed
all night. L. and I had quite a chat in the moonlight and I gave vent
to tears before sleeping.

December 15, 1886 Wednesday

L. called as he was going to the mill just as I finished a letter. I then did
some sewing. Nannie called as she came from Mr. James'. Jesse didn't
come home from the coulee. E. and I stayed alone.

December 16, 1886 Thursday

Nannie came and brought us some meat. I got some beef from Manford.
I did some sewing. Jesse came home from the coulee. L. spent the
evening here and brought us invitations to the Christmas <u>ball</u>. We
enjoyed some music.

December 17, 1886 Friday

Jesse went to the coulee again to take a cow to Gilmore. Mr. T.'s folks
went after their hogs so Emma and I went over and stayed over night
there; I learned to knit and helped milk the cows.

December 18, 1886 Saturday

At Mr. Titchenal's I read some. L. shaved his mustache off and he
and I had a visit which did me lots of good and also relieved him.
After supper we came home. I rode Frisk. In the evening did some
mending.

December 19, 1886 Sunday

I helped do up the work. L. came by in the wagon and we all went to the
Lake to church, came back to Jesse's for dinner. E. had the headache.
L. and I enjoyed a social visit but was not agreeable with all. I went to
bed early.

December 20, 1886 Monday

A very pleasant day but I did not enjoy it very well. I sewed most all day,
spent some time in thinking and in the evening did some writing. I
went to bed feeling bad and cried myself to sleep.

December 21. 1886 Tuesday
I had a slight headache but said nothing about it as there was a big wash to be done. Manford spent the evening here. I sewed some.

December 22, 1886 Wednesday
Mr. Will called before breakfast. Jesse went hunting with him. Emma and I mopped the floor. I walked and went to Mr. T.'s to make Nannie's dress and got it all cut before supper.

December 23, 1886 Thursday
At Mr. Titchenal's. Mr. Norton's folks moved to Lewis's house. I sewed on Nannie's dress but did not get it finished so stayed overnight there again.

December 24, 1886 Friday
I sewed until nearly noon then rode Frisk and went to Jesse's. He shingled my hair. I made Lewis a watch-pocket for his Christmas present. In the evening we popped some corn and Jesse and Emma and I spent a pleasant Christmas eve together.

December 25, 1886 Saturday
A very pleasant day. E. and I did some baking. Mr. and Mrs. Titchenal and John took dinner with us. I prepared a lot of presents for the tree. Norman came by in the bob-sled and we went to the Christmas tree at the Lake and back to Mr. Titchenal's.

December 26, 1886 Sunday
It stormed all day. Mr. Horing went to Okanogan and got drunk, came back to Mr. T.'s and he and Rachel stayed over night there again. We spent the evening singing and chatting and retired at 10:30 o'clock.

December 27, 1886 Monday
A more pleasant day. Mr. Horing and Rachel went home. I made me a dress skirt and after supper Norman brought me home in the sled. I enjoyed my visit there. L. was gone to the Columbia river.

December 28, 1886 Tuesday
I sprinkled the clothes and did a big ironing. Jesse spent the evening at Mr. Payne's. Emma and I wrote some letters. After I went to bed I got to thinking and gave vent to a few tears.

December 29, 1886 Wednesday
Emma was not very well so I did most of the house work, wrote a big letter and sewed some. In the evening I read some old letter and did some writing.

Letter Register

Name	Received	Answered
L. E. Roberson	Apr. 3	Apr. 6
L. E. Roberson	Apr. 14	Apr. 17
A. L. Robinson	Apr. 17	Apr. 20
J. Johnson	Apr. 22	Apr. 24
Alice Hays	Apr. 22	Apr. 26
L. E. R.	Apr. 22	Apr. 27
Mrs. Merriman	Apr. 29	May 7
Emma	Apr. 29	May 1
L. E. R.	Apr. 29	May 4
Katie Plaster	May 6	May 15
Albert Johnson	May 6	May 13
Minnie & F.	May 6	May15
L. E. R.	May 12	May 15
Alice Hays	May 12	May 15
Emma	May 12	May 15
A. Robinson	May 12	May 26
W. Johnson	May 6	May 14
L. E. R.	May 19	May 26
Alice Hays	May 27	June 1
L.E. R.	May 27	June 2

William Rodney Johnson and Nancy Adaline Beattie

MISCELLANEOUS.

John M. Johnson was born Nov 16th 1851
Ann Eliza Andrews.. ... June 2nd 1849.

William Rodney Johnson
(father of John M-)
was born Aug. 18" 1824
Nancy Adaline Beattie
(mother of John M)
was born Feb. 16" 1834

William Rodney Johnson
and Nancy Adaline Beattie
were married Jan 1- 1851

Probate Document Naming Heirs
for William Rodney Johnson
Cora's Father

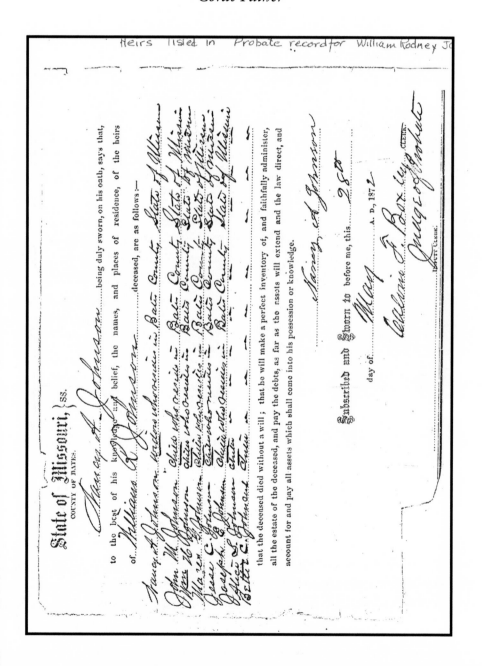

Heirs listed in Probate record for William Rodney J

Letter Declaring Nancy Johnson
Administrator
Cora's Mother

Bond

State of Missouri
County of Bates } sct

Know all men by these presents That we Nancy A. Johnson as principal and Moses Johnson and James H. Johnson as securities acknowledge ourselves indebted to the State of Missouri in the sum of Six Thousand dollars. for the payment of which we bind ourselves— our heirs Executors and administrators. Jointly severally and firmly by these presents. Given under our hands and seals this 28th day of May AD 1872

The conditions of the above Bond is such that if the said Nancy A. Johnson— as administratrix of the Estate of William R Johnson. deceased shall faithfully administer said Estate. account for and pay and deliver all money and property of said Estate and perform all other things touching said administration required by Law. or the order or decree of any Court having Juris= diction. then the above Bond to be void. otherwise to remain in force

Nancy A Johnson {Seal}

Moses Johnson {Seal}

James H Johnson {Seal}

Deaths as Recorded in the Johnson Family Bible

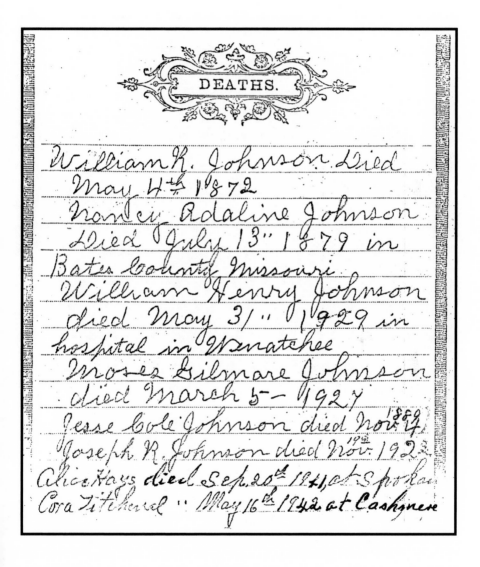

DEATHS.

William R. Johnson Died
May 4th 1872
Nancy Adaline Johnson
Died July 13" 1879 in
Bates County Missouri
William Henry Johnson
died May 31" 1929 in
hospital in Wenatchee
Moses Gilmare Johnson
died March 5 - 1927
Jesse Cole Johnson died Nov 24 1889
Joseph R. Johnson died Nov. 1923
Alice Hays died Sep 20th 1941, at Spokan
Cora Titchenel " May 16th 1942 at Cashmere

Births as Recorded in the Johnson Family Bible

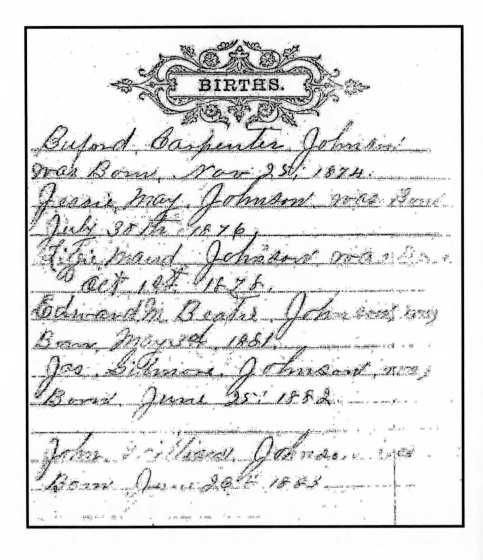

Sarah Alice Johnson Hay's
Family Tree

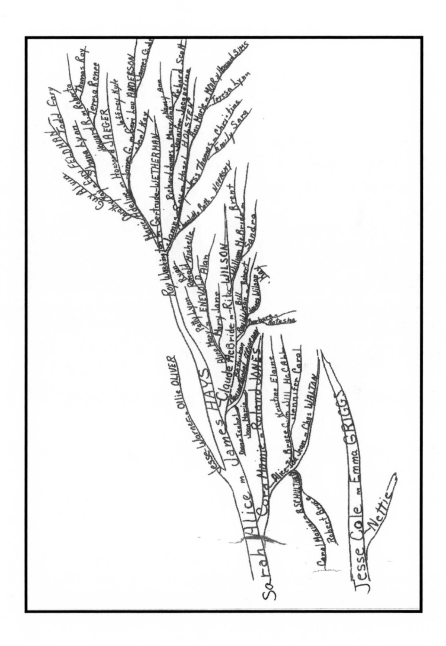

Betty Cora Johnson Titchenal's
Family Tree

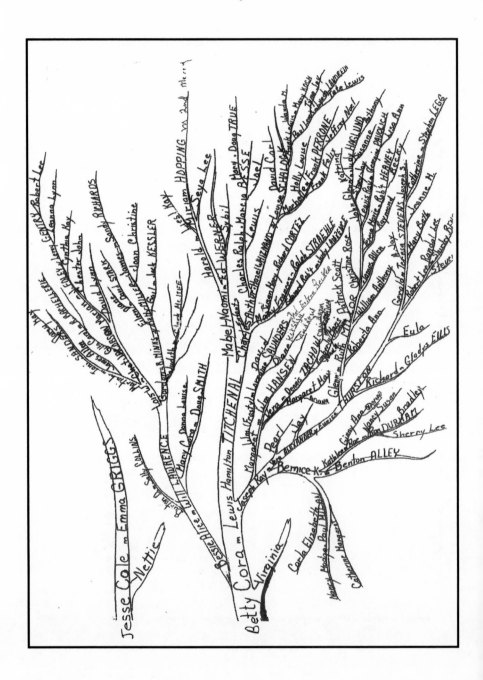

Cora Johnson's Brothers

Jesse Cole

William Henry

Joseph Rodney

John Martin

Moses Gilmore

Cora Johnson's Story
1887 Diary

January 1, 1887 Saturday

Stopping with Jesse and Emma in their little log cabin, with but one
room downstairs and one above with no window upstairs. But that
room served for my bedroom and was also used for a store room and
a closet. The snow was about twelve inches deep. I did not feel very
bright to enter upon the duties of a new year. Emma was sick and just
as I finished the morning work, Lewis came, just getting home from
the river and had laid out over night. I got him something to eat, then
Jesse and I went to Mrs. Payne's and enjoyed a nice dinner. Manford
spent the evening with us.

January 2, 1887 Sunday

I had a severe headache all day, commenced to read the new testament
through. Lewis called. I played some on my organ and sang some.

January 3, 1887 Monday

I was nearly sick all day, but sewed some and all went over to Mr.
Titchenal's in their sled and stayed over night.

January 4, 1887 Tuesday

I sewed some on the machine. Went to Mr. Norton's and back to Mr. T's
and was real sick for a while. We stayed there again overnight.

January 5, 1887 Wednesday

Le- brought us home in the sled and stayed all day. I mended his
overcoat. Jesse and Emma went to Mrs. Payne's. I retired early.

January 6, 1887 Thursday

I sewed most all day. In the evening. Gilmore came from the coulee.
Norman came and spent the evening and we had some pop-corn.

January 7, 1887 Friday

I helped mop the floor, wrote a letter to Alice and sewed some. Jesse went
to the post office and brought me two letters. Le – and Nannie spent
the evening here.

January 8, 1887 Saturday

I helped with the morning work and papered a part of the cabin, then
did some mending. Manford called and went with Gilmore to
Okanogan. They bought Emma and I some handsome valentines

which afforded us much fun. They spent the evening here and we enjoyed some music. Gilmore went home with Manford.

January 9, 1887 Sunday
Gilmore and Manford came in their new sled. J. and E. went to Mr. T's. Norman and Nannie came home with them. In the evening, L. and I went sleigh riding. Came back and enjoyed some music.

January10, 1887 Monday
Emma and I washed. In the evening I went with Gilmore over to Mr. Titchenal's. We spent a pleasant evening and stayed over night.

January 11, 1887 Tuesday
We came back to Jesse's. I wrote two letters and went to an oyster supper with Mr. Titchenal's young folks to Mr. Corbaley's. Had a very pleasant time.

January 12, 1887 Wednesday
Arrived at Mr. T's a little before sunrise, a little sleepy and awful cold. Gilmore went back to the coulee. In the evening Le and I went sleigh riding. Had a good time and I came home a little sleepy.

January 13, 1887 Thursday
I did not get up very early nor feel very well. I commenced to make my quilt but felt to bad to sew much and retired early and cried myself to sleep.

January 14, 1887 Friday
I was nearly sick but sewed all day. Jesse was helping Mr. T's folks with their cellar. Emma went over there too so I was alone awhile and read some.

January 15, 1887 Saturday
I sewed on my quilt all day. Le- came to get Jesse to cut his hair and we had a chat while Jesse and Emma went up to Mr. Will's.

Memoranda
I was not enjoying life very much at this time and was told of some things which were very unpleasant to hear.

January 16, 1887 Sunday
We went to church at the lake with Manford Payne, heard a good sermon. We went to Mr. Barnhart's to dinner, spent the evening at Mrs. Payne's. M came home with me.

January 17, 1887 Monday
I wrote two big letters and sewed some. Mr. Christinson called. Jesse went to the mountain with Lewis.

January 18, 1887 Tuesday
I sewed all day and finished my quilt. I was lonesome too. L spent the evening here. Jesse went hunting and Emma was sick.

January 19, 1887 Wednesday
I helped with the morning work, wrote another letter and went over to Mr. T's. It was Nannie's birthday. She was seventeen. I stayed over night.

January 20, 1887 Thursday
I ironed some shirts and collars and helped Nannie make Nim's birthday cake. Jesse and Emma came and we all ate and laughed until we had the "heart burn". Then we wrote Nim a letter.

January 21, 1887 Friday
Jesse commenced to dig my well. Emma and I came home and I read and practiced some. Mr. Will and Manford spent the evening here.

January 22, 1887 Saturday
I cleaned the house upstairs and down. I did some mending and a little writing. In the evening I read some, took a bath and retired.

Memoranda
I was not feeling very well but the time was spent a little more pleasantly than the week before was.

January 23, 1887 Sunday
A nice day, no snow. I spent some time in reading. Manford called. I played some for him. L. was here and I played for him too.

Jan. 24, 1887 Monday
Manford called on his way to the coulee. Mrs. T , L, Nannie, Pheobe were here. I cut some carpet rags. In the evening I wrote a letter and played some.

January 25, 1887 Tuesday
A very windy day. I did some writing. Then Emma and I went over to Mr. Titchenal's. Jesse was helping them on the new house and we stayed overnight.

January 26, 1887 Wednesday
I read and sang some. We came home about noon. Jesse went to the post

office and did not come back so Emma and I were here alone. I was reading, she was writing.

January 27, 1887 Thursday
A very disagreeable day, so Jesse did not come home until night. I cut carpet rags all day. Manford was here a few minutes in the evening. I read till late.

January 28, 1887 Friday
Jesse carried water for me and I washed. Mr. Norton called. I sewed carpet rags awhile, read some and went to bed feeling bad so gave vent to a few tears.

January 29, 1887 Saturday
I sewed two pounds of carpet rags. Manford came and we sang some for him. I walked to Mr. T's and L. came back with me. Jesse was quite sick for awhile.

January 30, 1887 Sunday
All sorts of a day with some snow. Mr. Will and Manford came and we all sang awhile. I was nearly sick and was in bed most of the day. L. came and we took a stroll and I felt better.

January 31, 1887 Monday
I was not feeling very well, but cut out my green 'Christmas' dress and got it ready for the machine. We spent the evening at Mrs. Payne's. M. came home with me.

February 1, 1887 Tuesday
The coldest day we have had this winter. I did some writing and in the evening I read until bedtime.

February 2, 1887 Wednesday
I sewed carpet rags awhile. Manford came and brought us some mail. I read some and in the evening Manford and Mrs. Will came. M helped me sew carpet rags. Then we sang some.

February 3, 1887 Thursday
I finished all of the carpet rags I had, then practiced awhile on some new pieces of music. In the evening we talked and I wrote a letter.

February 4, 1887 Friday
L. was here and helped me make the plating for my dress. I got dinner, sang and played some but had a severe headache in the evening.

February 5, 1887 Saturday
After helping with the housework, I took a bath. L. came by and we went

sleigh riding, which I enjoyed very much as well as a pleasant and profitable visit. I went to Mr. Titchenal's and stayed over night.

Memoranda

The weather was very cold all week.

February 6, 1887 Sunday
A pleasant day. I read some, then L. and I took a stroll. After dinner I sang several songs and stayed over night at Mr. T.'s again.

February 7, 1887 Monday
I made my new dress. L. went to the mill. Mr. Fitch spent the day at Mr. Titchenal's. I stayed there another night.

February 8, 1887 Tuesday
I helped with the morning work, then Nannie and I went up to the new house. L brought me home. I wrote a letter, which caused me to feel bad.

February 9, 1887 Wednesday
I was nearly sick so did some writing. In the evening Manford brought us some mail. I played and sang some for him

February 10, 1887 Thursday
I was too miserable for any use. I wrote two letters, read some and burned a few. Jesse went to the mill with Lewis. I practiced and read awhile.

February 11, 1887 Friday
Jesse and Emma went over to Mr. Titchenal's. I did not feel well enough to go. I wrote a letter and was reading over old letters when L came. We enjoyed a good visit and went sleigh riding. Nannie came home with J and E.

February 12, 1887 Saturday
I was not feeling any better but did my share of the housework and some mending. Mrs. Payne called. I cleaned out my trunk and did some writing.

Memoranda
I was very miserable all week and did not do much but think with a few tears to relieve me occasionally.

February 13, 1887 Sunday
Jesse, Emma and I went to preaching at the lake with Manford, to Mr. Barnhart's for dinner but did not enjoy the visit very much. Lewis and

Nannie spent the evening with us and I went home with them.

February 14, 1887 Monday
I bound Norman's coat. In the evening Lewis, Nannie, John, Phebe and I went coasting. I stayed overnight.

February 15, 1887 Tuesday
I cut Lewis's coat off and fixed it for him. Jesse and Emma were there. Phebe and I went up to the new house; in the evening "us children" went coasting.

February 16, 1887 Wednesday
I helped with the morning work, then L. and I went to the P. O. in his "new sleigh," came back to Jesse's. I got our dinner, then played and sang. L spent the evening here.

February 17, 1887 Thursday
I mopped the floor and did some mending. Emma went to the P. O. with Mrs. Payne and Mrs. Will. Jesse went to the mill with Lewis. Nannie was here. Mrs. Barnhart and Will, Manford, Mr. and Mrs. Will spent the evening here. We enjoyed some music.

February 18, 1887 Friday
I did some ironing and got some dinner. I sang and played until my neck was stiff, then I took a stroll all alone. Came back and read some and retired early.

February 19, 1887 Saturday
After helping with the usual housework, I did some writing and read over "Jem's" old letters which called back to memory the "days of yore". Manford called.

Memoranda
The weather was nice all week with from 2 to 3 inches of snow. I felt real well most all week, but not do much work.

February 20, 1887 Sunday
It snowed nearly all day. I read 333 verses in the Bible. Lewis and Nannie were here. I got dinner, played and sang some; in the evening L. and I took a sleigh ride.

February 21, 1887 Monday
A very nice day but cloudy. I washed some and cut out some sewing and got it ready for the machine. I read a while, retired early and gave vent to tears.

February 22, 1887 Tuesday
After helping with the housework, I did my ironing and wrote a letter.
I spent the rest of the day in reading over old letters and I burned
several.

February 23, 1887 Wednseday
A snowy day. Lewis and his Mother spent the day here. L. and I took
a sleigh ride. Manford and Mr. Owens spent the evening here. We
enjoyed some music.

February 24, 1887 Thursday
Manford and Jesse took my organ to the lake. I baked a cake, got ready
and went with Manford to a sociable at Mr. Barnhart's. Enjoyed lots
of music and a nice supper.

February 25, 1887 Friday
We got home about daylight and slept awhile, but I felt too miserable for
any use. Lewis and Phebe came. I went home with them.

February 26, 1887 Saturday
I spent a very pleasant day at Mr. Titchenal's and enjoyed a nice birthday
dinner. I fixed Nannies cloak for her. Gilmore came from the coulee.
I stayed over night at Mr. Titchenals. The Chinook wind blew all day
and it rained some in the evening. The snow is fast leaving.

February 27, 1887 Sunday
I was nearly sick all day but went to preaching at the lake with L. Back to
Mr. T's and in the evening L. brought me back to Jesse's.

February 28, 1887 Monday
A nice warm day, but I was too miserable to enjoy it. After helping with
the morning work I finished reading the book downgrade, played
some, wrote a letter; had a big cry.

March 1, 1887 Tuesday
I felt lots better and wrote two letters. Gilmore went back to the coulee.
Manford and Mr. Owens spent the evening with us.

March 2, 1887 Wednesday
I went to Mrs. Payne's and came back and did some mending and got
dinner. Mr. Norton called. I read and played some and we chatted
then had prayer and retired early.

March 3, 1887 Thursday
I wrote to Edna. Emma and I spent the day at Mrs. Payne's. They were
building their new house. Manford, Charlie and Mr. Owens spent the

evening with us.

March 4, 1887 Friday
I went over to Mr. T's and made my bonnet. Jim Owens was there. Lewis came home with me and spent the evening.

March 5, 1887 Saturday
I mopped the floor and sewed some. Emma and I entered into conversation which caused me to give vent to some burning tears. Manford and Mr. Owens spent the evening again. I was very miserable all week and cried a little more than usual. The weather was very pleasant all week.

March 6, 1887 Sunday
A beautiful day but windy. Mr. and Mrs. Norton and Lewis spent the day with us. In the evening L and I enjoyed a horseback ride and also a pleasant visit.

March 7, 1887 Monday
I was nearly sick but went to Okanogan with Manford and Mrs. Payne. We took dinner at Mrs. Barnhart's and did not get home until dark. Mr. Titch stayed overnight here.

March 8, 1887 Tuesday
A rainy morning. Mr. Titch stayed a while. I sewed some and wrote a letter. Mr. Owens and Manford were here and I had a good talk with Manford. Lewis and Norman called.

March 9, 1887 Wednesday
Manford and his brother called to say good-bye. I wrote a letter and after dinner went to Mrs. Payne's. Nannie called. Mr. Wills spent the evening with us.

March 10, 1887 Thursday
I cleaned the house upstairs and down, went to Mrs. Payne's after milk and to take their mail. Gilmore came up from the coulee to stay.

March 11, 1887 Friday
I washed mine and Gil's clothes and mopped and painted some book marks. Then mended our clothes and put them away. Emma and I went to Mrs. Titchenal's.

March 12, 1887 Saturday
Came home and made some cookies. Then I mended Gilmore's clothes and read some. I helped get supper.

Memoranda

Jesse and the Titchenal boys made their shingles. The weather was
pleasant and I felt pretty well and did not cry all week.

March 13, 1887 Sunday

I got breakfast and cleaned up the house alone. I got ready and went to
church. Horse back with L., came back to Jesse's, sang some, then
went home with L.

March 14, 1887 Monday

Started from Mr. Titchenal's on Frisk. Came by Jesse's and Gilmore went
with me to Mr. Snow's. I called to see Mrs. Nixon, then to see about a
school and to Okanogan and back to Jesse's. Nearly sick.

March 15, 1887 Tuesday

I did not feel very well or do anything except write two letters. I laid
down to read some and woke up real sick and was sick all night.

March 16, 1887 Wednesday

I felt some better and helped with the morning work and wrote a letter.
Nannie spent the afternoon here and L. was here to supper. I took a
big cry.

March 17, 1887 Thursday

I rode Frisk and went to Okanogan, took dinner at Mr. Barnhart's and
called on Mrs. Wallace; rained on me all the way home. The boys
were on the mountain. Nannie stayed with us.

March 18, 1887 Friday

Phebe brought Frisk and Laura and we all went to Mr. Titchenal's. I
sewed some and stayed there over night.

March 19, 1887 Saturday

I helped with the morning work then made two aprons and gave Nannie
one. I stayed there again that night.

Memoranda

I rode about 45 miles on horseback and did not feel very well the
remainder of the week.

March 20, 1887 Sunday

At Mr. T's I read some, then L. and I walked up to the new house for a
visit. In the evening we walked over to Jesse's.

March 21, 1887 Monday

I helped Emma with the morning work and sewed nearly all of the day.

In the evening we all went to Mr. T's and "worked" the new horse.

March 22, 1887 Tuesday
Gilmore helped Lewis build fence; Emma went with Jesse to the mill. I did some writing. Went to Mrs. Payne's, came home and got supper.

March 23, 1887 Wednesday
Emma and I rode Laura to Mr. Titchenal's. I worked a pair of pillow shams for Mrs. James and trimmed a hat for Nannie. I stayed all night there and we had popcorn.

March 24, 1887 Thursday
Mr. Norton started to Spokane. I had a severe headache most all day and did not do much. I cut Lewis' hair and walked to Jesse's. I retired early.

March 25, 1887 Friday
I did not get up until after breakfast and was miserable all day. I wrote a letter and mended some of Gilmore's clothes.

March 26, 1887 Saturday
I felt some better and helped Emma with the housework and did some mending.

Memoranda
We were receiving some of the calm March winds and the nights are cold.

March 27, 1887 Sunday
A nice day. I rode Snip and went with L. to preaching at the lake. Nannie spent the afternoon with us at Jesse's. Gilmore went home with her.

March 28, 1887 Monday
I walked over to Mr. T's and sewed all day on Nannie's gingham dress. It rained, so I couldn't come home.

March 29, 1887 Tuesday
I rode "Bragg" home. L. came with me and stayed awhile. I sewed some. Emma told me some news, which caused me to shed some bitter tears.

March 30, 1887 Wednesday
Emma and I did a big washing. I ironed some and sewed a little. I was very tired and retired early.

March 31, 1887 Thursday
I mended Gil's clothes and got things ready for him to go back to Snake River. Mr. Kenney was here to dinner. Nannie was here in the afternoon.

April 1, 1887 Friday
A very windy day. Gilmore started away to work for Mr. Hughs. I ironed nearly all day. Emma was taken sick.

April 2, 1887 Saturday
Another windy day. I cleaned the house all over and after dinner went to Okanogan with L. We called at Mr. Barnhart's and came home by moon light. I was very tired and cold.

Memoranda
I weighed 138 pounds

April 3, 1887 Sunday
A nice day. Emma was better. Mrs. Titchenal and Lewis were here to dine. Mr. and Mrs. Will called. L and I took a stroll and had quite a chat.

April 4, 1887 Monday
After I finished morning work I spent some time in writing and sewed a little. Nannie T- came and brought us the Okanogan mail.

April 5, 1887 Tuesday
I did the housework and walked to Mr. T's and back. Wrote a letter and went to Mrs. Payne's after milk. Came back and got supper. L. spent the evening here.

April 6, 1887 Wednesday
Went to Mr. T's after a horse to ride to the post office. Called at Mr. Corbley's and at Mrs. Jefferson's. I waited late for the mail and got home about dark. Got supper and made light bread. I was real tired.

April 7, 1887 Thursday
I went to Mr. T's to do some sewing: just after dinner Johnny Payne came after me so I went home. Mrs. Luber, Mrs. Hayes and Mrs. Cox were at Jesse's.

April 8, 1887 Friday
Jesse worked for Lewis so Emma and I spent the day at Mr. Titchenals. I finished Nannie's dress and fixed Mrs. T's dress: after supper we came home.

April 9, 1887 Saturday
I did the housework and some baking. In the afternoon I read some, swept the yard and got supper.

Memoranda

Emma was not well so I did the housework all week and was feeling lots better than I had for some time.

April 10, 1887 Sunday

Easter Sunday and a very lonesome one. Rained all day. I did the housework, read some and played some. L called in the evening.

April 11, 1887 Monday

After doing the morning work, I went to Mr. Titchenal's to do some sewing. I rode "Old Gray" and went to Mrs. Norman's for a dress pattern and cut and fit Mrs. T's dress. I stayed all night.

April 12, 1887 Tuesday

I sewed on Mrs. T's calico dress and cut out her brown worsted. Us girls went up to the new house and stayed awhile.

April 13, 1887 Wednesday

Nannie and I went to Okanogan on horseback, came back to Jesse's and sewed some. I had a severe headache. I retired early and gave vent to some big tears.

April 14, 1887 Thursday

Jesse and Emma went to Mr. Titchenal's. I did the morning work. Phebe came after me on "Old Gray". Mr. Will brought the mail. We stayed all night at Mr. T's.

April 15, 1887 Friday

I finished Mrs. T's calico dress and mended her old one and made a dress skirt for Phebe. Mr. Smith was there. We came home in the evening.

April 16, 1887 Saturday

I cleaned the house and sewed a little. L. was here to dinner and in the afternoon they moved my house. L. and I had quite a chat there.

Memoranda

Windy most all week. I was feeling pretty well most all of the time but had the headache Saturday.

April 17, 1887 Sunday

A nice day with some wind. I went to Mr. T's in the afternoon. L. and I went to the new house where we enjoyed a visit long to be remembered.

April 18, 1887 Monday

I walked home and Emma and I washed. I was nearly sick too and after dinner rested and slept a little. I got supper and L. spent the evening with us.

April 19, 1887 Tuesday
I did not get up very early and felt bad all day, but helped with the work and ironed my clothes. Jesse went to look for Gilmore's horses. Nannie stayed overnight with us.

April 20, 1887 Wednesday
I finished working an apron for Alice: borrowed John Payne's pony and went to the post office. Called at Mr. Corbley's and L. came back with me. He and Mrs. Norton were here to supper.

April 21, 1887 Thursday
I wrote 2 letters, then L. came after shingle bolts and I went home with him. In the afternoon we all went up to the new house and I went back feeling bad.

April 22, 1887 Friday
I had a sore finger and was feeling very miserable. I came home on the wagon with L. as he went to the mill. In the afternoon I read old letters and had a fever and headache.

April 23, 1887 Saturday
Was feeling lots better. Washed some and spent the rest of the day in getting ready for our trip to Spokane. L and Jesse took my organ to Mr. T's. Mr. Redfield called.

Memoranda
We enjoyed nice weather all week but had our share of wind and a nice rain Wednesday night.

April 24, 1887 Sunday
I helped do the morning work, then read a little. L came by and we went to preaching then to Mr. T's. We enjoyed some music. L and I had quite a talk but not a very pleasant one.

April 25, 1887 Monday
I bade Mr. T's folks good-bye and rode "Bauly" to Jesse's, got ready and we started for Spokane Co. Traveled 28 miles and camped in Moses Coulee.

April 26, 1887 Tuesday
We started early the next morning, ate dinner on the coulee hill and camped at the "Blind" spring a little before sundown. Windy and cold all day.

April 27, 1887 Wednesday

Started a little after sunrise and reached Wilson Creek at half past ten o'clock. We ate dinner out on the prairie in the wind and camped 15 miles from Cottonwood.

April 28, 1887 Thursday

Emma walked quite a ways. We met Mr. and Mrs. Will and reached Cottonwood at noon. Camped at "Caps Post Office" and I went after some milk.

April 29, 1887 Friday

Windy and cold again. We took dinner at Mr. Merriman's and had quite a visit there. Came on by Marshall and camped a little this side of there.

April 30, 1887 Saturday

I walked a ways and it snowed on us for some time. We took dinner at Spangle then went on and stopped to see Mrs. Davies a while. She was very sick. Emma stayed overnight there. Jesse and I went on to Mr. Hayes. I met Mr. Thayer's folks at the schoolhouse and found all glad to see me. I stood the trip very well but was very tired.

May 1, 1887 Sunday

A rainy, disagreeable day. I read some and in the afternoon we all went to S. S. at Waverly. Only a few there but we had a good school. I wore Alice's dress.

May 2, 1887 Monday

At Mr. Hays's. Did not get up very early nor do very much. In the afternoon I did some writing.

May 3, 1887 Tuesday

A rainy day. I finished my letter and in the afternoon I did some sewing.

May 4, 1887 Wednesday

I helped Alice some, in the afternoon Jesse took Alice, Emma and I to see Mrs. Tryon, had a very pleasant visit and in the evening we attended prayer meeting at A. D. Thayer's. Had a good meeting.

May 5, 1887 Thursday

I got up early and went with Emma to Mrs. Davis's and then went with Mr. and Mrs. Ligget to Spokane Falls. Brother Moore rode with us part of the way.

May 6, 1887 Friday

At Prof. Westfall's. Had a splendid visit with Katie and in the afternoon we went downtown. In the evening we went to the literary.

May 7, 1887 Saturday
Started from Spokane early and had a very disagreeable time to travel. I reached A. D. Thayer's about sundown and stayed overnight there. We enjoyed some music and a pleasant visit but I was tired.

Memoranda
The weather was cold and it rained some every day in the week.

May 8, 1887 Sunday
Minnie and I did not get up until late. I went to S. S. and from there to see Mrs. Davis and from there to Mr. Hays's.

May 9, 1887 Monday
I worked on Mrs. Titchenal's dress until noon. In the afternoon I went with Eliza, Alice and the children to Mr. Thayer's. Had a pleasant visit but it rained on us as we went home.

May 10, 1887 Tuesday
Another rainy day. I did not do much but help Alice a little with some sewing.

May 11, 1887 Wednesday
I walked from Mr. Hays's to Mr. Sander's and had a very pleasant visit there: then walked to Waverly. Called to see Mrs. Roberts. I took supper at Jesse's and we went to the prayer meeting at Mr. Thrall's.

May 12, 1887 Thursday
Went on the stage to see Mrs. Davis and found her no better. Went back to Waverly on the stage, then walked to Mr. Hays's in the rain and sleet and got wet to the skin.

May 13, 1887 Friday
I was in bed all day and suffered a good deal but wrote a letter and read some and did lots of thinking.

May 14, 1887 Saturday
I was able to get up at 9 o'clock after being in bed for 38 hours the longest time that I had to be in bed for two and one-half years. I sewed some and in the afternoon Dr. Allison called as he was passin.

Memoranda
The weather was cold and rainy nearly all week.

May 15, 1887 Sunday
I felt some better and went with Alice's folks to preaching at Waverly and

back there. In the afternoon to S. S. to see Mrs. Davis and back to
Mrs. Hays's. Geo. Genot was there.

May 16, 1887 Monday
I mended some of my clothes and in the afternoon Mrs. Thayer and
Minnie came and I went with ... to "Uncle Jack's". We had a nice time
but I cried myself to sleep that night.

May 17, 1887 Tuesday
I fixed my alpaca dress and made me a white apron in the afternoon,
helped get things ready for our trip to Spokane. Mrs. Tyree and Dollie
called.

May 18, 1887 Wednesday
Alice, Mrs. Thayer and I went to Spokane Falls alone in Jim's hack. We
stopped with Grandma Mc Ginney and went to church that night.

May 19, 1887 Thursday
Alice went with me to see Dr. Allison. In the afternoon we went to the
Temperance Conference where I met several friends. In the evening
we went to the conference again.

May 20, 1887 Friday
Went to the conference again and in the afternoon did some trading.
Went for a drive and we all took supper at Mr. Keats's. Lucy and I
went to church.

May 21, 1887 Saturday
We rose early and started for Waverly. Had a very pleasant ride and I
drove all and we reached home early in the evening all tired out. I
found Jodie's picture and three letters awaiting me – one of which
caused me to shed some bitter tears. Thus ends another week of
miserable existence.

May 22, 1887 Sunday
At Mr. Hays's I felt bad and slept awhile. We went to S. S. and preaching
with the rest of the folks and wrote part of a letter when I went home.

May 23, 1887 Monday
I did not do much except write some letters and post some accounts in
my diary, ect. I read some. Jesse and Emma stayed over night at Jim's.

May 24, 1887 Tuesday
I put out some houseplants and commenced to make a chair tidy. In the
afternoon Alice, Emma and I went to Mr. Huffman's then to the P. O.
and home.

Waverly, May 22, 1887

My Dear Friend Lewis:

On my return from Spokane yesterday evening I found three letters awaiting me; one of which was addressed in Nannie's writing but I felt quite sure that it was written by a hand much dearer to me than any other earthly hand; so the seal was soon broken & I tell you I did really enjoy what it contained But one thing I would enjoy better and that is that you could be here this beautiful Sabbath evening & assist me in spending the time more pleasantly. I have just returned from Sunday school & preaching – both were very good, but I cannot help feeling lonely here. No, Lewis, I do not think it is any harm for you to write to me on Sunday especially when you have no other time: of course if you had plenty of time during the week I should not think it just right to put it off for a Sunday job but under the circumstances I cannot think it any harm. I do not want you to stay away from church to write to me but if you cannot conveniently go, you can perhaps spend the time as well in writing as in something else you might find to do. If we're together we would talk on Sunday the same as we write & I think neither our talking or writing will harm us.

Lewis, I am so glad to hear of you having good luck & sincerely hope your luck has changed and will continue so. You remember I told you once that perhaps if you would change your ways your luck would change too? Or do you ever think of what I have told you about these things? I believe you will be reminded of me in that way occasionally as you journey through life and I trust it will be of some benefit to you. I have just cause to feel that it has already benefited you by some things that I have said & done. On the other hand I know you have been greatly hurt by things that I have said & done many times; but I do not feel as if you hold any thing against me now; if you do I want to know it immediately. We all make mistakes & many times good comes from what we thought at the time was a mistake; so let us not be discouraged when we have such trials but be firm to the end & we will receive our reward.

I finished your other letter last Sunday morning when I was hardly able to sit up but felt better & went to Sunday school in the afternoon. I was real miserable for several days & was in bed 38 long hours. Alice went with me last Wednesday to Spokane & I went to see Dr. Allison. He gave me medicine to last me about three weeks then I have to go & see him again. Now Lewis you asked me not to work: it is awful hard for me be quiet & not do much but I will have to be for a while, and perhaps all summer for the Dr. told me not to touch a sewing machine nor ride horseback, nor walk but a short distance at a time. I think he is real cruel to deprive me of so much for I do not know how I can stand it; but he said if I would be careful of myself this summer & change climates this fall for a few months that I would be able to enjoy good health again. I shall try to obey him as near as I can for I want to be able to enjoy good health again. I want to enjoy life & not make every body about me miserable because I am.

The Christian camp meeting is to begin at Medical Lake the 17th of next month & I expect to be there during that time. Now Lewis I have just been thinking how nice it would be for you to attend the meeting & be immersed there; don't you think so? I hope you can be there at that time.

I had a real nice time at the Falls & met with Mrs. Merriman & several of my Cheney friends who were there attending the convention of the W.C.T.U. We came home Saturday. I drove all the way & was real tired when I got here. While in Spokane several of us went for a drive Friday eve. I drove the team & we came back over the bridge that you & I crossed on the evening of the 6th of July & I thought of some things that were said as we sat on the log near the bridge & of the bitter tears I shed that night after I went to my room. I could also recall the feelings I had next morning when I opened my eyes. But tongue nor pen cannot express them. I had then began to realize what a good friend you was to me although I sometimes felt as if all my friends had forsaken me. But I must change the subject or you will think I feel that way now; but I do not.

Monday Morning

I feel lots better this morning than I did yesterday & hope I will continue to improve. No Lewis I have not been with Mr. Thrall since I came back or with any other young man except with Mr. George Thayer from the school house to Mr. Davis's last Sunday. I do not care for your men's company very much any more and shall offer excuses when I can. I will send you the Waverly items which were published the next week after we came.

We got a letter from Jodie last week. He is well & sent to u – Alice, Emma & I each a photograph of the engine & the men that work on it. Jodie's picture is just splendid. Jesse has come by going to Rockford so I will close & send this by him so you can get it this week. Address me at Waverly.

Yours with love

Cora J.

May 25, 1887 Wednesdaay

Mrs. Davies was worse and Alice and I went to see her. In the afternoon
    I read some and wrote a letter. Mr. Graham was here to supper. Elza
    Rothget died.

May 26, 1887 Thursday

I ironed a few pieces and helped Alice a little. In the afternoon went to
    attend the funeral of Elza Rothget. Came back by the P. O. and by
    Mr. Tyree's.

May 27, 1887 Friday
I helped Alice some and in the afternoon went with Mr. Thrall to Mr. Thayer's, enjoyed a nice visit, some music and a pleasant moonlight ride.

May 28, 1887 Saturday
As Eliza was away, I helped with the morning work, I baked a cake, and in the afternoon I cut out my black cloak, helped Alice and to bed late feeling real bad and cried myself to sleep and had a dream which was partly realized next day. I felt bad all week and could not work much.

May 29, 1887 Sunday
I helped Alice with the work, read some and while we were eating dinner Lewis gave me a pleasant surprise and we enjoyed a pleasant visit of several hours.

May 30, 1887 Monday
I got up earlier than usual and helped Alice with breakfast. L. stayed til evening and we enjoyed the day together but he did not let me work much.

May 31, 1887 Tuesday
I helped some with the housework and sewed some on my cloak. Mrs. Thayer and her children came and Fannie stayed all night.

June 1, 1887 Wednesday
A windy, cold day. I helped Alice some and sewed a part of the day. Emma and Fannie went to prayer meeting at Mr. Brittondall's.

June 2, 1887 Thursday
Wash day. I helped some with the washing. In the afternoon, Ada Lane made us a nice visit and I made a chair tidy. Was real tired at night.

June 3, 1887 Friday
I did not feel very well. Read some, wrote a letter and in the afternoon I rode "Dollie" went to see Mrs. Davis and back home by the Post Office

June 4, 1887 Saturday
I helped with the work, swept the house all over, finished my cloak and cut out my gingham dress. It rained all the afternoon and I felt lonesome. I retired early and cried myself to sleep.
At Mr. Hays's all week and felt some better than usual.

June 5, 1887 Sunday
George Allen took Alice, the girls, and myself to see Mrs. Davis. In the afternoon we went to S.S. at Waverly and had a good school and full attendance.

June 6, 1887 Monday
I felt much better and sewed nearly all day. Made my gingham basque but did not feel so well at night.

June 7, 1887 Tuesday
I was nearly sick all day, but made the overskirt to my dress and Dolly Tyree went with me to Waverly. Winnie and Vada came home with me and we all went to take Dolly home.

June 8, 1887 Wednesday
I was hardly able to be up in the forenoon. Winnie and Vada went to school. Mr. Mower called. I sewed and read some and was feeling better.

June 9, 1887 Thursday
I received a letter which caused me to feel very bad all day and cried about half the time. I helped Alice some and sewed awhile. I read some too.

June 10, 1887 Friday
I helped Alice some then wrote a letter and went to Mrs. Davis funeral and burial at Spangle, returned at 9 p.m. real tired and Alice was quite sick.

June 11, 1887 Saturday
I finished my gingham dress and helped some with the housework.

Memoranda
The weather was cold and rainy. I was real miserable most all week.

June 12, 1887 Sunday
It rained all day and I never felt more lonely in my life; In the evening I sat in the hammock and sang until late.

June 13, 1887 Monday
It rained all of the forenoon. George helped me and we washed until noon. I rested awhile then cut out the lining for my new dress.

June 14, 1887 Tuesday
I did not get up til late but started the clothes and hung up 120 pieces then cut out my new dress and sprinkled my clothes.

June 15, 1887 Wednesday
I helped with the morning work, ironed my clothes and sewed some.
George, Emma and I went to prayer meeting at Mr. Thrall's; then I
went home with Mr. Thayer's folks.

June 16, 1887 Thursday
I went with Mr. Thayer to Cheney, had a very pleasant ride but was real
tired. We took dinner at the restaurant and I stayed overnight with
Rena Hall.

June 17, 1887 Friday
I wrote a letter then went to Spokane on the morning train. Found C.
Will at the depot. I took dinner with Grandma Mc Kinney, did some
trading and in the evening went to Mr. Cannon's and then to Mr.
Robertson's and stayed there all night.

June 18, 1887 Saturday
I went with Mr. Robertson, John, Lucy and Ollie to Spokane river a
fishing but I did not catch any fish nor enjoy myself very much, but
felt some better in the evening.

Memoranda
The weather was quit cool all week with some rain and wind. I was
feeling much better than usual.

June 19, 1887 Sunday
A very pleasant day. John Robertson took me to Spokane and I spent
a part of the day very pleasantly with Mrs. Will. Returned to Mr.
Robertson's in the evening.

June 20, 1887 Monday
I went to town with Mr. McDonnell. Did some trading for Mrs. Norton
and sent it to her by Mrs. Will. Then went back to Mr. Robertson's
and Lucy and I sewed on my dress. Jesse and Emma stayed overnight
there.

June 21, 1887 Tuesday
Jesse and Emma started to Waverly before 6 o'clock. Lucy and I sewed all
day and after supper we took a walk. Went over to John's house and
did some mischief while he was in town. We went back and washed
the dishes.

June 22, 1887 Wednesday
We finished my dress in the forenoon and in the afternoon made my
ulster. After supper, Lucy and I made a very pleasant call with Miss

McDonnell.

June 23, 1887 Thursday
I made 12 buttonholes in my basque and 12 in my ulster. In the afternoon, John took Lucy and I to Spokane. I was nearly sick when night came and stayed with Mrs. McKinney.

June 24, 1887 Friday
I woke at 4 o'clock and started for Medical Lake at half past six in an old stagecoach arrived there before 9 and was very tired but went to the camp meeting and found several friends there. I took dinner at Brother Dean's and supper with Mrs. Merriman.

June 25, 1887 Saturday
I wrote a letter and walked over to the post office and came back in a boat, then went to meeting in the forenoon and to the women's meeting in the afternoon and evening. I took supper at Brother Dean's but stayed with Mrs. Merriman again over night. Edna Forrey, Mrs. Turner, Mrs. Lockheart, and I went in bathing and I enjoyed it very much. In the afternoon Mr. Moody took Edna and I boat riding.

June 26, 1887 Sunday
A cold, rainy day and I was nearly sick but went to the meeting and heard a good sermon also a good one in the afternoon and in the evening. Brother Oaisley preached in the church. Mr. Sanders walked back to the tent with me. As the meeting closed Sunday night, we broke up the camp and I went home with Mrs. Merriman and was nearly worn out when we reached Deep Creek.

June 28, 1887 Tuesday
I was real miserable all day, but helped Mrs. M some and "Bossed the Squaw." In the afternoon, I rested and had a big cry. In the evening I played some.

June 29, 1887 Wednesday
In the forenoon I wrote a letter and some in my diary that I had neglected. In the afternoon, I went with Mr. and Mrs. Merriman to see Mr. Stroup who was sick.

June 30, 1887 Thursday
I wrote a letter and finished the basque that Lucy made for me. I read some and in the evening went downtown with Edna Forrey.

July 1, 1887 Friday
I made a cake for Mrs. Merriman, then rested and read quite a while. In

the afternoon I was real miserable and slept some and felt better in the evening.

July 2, 1887 Saturday

I was quite sick all morning but felt better in the afternoon. Lewis and Nannie came from Badger and L. and I went for a buggy ride that we enjoyed very much. I also wrote a letter, read some and shingled Mr. Merriman's hair.

Memoranda

The weather was warm most of the week.

July 3, 1887 Sunday

I did not feel very well but in the P. M. went with Lewis and Nannie from Deep Creek to Spokane Falls and stayed overnight with Miss McKinney.

July 4, 1887 Monday

I went with L to Mr. Corbley's then downtown to see the doctor. Took dinner at the restaurant. Went to Spangle with L. and Nannie. Reached Mr. Hays's at one o'clock at night. Very tired and sleepy.

July 5, 1887 Tuesday

We all felt too bad to do much but I sewed a little. Mrs. Thayer and her children and Vada Cobb called in the evening.

July 6, 1887 Wednesday

Jesse and Emma went after a girl but did not get any. Lewis got some gooseberries. Nannie and I helped Alice with the work and I sewed some. John Tryon called. I cried and Nannie got mad.

July 7, 1887 Thursday

All at Alice's yet. Nim T. called and went with Lewis to Cabbage Flat. I sewed all day and helped Alice get supper, then went with L for a buggy ride until 10 P. M.

July 8, 1887 Friday

I helped Alice with the work and sewed some. Mrs. Tyree came to sew. Nannie, sewed some for Alice. I was there all day; also Jesse and Emma.

July 9, 1887 Saturday

I helped with the work and sewed on Mrs. Titchenal's dress. In the afternoon, L., Nannie, Edna and I went to Mr. Tyree's; had a pleasant time stayed until late. Cicero Roberts was there, too.

Memoranda

Bill told L something that caused me to feel bad for a while. Jesse and Emma went to Mr. Henry's. I was feeling much better than I had for some time.

July 10, 1887 Sunday
I helped Alice with the work. L. and I went to S. S. and to preaching at Waverly, then to Mr. Tyree's after Nannie and back to Mr. Hays's for supper. Nim was there and stayed late.

July 11, 1887 Monday
Lewis and Nannie started home. I did not feel very well but helped do a big washing and rested and read and slept some before I helped get supper.

July 12, 1887 Tuesday
I was nearly sick and did not do much. In the afternoon I sewed some. Mrs. Smith was here and Minnie stayed all night with me.

July 13, 1887 Wednesday
I sprinkled and ironed my clothes. Alice and Emma went to Mr. Henry's funeral and I kept the children and was alone with them most all day.

July 14, 1887 Thursday
I ironed until noon for Alice and in the afternoon Emma, Alice and children and I went to Mr. Thayer's. We had a very pleasant visit and returned late.

July 15, 1887 Friday
Spent another forenoon ironing for the children. In the afternoon I commenced making my lawn skirt. In the evening I took a horseback ride and went to Mr. Tyree's after the fluter.

July 16, 1887 Saturday
I made a cake, then cleaned both rooms upstairs and the front room. After dinner I shingled Willie Dawson's hair and finished my dress skirt. In the evening I wrote three letters and helped Alice with the work. Billie and I killed some chickens. I worked harder and felt better than usual.

July 17, 1887 Sunday
I helped with the work and read until dinner. I went to S.S. at Waverly and from there to Mr. Cobb's with George Thayer and had a pleasant time.

July 18, 1887 Monday
Alice and the children and I were here alone most all day and we sewed all day. I made two garments and was very tired when night came.

July 19, 1887 Tuesday
I made another garment and helped Alice some with her sewing but did not feel well all day. I rested some and wrote a letter. Mr. and Mrs. Thayer and Eliza called. I retired early.

July 20, 1887 Wednesday
I cut out some sewing for the children and made an apron for May. Did some sewing for myself and helped with the work. Joe Kelso was here cutting grain.

July 21, 1887 Thursday
Another wash day but we got through before dinner. In the afternoon I visited Vada's school and went from there to Waverly and cried as I came home.

July 22, 1887 Friday
I ironed all of the white clothes and finished two garments for myself and made little Jesse a collar, besides helping with the housework.

July 23, 1887 Saturday
I did not feel very well but said nothing about it and ironed until one o'clock. Bro. Mouer was here to dinner. We moved the stove and dishes out and Jesse painted the kitchen floor. I read some and did some writing.

Memoranda
The weather was very warm all week.

July 24, 1887 Sunday
I read some and studied my S. S. lesson, rode to the schoolhouse with Jim as he went to Cheney, but was too late for S. S. Bro. Mouer preached and I went home with Mr. Thayer's folks.

July 25, 1887 Monday
I helped Mrs. Thayer with some sewing and in the afternoon went back to Mr. Hays's and got there just before a hard rainstorm. Jim brought Miss Tompson with him.

July 26, 1887 Tuesday
I had a severe headache all day but made Alice and Becca each a new bonnet. I slept most of the afternoon and woke up feeling worse than I did before I slept.

July 27, 1887 Wednesday

I did not feel very well but had no time to rest. Bro. Mouer came to do some papering and I had to help him. We papered Alice's room, put the carpet down and went to a prayer meeting.

July 28, 1887 Thursday

We papered the bedroom and halls, and put things to rights again. We had quite a visit too. I was very tired when night came.

July 29, 1887 Friday

I wrote a letter. Eliza T. and Mr. Davis and Clide came. In the afternoon we all went to the closing exercises of Vada's school. They were very good. We called at Jeff's.

July 30, 1887 Saturday

I was nearly sick all day and did not do much. I made Jesse a birthday cake and did some writing, felt better in the evening and sewed a little.

Memoranda

I did not feel quite so well this week. The weather was real cool all week.

July 31, 1887 Sunday

Sate and Lant came by and Alice and Jim went with them to Mr. Smith's. I was here alone most all day. I read some and wrote some letters. Minnie came and stayed all night.

August 1, 1887 Monday

I was not very well. I ripped up my cashmere dress to color it and did some writing. I felt better in the evening.

August 2, 1887 Tuesday

I did not feel able to do much but in the afternoon Mrs. Tyree helped me and we colored my dress and some things for Alice.

August 3, 1887 Wednesday

I pressed my dress and sewed some on it. In the afternoon I helped Eliza wash the white clothes and was very tired at night.

August 4, 1887 Thursday

I helped finish the washing. Herb Goffgues here to dinner. Mr. Toll called. Alice and Emma went to Mr. Thayer's and Eliza got hurt. I did some writing and sewed some.

Thursday Evening
August 4, 1887

Dear Lewis:

    I feel very much disappointed that I have not received any letter from you this week, but feel sure that there is one at the office for me. I heard from the office Tuesday and should have received your letter that day and did not hear from there yesterday. But Alice and Emma have gone to Mr. A.D. Thayers this afternoon & I think they will bring me a letter this evening.

    The summer is half spent & I have not visited Jodie and the mining region yet. I should have been there ere this but you know I am a dependent little creature and have only been waiting for some way to be provided for me to go, and at last think I am able to see my way through. I had fully made up my mind to go to Kingston if it was possible for me to go and have silently been listening to hear of some body going to the landing that I could go with them but I was afraid to say very much about it and have been quite impatent about it for the last week; but consoled myself with the thoughts that if it were best for me to go, there would be a way provided. So today, as I was busy with my work & thinking of what I had to do, Herbert Goff came to see Mr. Hays and engaged a load of potatoes to take to the mines. He was here for dinner & I had quite a chat with him. He was telling me about Jodie & that country & said that I ought to go up there so I made arrangements to go when he comes after the potatoes which he said would be next Tuesday morning. I will get on the boat about 9 o'clock Wednesday morning & get to Wardner Junction about one. I do not know how long I will stay there but can tell you more about it in my next letter which I will write soon as I get there and tell you about my trip.

    I was here alone most all day Sunday; the first time that I have been entirely alone since I left Douglas Co. I enjoyed myself fine for awhile, for I was feeling just like I wanted to be alone, but about 4 o'clock I began to feel like I would rather have the company of some good boy that I know was thinking about me. Lewis, I would have given a good deal if you and my organ had been here. I was not feeling very well & know you would have cheered me up some. It has been nearly four weeks since you were here & I have only cried twice since then & and only for a few minutes each time. So you see I am in much better spirits than I was before you came to see me. I wish you could come oftener, but one consolation I have is that we will not always be so far from each other & if we live the time will not be far distant when we will be happier than we are today and I hope our happiness will last forever.

    I will wait to see if I get a letter. (by-by.)

Alice and Emma did not get here until 10 o'clock last night but I was still waiting for my letter and you can imagion my disappointment when they said there was no mail for me. I did not know what to think but imagioned a whole lot and gave vent to my feelings by sheding some big tears. In your last letter you said you were not very well but would be all right in a few days. Now Lewis we can not always tell what will take place in a few days and I am very much afraid that you have been sick & could not write. I sincerely hope, however, that such is not the case and I am going to the office this evening in hopes of hearing from you & will not seal this until I know, & if I do not hear from you this week I will think that something is the matter. Perhaps Gilmore will come & bring my letter. I hope he will, but did not expect him quite so soon; and perhaps you are coming again, but can hardly think that, for you did not think you could come until this fall. I can only know by waiting.

The reason that they were so late coming home last night they happened to a serious accident. Eliza was at Mr. Thayer's & had no way to get to Mr. Davis's so they started to take her and Clide home and as they were passing the bridge the team got sacred & ran away and threw the back seat off the hack & Eliza and Alice's baby with it. Alice, Emma & Clide were on the front seat & as soon as they could stop the team they went to Eliza & she couldn't speak & did not know anything. Jeff & Mr. Crabtree went & helped her in the hack & then took her back to Mr. Sanders house & sent for the new Dr. & for Mr. Thayer's folks. She was badly hurt but I hope not fatally. I have not heard from her today but if I can will go to see her this evening. The rest of them were scared but not hurt any.

If I do not get a letter from you or Gilmore this evening I shall look for Gilmore this week & may not go to Kingston next week. Jesse is working for Mr. Leack. Emma went to see Eliza this morning & has just now come back. She says Eliza is better.

Cora

August 5, 1887 Friday

I ironed my clothes and in the afternoon went to Jeff's to see Eliza and to the P. O. I rode "Laura" and returned to "Haysburg" about dark. "Pass the Jelly H. G."

August 6, 1887 Saturday

I washed and colored my blue sack but it did not suit me and I made it over for Edna. Minnie called also Mr. Witter. I ironed some for Alice.

Memoranda

I did not feel very strong all week but I kept my spirits up pretty well. Warm weather again.

107

August 7, 1887 Sunday
I read and studied my S. S. lesson. Emma was sick and I went to S. S. with Jim and Alice and home with Mr. Thayer's folks. It rained while I was there and "Uncle Gil" brought me home in the hack.

August 8, 1887 Monday
Alice's girl went home and I had to help with the work. Bro. Mouer called to tell us good-bye as he was going east on a visit. H. Hays spent the afternoon and stayed all night and we had quite a long chat.

August 9, 1887 Tuesday
I was feeling bad because I could not go to Kingston and I had a talk with Emma which caused me to feel worse. I tried to sew some but was very nervous and cried myself to sleep at a late hour.

August 10, 1887 Wednesday
I was nearly sick but said nothing about it and helped with the work. In the afternoon, Mrs. Tyree and Dollie helped me and we washed 150 pieces.

August 11, 1887 Thursday
I helped Alice make some raspberry jam and helped with the work. Afternoon we went to the P. O. and to Mr. Davis's after currents and I was sick all night.

August 12, 1887 Friday
I felt bad all day but ironed my clothes and cleaned the rooms upstairs. In the afternoon I sewed some and helped with the housework.

August 13, 1887 Saturday
I picked berries for a while, then did some baking, mopped the kitchen floor and went to Mr. Tyree's after the clothes. I expected Lewis but he did not come so I retired early and was very tired.

Memoranda
I felt bad all week over some things that I heard and cried more than usual. (Still near Waverly)

August 14, 1887 Sunday
I had just finished my morning work when Mr. and Mrs. Langhan came, then Lewis and Mr. Engle from Badger. I went to S. S. with L. and we had a good visit.

August 15, 1887 Monday
I was nearly sick again but helped do up the morning work. L. helped me then we spent the forenoon in chatting. In the evening we gathered

raspberries.

August 16, 1887   Tuesday
I took Emma, Edna, Mamie and me to A. D. Thayer's where I spent a very pleasant day and I enjoyed a nice birthday dinner. I weighed 130 and was 22 years old.

August 17, 1887   Wednesday
I was sick all day but L. stayed and cheered me some and in the afternoon I read some to him. We enjoyed a great visit.

August 18, 1887   Thursday
I felt some better and helped Jesse, Emma and Lewis get started to the Falls. Then wrote a letter and sewed some. Mr. Richardson stayed overnight at Mr. Hays's.

August 19, 1887   Friday
Mrs. Tyree and Dollie were here and washed for us. I helped some and wrote a letter; did some sewing and sprinkled my clothes.

August 20, 1887   Saturday
I ironed until noon. In the afternoon sewed a little, made a cake then went to see Pauline Tryon and home via P. O. Jim's team ran away.

Memoranda
I was very miserable all week and could not do much work. It was very warm.

Thrashing grain with horses

August 21, 1887   Sunday
I helped with the work, studied my S. S. lesson, wrote a letter, went to S.

S. in the hack, called at Jeff's a while and returned to the ranch about dark.

August 22, 1887 Monday
I wrote a letter and Edna went with me to Waverly in the wagon on errands. I sewed some and filled 45 glasses with jelly. The "tin man" was here.

August 23, 1887 Tuesday
Mr. Hays's started his header Mrs. Braman was there. I finished my old cashmere dress skirt, wrote a little and helped some with work.

August 24, 1887 Wednesday
Went to the P. O. in the forenoon, helped with the work and Alice and I put away 88 glasses of jelly.

August 25, 1887 Thursday
I swept the house and got ready to go to Spokane. After dinner I rode "Nellie" and went to Mr. Huffman's. From there to Spangle on the stage and stayed at the hotel.

August 26, 1887 Friday
Ed Gimble went with me to Spokane on the train. I stayed with Emma but was sick all day and went to the show with Lewis at night but did not feel well enough to enjoy it very much.

August 27, 1887 Saturday
I felt bad all day. L. went with me downtown to see the doctor. In the afternoon we wrote some letters then went for a ride which I was able to enjoy.

Memoranda
The weather was warm and I was not able to do much so I went on a pleasure trip and left Mrs. Tyree and Dollie to help Alice.

August 28, 1887 Sunday
I felt so bad that I had a big cry before breakfast. I went with Mrs. Robertson to the telephone office, then with L. to hear Mrs. Jones preach in the morning and eve.

August 29, 1887 Monday
I was not better and went to see the doctor again and did some trading and went to Spangle on the afternoon train and stayed overnight at the hotel.

August 30, 1887 Tuesday
I was able to eat quite a breakfast but had a cold ride on the stage to

Waverly, then over to Alice's on horseback and found her in bed. Dollie was there, Mrs. Smith came. It rained.

August 31, 1887 Wednesday

A rainy morning. I had a severe headache all day and lay on the lounge most of the afternoon with a hot fever, but was better at bedtime.

September 1, 1887 Thursday

As it was raining and he could not work, Billy helped us wash the white clothes. After dinner I wrote a letter and as Dollie went home I helped Alice.

September 2, 1887 Friday

I helped finish the washing and as I got the white clothes on the line, it broke and let them down in the dirt. I wrote another letter. Mary Goffinet and Fannie T. called in the afternoon.

September 3, 1887 Saturday

I ironed until 2 o'clock, then I papered the hall and cleaned the rooms upstairs besides helping some with the other work and was very tired when night came and retired early.

Memoranda

The weather was cold and rainy all week. I was real miserable and commenced taking medicine again.

September 4, 1887 Sunday

A very disagreeable day and I was lonesome all day, but read some and drove the team to S. S. and they broke the hack. Mr. and Mrs. Thayer came home with us and we enjoyed a nice little visit.

September 5, 1887 Monday

I had a headache all day but sewed some and cut out my red dress. Mr. Tyree and "Uncle Jack" called. I was real tired and retired early and cried a while.

September 6, 1887 Tuesday

I helped with the housework and wrote two letters. In the afternoon Jim and Billie went to Mr. Dawson's to work and I sewed on my dress.

September 7, 1887 Wednesday

I helped milk the cows and some with the other work and sewed some. George Yount and Frank D. were here to dinner. Alice went to Mr. Dawson's to see Jim.

September 8, 1887 Thursday

I helped Dollie wash. Mrs. Tyree was here all day. Edna fell offf "Nellie" and hurt her arm, and Alice took her to the doctor. Dollie and I milked.

September. 9, 1887 Friday

Dollie helped me milk. Then she went home. Lizzie Cable to help us. I wrote some letters and went to Waverly and called at Mr. Braman's.

September 10, 1887 Saturday

I walked after the cows but Frank Dashiell helped me milk. I worked hard all day preparing for company tomorrow. Frank and Link went to the orchard with me after plumbs. Jim and Billy came home late. I took my bath and retired at 9:30 very tired.

Letters Cora received from the bank in Butler, Missouri

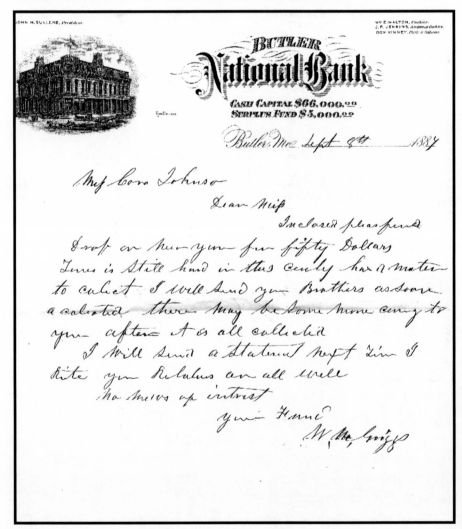

Memoranda

The weather was cool all week and I was feeling much better.

September 11, 1887 Sunday

A rainy day and no company except Mr. McGhee and Mr. Thrall were here to dinner and I went to S.S with Mr. T and rode "Win". In the evening, we enjoyed some vocal music.

September 12, 1887 Monday

Mrs. Thrall spent the day here and told Alice and I of her troubles. She went to the orchard with me. I helped get dinner and sewed some on my dress. Lizzie was there.

September 13, 1887 Tuesday

I sewed awhile, then went to the post office and got 29 letters and 3 cards, which had been forwarded from Badger. In the afternoon I sewed some and the men went away to work so Alice and I did the milking.

September 14, 1887 Wednesday

Ada called. I wrote a letter and went to the post office and received 3 letters. In the afternoon I sewed some and helped do up the work.

September 15, 1887 Thursday

I walked after "Nellie" to ride after the cows and did not feel very well after the milking was done. Minnie and Fannie spent the day and Lee Beaure and Ada and Bill and Dollie the afternoon.

September 16, 1887 Friday

Mrs. Thayer and Minnie came after some plums and we gathered about 24 gallons and canned some and put some up to dry. George Gount called. I told Minnie something which caused to feel bad.

September 17, 1887 Saturday

The cows were to the back of the pasture again and I rode "Nellie" after them. Helped do the milking, strained away the milk and skimmed some, then made a big cake and finished my red dress. In the afternoon, I went to Mr. Thayer's after Marnie and Minnie came home with me. We went after the cows but the men were there to milk. I helped with the evening work and Minnie and I talked until late.

September 18, 1887 Sunday

Billy and Link hurt my feelings and I had a big cry and helped do up the work. George Thayer came after me and we went over there and spent a pleasant time singing and went to S.S and back to Mr. Hays's. A.B. Robinson and Nim called.

The September, 19, 1887 Monday

The header's were here and I helped do the work. After dinner I wrote three letters and went to the post office. Gilmore and Emma came from Spokane and it was late when we finished the work.

September 20, 1887 Tuesday

Emma went to Waverly. Gilmore drove the Header wagon. Lizzie went home and I helped Alice with the work. Emma brought me six letters.

September 21, 1887 Wednesday

Gilmore and Emma went to Waverly to clean Emma's house. Mrs. Thayer and Fannie called and I went with Fannie to the field. They finished heading. I went to Mr. Covington's on an errand and helped with the work.

September 22, 1887 Thursday
Bill Tyree was there to help Alice, so I went to Spangle with Jim and Mrs. Thayer. We called to see Mrs. Spangle and did not get home until dark. I had a headache and was tired.

September 23, 1887 Friday
Gilmore helped me gather some plums and I made 2 gallons of plum butter. Emma made some too. It was a very warm day. Alice and I went to Waverly late.

September 24, 1887 Saturday
I helped Alice get Edna ready to go to Spokane with Gilmore and Emma. I felt real bad for awhile but helped do the Saturday work and did my ironing but retired early.

Memoranda
The weather was nice and I was feeling better during the last two than I had for a long time.

September 25, 1887 Sunday
A nice warm day. I did some writing and went to S.S with Mr. Hays's family at Waverly and after S.S we called at Mr. Fred Dashiell's a little while.

September 26, 1887 Monday
Bill and Dollie Tyree washed for us. I was sick all day but helped some with the work and sewed some for myself. Gip came and brought me some medicine.

September 27, 1887 Tuesday
I helped with the housework and rode "Dollie" to Mr. Tyron's to see if the thrashers were coming and she came near throwing me. Mrs. Thrall helped us for three days.

September 28, 1887 Wednesday
The thrashers were at Mr. Hays's and Alice was sick all day but Gilmore helped Mrs. Thrall and me and there was plenty to keep us busy.

September 29, 1887 Thursday
A warm day. I helped with the work and sewed some in the afternoon, until time to help with supper and wait on the tables.

September 30, 1887 Friday
A rainy day but they did not stop work. In the afternoon, Mr. Thrall came after his mother so I worked till late and was very tired.

October 1, 1887 Saturday
A cold, windy day. Mrs. Black called. I helped Alice with the work. The thresher's finished at Mr. Hays's about 5 o'clock. We all went out to the field awhile, then came back and worked until bedtime. I was nearly sick.

Memoranda
Thus ends another week of this busy life.

October 2, 1887 Sunday
Gilmore took Alice and the children and me to S. S. at Waverly. Eliza Thayer went home with us. H. Goff spent the evening with us.

October 3, 1887 Monday
Gilmore and I put out a big washing, then I canned 4 gallons of crab apples and was very tired when I quit my work without being finished.

October 4, 1887 Tuesday
A rainy morning. I got breakfast and helped Gilmore get his things ready to move to the Ben. After dinner we went to Spangle. I stayed with Mrs. Spangle.

October 5, 1887 Wednesday
We started for Spokane about 8 o'clock and reached there at ten o'clock. Found Jodie there. Was glad to see him. Lewis was hauling lumber and did not get in until late.

October 6, 1887 Thursday
A rainy morning so Lewis did not work and helped me can some fruit for Gilmore. In the evening we enjoyed a nice visit while walking by the electric light.

October 7, 1887 Friday
Lewis and Jesse hauled lumber. Gilmore and Jodie went with me downtown and Jodie and I had our pictures taken. The boys were late getting back. Jim was there.

October 8, 1887 Saturday
Lewis and I went downtown and bought us a lounge and did some trading for Mrs. Titchenal. Jesse and Gilmore started for Badger about 2 o'clock P. M. Emma and Jodie rode a ways with them. L. stayed with me and we had quite a visit. None of us were feeling much like talking so we retired early.

October 9, 1887 Sunday
I was not very well but went to church with Edna and Lewis and to the YMCA. In the afternoon to the Baptist church and in the evening heard a good sermon by Mrs. Jones.

October 10, 1887 Monday
Jodie left us for his work at Wardner. L. took breakfast with us then went to work, Edna went to school and I went to bed but after dinner went with Emma to the court house. L. came late.

Edna Hays Oldest daughter of James and Alice Hays.

October 11, 1887 Tuesday
The fair commenced at Spokane. I went downtown to see the street parade and to see Dr. Allison. I got some medicine and was in bed all the afternoon but L. was there most all evening.

October 12, 1887 Wednesday
After spending a miserable night I was not able to get up until 3 O'clock. I went after my pictures and found Alice and her family at Grandma's when I got back there then I was better.

October 13, 1887 Thursday
I was feeling much better and went down to see the street parade. Mrs. Merriman and Maud took dinner with me and after dinner Lorenzo took me to the fair grounds. We had supper at the Arlington Hotel. Lorenzo and I had a great visit.

October 14, 1887 Friday
A rainy day. I used Jim Hays's hack and team and took Mrs. Merriman over the city. Then went to the depot in the rain, then bought my wedding dress and in the evening Lorenzo and I had a farewell visit.

October 15, 1887 Saturday
I felt real miserable, but left the city and "my boy" and went with Mrs. Hays and family to their home near Waverly. A cold windy day and I was very tired when we reached there at 6:30 P. M. George Leach and Henry Helm were there. Bill and Dollie Tyree had got supper but were gone home. I helped Alice with the wash and retired early.

October 16, 1887 Sunday
I helped Alice with the work, studied my S. S. lesson and went to S. S. with George Allen and Alice and her children. I then called to see Mrs. Thayer as she had been quite sick but was better.

October 17, 1887 Monday
I wrote some letters and did some sewing and helped with the housework. Bill and Dollie Tyree called.

October 18, 1887 Tuesday
I sewed some but had a headache and sore throat besides a very bad cold.

October 20, 1887 Thursday
Henry Helm helped me wash for myself and Alice. Mr. Jackson was there to dinner and Bro. Mouer called.

October 21, 1887 Friday
I starched the clothes and hung them out, but was too sick to do much else. I wrote a letter and helped Alice.

October 22, 1887 Saturday
I made a cake and helped with the work preparing for company next day. The boys moved the stoves for us.

October 23, 1887 Sunday
I helped with the morning work and read some. Mr. Cobb's folks got there about noon, then I helped get dinner and wash up the dishes after supper.

October 24, 1887 Monday
I helped with the housework and made some jelly and crab apple butter and ironed some. Alice went to Waverly to see Mrs. Thayer. I was very tired at night.

October 25, 1887 Tuesday
I finished my ironing and helped with the other work then sewed some in the afternoon.

October 26, 1887 Wednesday
A rainy day so the boys could not work and Henry Helm helped us wash.

I was nearly sick with my cold besides other ailments.

October 27, 1887 Thursday
I hung the clothes out, then got ready and went with Alice and the
children to Mr. A.D. Thayer's on a visit; she was sick. We helped
make Minnie and Fannie some aprons.

October 28, 1887 Friday
A nice, warm day. I helped Alice move the things in the cellar and
kitchen and cleaned the room upstairs. Then went to Mr. Covington's
and Mr. Tyree's and found Mr. McGhee and family there on my
return. Lewis got there late.

Mr. Cobb, and his family who traveled to Washington Territory
with Cora and her brother's family.

October 29, 1887 Saturday

Mr. McGhee's folks went to Mr. Cobb's. I helped do the housework and Lewis helped me get ready to move "home" and in the evening we called at Mr. Black's and at Mr. Thayer's. I had a big cry, which was the first for two weeks, but I could not help feeling bad to leave Alice and the place that was once my <u>home</u>.

October 30, 1887 Sunday

I helped with the work and was busy most of the day getting ready to leave. Lewis was there all day. Nim and Mr. Norton called and Mr. Davis stayed overnight there.

October 31, 1887 Monday

I told my sister goodbye and went with Lewis to Spokane Falls in the wagon. We reached there at 7 o'clock and found all glad to see us. Minnie was there very sick.

November 1, 1887 Tuesday

A nice day. I had the headache and was tired but went downtown and did some trading. Moved my things and fixed up my room at Mrs. Thompson's house.

Lewis and Cora's Wedding photograph

November 2, 1887 Wednesday

My wedding day. I did some trading and took dinner at the restaurant with Lewis, Emma and Minnie and was married at Mr. Corbaley's at 8 o'clock and came home happy.

November 3, 1887 Thursday

L and I went to the train to meet Alice but she did not come. We went downtown with Mrs. Braman and to the train with Minnie, then had our photographs taken.

November 4, 1887 Friday

L hauled lumber and did not get home until half past 7 o'clock. I went downtown with Mr. Cobb, ate dinner alone, wrote some letters, and got supper for my boy.

November 5, 1887 Saturday

I got breakfast for Lewis and he went to the mill again. I cleaned up my room and did some writing in my diary that I had neglected. I went to the train again, but Alice did not come. After dinner, I slept an hour then went downtown and had to come back in the rain. Lewis did not get home til half past 7 o'clock.

November 6, 1887 Sunday

We had late breakfast and went to hear Mr. Corbaley preach. I read some then we called at Mr. Corbaley's and went to hear Mrs. Jones preach in the evening.

November 7, 1887 Monday

Lewis went to the mill. I wrote a letter and in the afternoon went to Cheney on the train, stayed overnight at Bro. Dean and had a nice visit with them.

November 8, 1887 Tuesday

I saw some of my old Cheney friends and returned to Spokane and found Emma and "my boy" to meet me. In the afternoon we did some trading and spent the evening at "Grandma's"

November 9, 1887 Wednesday

We did not get up till late but Lewis went to the sawmill and Emma stayed with me until afternoon, then I went downtown.

December 4, 1887 Sunday

A snowy day. Gilmore came and I sang until I was hoarse. In the evening I was writing a letter when Nim, Norman and Mr. Norton came from Spokane.

December 5, 1887 Monday
A very disagreeable day. The boys went after their wagon they left at Mr. Whimry's. I wrote some letters and in the evening played some.

December 6, 1887 Tuesday
Mr. Norton's folks moved over to Lewis' house again. I helped some with the housework and wrote another letter.

December 7, 1887 Wednesday
I helped some with the work and wrote some more letters after finding that we had a band-box on our trip from Spokane. I had a visit with Nim.

December 8, 1887 Thursday
I washed my white clothes and helped Mother and Nannie a little with their washing and made some mush for supper and washed the dishes.

December 9, 1887 Friday
Lewis helped me and I washed our colored clothes. I was tired and retired early in the evening.

December 10, 1887 Saturday
I did not feel very well nor do much except mend some of our clothes.

Memoranda
The weather was cold and the snow was about 14 inches deep a part of the week.

December 11, 1887 Sunday
A rainy day. I washed the dishes and I went upstairs and read some. Gif came. I played and sang some and in the evening read some and Gif, Nim and Norman played cards in the kitchen.

December 12, 1887 Monday
I washed the dishes, cleaned up my room and mended some clothes, then went with Lewis to haul some lumber over to our house. He and John hauled some wood.

December 13, 1887 Tuesday
I patched Lewis's pants while he went after the horses, then I went with him and John over to my shanty and we hauled part of it away. Mr. Konkle stayed overnight there.

December 14, 1887 Wednesday
I helped some with the morning work and wrote a letter while Lewis went after the rest of my house. Then went with him over to our place.

December 15, 1887 Thursday
I commenced sewing on my black basque. I am making it over. The men folks killed a beef and I went over to where they were and took a severe cold.

December 16, 1887 Friday
I finished my basque and helped some with the housework. In the evening we all read and talked till bedtime.

December 17, 1887 Saturday
I had a headache all day but cleaned up our room and washed the kitchen windows and patched my dress. Mr. E. D. Nash was here to dinner. Lewis was working on his bob-sleds. The weather was nice all week with some wind. We were still staying at father Titchenal.

December 18, 1887 Sunday
A very windy day. I was nearly sick and was in bed a part of the day. Mrs. Norton and her children, Mr. Bliss, Mr. Kunkle were here over night.

December 19, 1887 Monday
I was not able to get up until noon and did not do anything but clean my room and write some letters. Mrs. Norton and her children were still here.

December 20, 1887 Tuesday
I was not feeling well and wrote some letters, just for a change. Nim moved Mrs. Norton and her children to the saw mill.

December, 21, 1887 Wednesday
I was feeling some better and mended my black cloak and Nim's pants and in the evening did some writing.

WEATHER RECORD

Date	Remarks	Therm.
Feb. 1	The coldest but the Sun shone bright	4 degrees below zero
Feb. 2		10
Feb. 3	A little more snow	14

The weather was cold, windy and rainy till the middle of May. A nice rain June 4th. A thunder storm and hard rain July 25th and a real cold spell for a week in the middle of October.

123

Memoranda

Date	Bought	Dolls. Cents
Jan. 26	stamp	.25
Feb. 16	postal cards	.05
Feb. 24	corset cover	.72
	Shawl	.75
	Paper and envelops	.16
March 7	soap	.25
	Stamps	.35
April 6	songs	.10
	Dried fruit	.50
April 20	Stamps and envelops	.30
April 28	Milk	.10
April 30	Hotel bill	.75
May 6	Buttons	.40
	5 yards of lace	1.00
	Thread	.10
	1 yard of lace	.25
	10 yards of gingham	2.00
May 12	Patterns	.70
May 20	7 yards of muslin	.50
	2 yards of wiggan	.20
	1 ½ yards of dress lining	.20
	8 yards of cambric	.65
	10 yards of dress goods	3.75
	8 yards of lawn	.40
	Hat	3.25
	2 dozen buttons	.50
	Silk and twist	.15
	2 ½ yards of ribbon	.50
	Stamps	.50
	Pencil tablet	.50
	Riding gloves	1.50
	Medicine	1.50
May 21	Watch mended	2.00
May 24	A doctor book	1.55
June 3	Envelopes	.25
June 7	Song book	.55
June 17	Ticket to Spokane	.80

Date	Bought	Dolls. Cents
June 17	Shoes	3.25
	Velvet	1.55
	Dress binding	.10
	Veiling	.75
	Hooks and eyes	.05
	Jersey	2.00
June 20	Book for Phebe	.40
	Candy	.20
	Slippers	1.35
	Shoes mended	1.00
	Goods for ulster	1.00
	Buttons	.50
	Thread	.10
June 23	Collars and cuffs	.35
	Shoe polish	.25
	Pin mended	.25
	Glycerine	.15
	Pencil tablet	.10
June 24	Envelops	.25
	Stage fare	1.00
	Knife	.50
June 26	Donated	.50
July 4	Doctor bill	4.00
	Medicine	1.75
July 5	Corset waist	1.50
July 21	Writing paper	.15
	Coloring dye	.10
Aug 5	Envelops	.50
Aug 25	Hotel bill	.50
Aug. 26	Ticket to Spokane	1.00
Aug. 29	Doctors bill	2.00
	Medicine	1.50
	Dress goods	1.80
	Calico	.45
	Muslin	1.00
	Morine	2.60
	Lace	.50
	Shawl	1.75

Things to be Remembered.

Lewis H. Gatchenal and Cara Johnson were married at the residence of R. Gatchalay in Spokane Falls, on the 2nd of Nov. 1887.

We remained in Spokane till the 14th when we started in a wagon with a four-horse team for our home at Badger Mountain. We reached Lewis' father's place on the 21st, and remained there until the 2nd day of March 1888 when we moved to our log cabin home. Another room built of lumber was not finished

Our rooms were rather limited at that time, as we had but little to go to housekeeping with; though we much our most of the slight in this country had to begin with. We had a new cook-stove which we paid $28 for, in Spokane, a lounge that cost $10, and three chairs, one being a rocking-chair. I sure made a lounge, a table & a bedstead which I stained with Burnt Umber & made them quite respectable. The old cabin was 12 x 14 feet & the other room was 14 feet square, could over head & the walls were papered. I had an old rag

2

carpet and chairs. mother gave us a new one. My sister got up a knitting club school. Organ, a stove-table, some pictures, etc. which fitted us out and thus are "set out" to house-keeping, happy and contented with our lot.

Our home consisted of a homestead and a timber-culture of 160 acres each. About half of it was fenced and about eighteen acres in cultivation.

We had eleven head of cattle (all were females except one); and nine head of horses.

The David Jackson Titchenal Homestead

DJ Titchenal Ranch
9 miles South of Waterville
June 26 1896
1883-1902

The David Jackson Titchenal Family

David Jackson Titchenal	b. 11/19/1827	d. 6/30/1911
Married Mary Moore 12/04/1856		
Mary Moore Titchenal	b. 10/31/1834	d.1/29/1929

Daniel B.	b. 1/24/1858	d. 6/5/1867
Lewis Hamilton	b. 2/27/1860	d. 10/14/1951
Norman Stanley	b. 2/25/1863	d. 11/8/1947
Nimrod David	b. 1/20/1865	d. 3/27/1949
Nancy Moore	b. 1/19/1870	d. 12/28/1930
John David	b. 1/1/1872	d. 5/13/1933
Phebe Ellen	b. 6/26/1874	d. 6/21/1958

"This clock was purchased from Sol Caninsky by D. J. Titchenal Jan. 8th 1883 at Cheney, Washington ter. Repaired by N. S. Titchenal April 11th 1904."

The David Jackson Titchenal Family

David Jackson and Mary Moore Titchenal,

Lewis Hamilton   Norman Stanley   Nimrod David,

Nancy Moore   John David   Phebe Ellen

Titchenal June 10, 1883 Homestead Claim

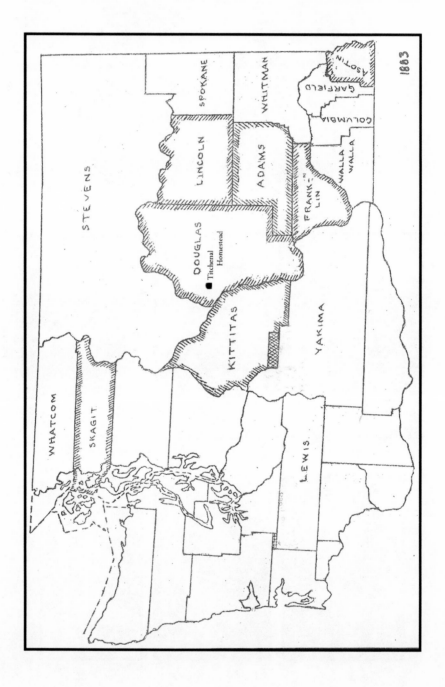

Map Showing the Wagon Roads

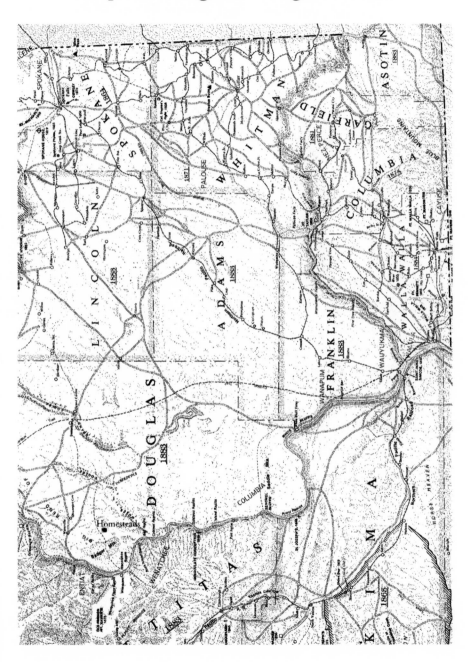

1886 Homestead Claims of Jesse Johnson and Cora Johnson
Map Circa 1886-87

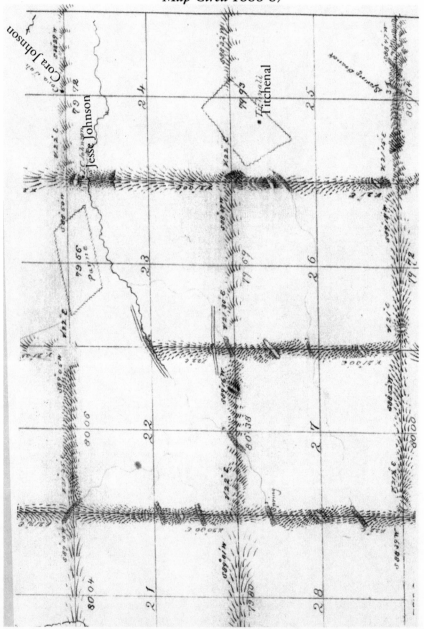

*Township 24 N, Range 22, E. W. M. Washington Territory
near the established claims of the Titchenals*

Lewis H. Titchenal's 1887 Diary
Badger, Douglas Co.
Washington Territory

Memoranda

The snow 14 inches deep.

I am 26 years old and still living with my parents in their log cabin near Badger Mountain. I have formed a new resolution at the beginning of this year to live a better life than I have in the years that are past.

January 1, 1887 Saturday
I returned from the river where I had been on a cold trip for several days: laid out in the snow the night before and was about sick when I reached home.

January 2, 1887 Sunday
I was not feeling very well but walked over to see Cora and found her nearly sick.

January 3, 1887 Monday
Several of us went to the "road election" at the Lake, came back by Jess's and they all went home with us and stayed over night.

January 4, 1887 Tuesday
I mended my whip and walked over to Mr. Norton's with C. and made them a short visit.

January 5, 1887 Wednesday
Took Emma and Cora home in the sled and stayed there most all day. The snow was deep and the wind blew cold.

January 6, 1887 Thursday
I went to the mill after a load of lumber for the new house but had to leave part of it on the hill.

January 7, 1887 Friday
I went back after the rest of my lumber and in the evening Nannie and I went to Jesse's. We had pop corn.

January 9, 1887 Sunday
I read some of Sam Jones' sermon then went to see C. and in the evening we enjoyed a sleigh ride in the Manford's "sled".

January 10, 1887 Monday
I did not do anything of much importance. Gilmore and Cora came over and stayed all night.

January 11, 1887 Tuesday
About 4 o'clock Norman, Nanny, Phebe and I started to P. M. Corbaley's to an oyster supper. Went by for Gilmore and Cora and had a very pleasant time.

January 12, 1887 Wednesday
We arrived at home a little before sunrise a little sleepy and cold. In the evening C. and I went for a sleigh ride and had a good visit. I took C. to Jesse's.

January 13, 1887 Thursday
I did not get up very early but helped dig the cellar the rest of the day.

January 14, 1887 Friday
Jesse helped us work on the cellar.

January 15, 1887 Saturday
In the afternoon I went over to get Jesse to cut my hair. He and Emma went up to Mr. Wills and Cora told me something which caused me to feel bad.

January 16, 1887 Sunday
I took the folks to preaching at the Lake but was feeling too bad to enjoy the sermon.

January 17, 1887 Monday
Jess and Will went to the mountain with me after logs to fix the cellar. I had some bad luck, as usual.

January 18, 1887 Tuesday
I spent the evening with C. She was lonesome and feeling bad. Emma was sick.

January 19, 1887 Wednesday
I worked on the new house. C. came over. I gave Nannie a gold ring for a birthday present. She was 17.

January 20, 1887 Thursday
I was in the house most all day. Jesse, Emma and C. were there and we enjoyed a birthday dinner. I read some and wrote to Nim. Jess, Emma and C. stayed all night.

January 21, 1887 Friday
I helped Norman work on the house.

January 22, 1887 Saturday
I went to the mill after lumber but had to leave part of my load 4 miles from home.

January 23, 1887 Sunday
A nice day: no snow. I went to see Cora. She played and sang some for me.

January 24, 1887 Monday
I went after the lumber that I left on the road Saturday. Took Mother and the girls to Jesse's as I went by there.

January 25, 1887 Tuesday
Jess helped us work on the new house. Emma and Cora came over and stayed all night.

January 26, 1887 Wednesday
I read some and then helped Norman work on the house.

January 29, 1887 Saturday
I worked on the house. In the evening C. came over and I walked home with her. Jess was quite sick for a short time.

January 30, 1887 Sunday
A very disagreeable day. I read several of Sam Jones sermons and went over to see C a little while and found she had been sick most all day.

February 4, 1887 Friday
I went to help Jess work in Cora's well and as he did not work I spent the day at his house and helped C. sew on her new dress.

February 5, 1887 Saturday
I made a "sleigh" then went after C. and we enjoyed a nice sleigh ride and a pleasant and profitable visit. She went home with me.
The weather was very cold all week.

February 6, 1887 Sunday
A pleasant day. C. and I took a strole and had quite a chat. She stayed here over night again.

February 7, 1887 Monday
I went to the mill after another load of lumber.

February 8, 1887 Tuesday
I took my lumber to the new house and C. helped me unload it, then I

took her home on the sled.

February 10, 1887 Thursday
Jess went to the mill with me and I had some more bad luck.

February 11, 1887 Friday
I went over to cheer C. up and we went for a sleigh ride.

February 13, 1887 Sunday
I took the folks to preaching at the Lake. In the evening Nannie and I
went over to Jesse's. C. went home with us.

February 14. 1887 Monday
I worked on the house all day. Cora, Nannie, Phebe, John and I went
coasting by moon light.

February 15, 1887 Tuesday
C. was here and cut my coat off and fixed it for me. Jess helped us raise
the new house.

February 16, 1887 Wednesday
C. and I went to the P.O. in my "new sleigh" came back to Jesse's and I
spent the evening there. C. played and sang.

February 17, 1887 Thursday
Jesse went to the saw mill with me again.

> The above entries appear to be written in Cora's handwriting
> possibly as dictated by Lewis. The Feb. 18th entry is in pencil and
> harder to read as are all the entries starting on March 20th written
> by Lewis

February 18, 1887 Friday
I went after the rest of my load that I left on the hill at me coss and
brought it home. A mistake no.

February 20, 1887 Sunday
It snowed nearly all day. Nannie and I were at Jesse's. We enjoyed some
music then C. and I took a sleigh ride.

February 23, 1887 Wednesday
I took Mother to Jesse's and we were there most all day. I helped C. fix
her organ.

February 24, 1887 Thursday
I went to the mill and in the evening Norman, Nannie and I went to a
sciable at Mr. Barnhart's; enjoyed a good supper and lots of music.

February 25, 1887 Friday
I was too sleepy to do much. Phebe and I went over to Jesse's and C. went home with us.

February 26, 1887 Saturday
I went after Emma in my "little bob". Jess helped us work on the house and we enjoyed another birthday dinner. I took Jess and Emma home but C. stayed all night. The Chinook wind blew hard all day and the snow was fast leaving.

February 27, 1887 Sunday
I am 27 years old today. We went to hear Mr. Fitch preach. I took C. home which was our last sleigh-ride this winter.

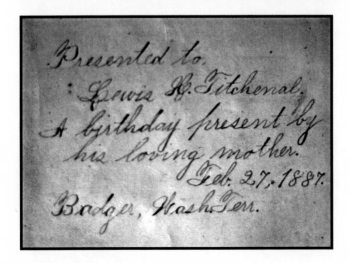

March 6, 1887 Sunday
A beautiful day but windy. I was at Jesse's and C. and I enjoyed a horseback ride also a pleasant visit.

March 7, 1887 Monday
I went to Okanogan after some nails, called at Mr. Barnhart's and the evening with C.

March 8, 1887 Tuesday
Norman and I worked on the house all day and spent the evening at Jesse's.

March 9, 1887 Wednesday
Norman and I went on the mountain to make shingles.

March 10, 1887 Thursday
I sawed all day, Jess came at noon and helped me som in the eavening and he went home at night.

March 11, 1887 Friday
Jess came and helped me all day and we worked hard all day.

March 12, 1887 Saturday
Worked till noon and John and John Norton brought the horses and we all went home.

March 13, 1887 Sunday
C. and I went to preaching horseback: heard a very good sermon: came back to Jesse's to dinner and C. went home with me.

March 14, 1887 Monday
I went to the mountain after shingle bolts.

March 15, 1887 Tuesday
I went to the mountain again and Mr. Rowell came in the eavening and stayed all night.

March 16, 1887 Wednesday
I went with Gilmore to "Nashland" and took supper at Jesse's and went home feeling a little discouraged.

March 17, 1887 Thursday
I made a trade with Mr. Rowell and bought "Black Hawk" then went with the boys to the mountain and brought back a load of shingle bolts for Jess.

March 18, 1887 Friday
I went to the mountain after another load and sold one of my cows to

Mr. Cox.

March 19, 1887 Saturday
I went to the mountain again; came back and went to Okanogan to see Mr. Rowell, but he was not there. I didn't get home till late.

March 20, 1887 Sunday
I read some then C. and I went to the new house for a visit. I walked home with her in the evening.

March 21, 1887 Monday
Nailed shingles on the new house. In the evening Gilmore, Jesse, Emma and Cora came over and stayed awhile.

March 22, 1887 Tuesday
Gilmore and Norman helped me build fence on my ranch.

March 23, 1887 Wednesday
The boys helped me with the fence again. Emma and Cora were there. C. stayed all night and we had pop-corn.

March 24, 1887 Thursday
I helped Mr. Norton start to Spokane Falls. Then I went after the cattle. C. shingled my hair - a very good "job".

March 25, 1887 Friday
I nailed on shingles and in the afternoon went after the cows and spent the evening at Jess's.

March 26, 1887 Saturday
I nailed on shingles and then went to Okanogan and rode Bragg.

Memoranda
We were enjoying some of the calm March winds during the week.

March 27, 1887 Sunday
C. and I went to the Lake to church. Mr. Fitch preached. It was a very windy day. Cora was nearly sick.

March 28, 1887 Monday
Went after the horses. Cora and Emma came over in the morning. I went after the cattle and Gilmore's horses and got met. Cora stayed all night.

March 29, 1887 Tuesday
Cora and I went over to Jesse's. C. was sick and she rode Bragg. I came back and worked on the fence. In the eavening I plowed.

March 30, 1887 Wednesday
I plowed all day and was some tired when night came.

March 31, 1887 Thursday
I hunted cattle untill noon and plowed in the eavening and Gilmore
   brought his horses up to cach his horses to start.

April 1, 1887 Friday
I went over to Jesse's after the yearling calf that Father traded for and saw
   Gib start.

April 2, 1887 Saturday
I looked for Gib's horses and Cora and I went to Okanogan in the
   eavening and came back by Mr. Rosnharts' and had a very nice visit.
   Very windy.

Memoranda

It was very windy most all week.

April 3, 1887 Sunday
Mother and I went over to Jesse's. Emma was sick. Mrs. Wills and Mr.
   Will were there too. Cora and I had a fine visit in the eve.

April 4, 1887 Monday
I went to look after Gillmore's horses. In the evening I plowed.

April 5, 1887 Tuesday
We planted seeds on the timber culture Father, Phebe and me. Jess
   harrowed for me.

April 6, 1887 Wednesday
We planted seeds again and John Norton helped. I caught Bragg for
   Cora. She went to the post office. Jess worked for me again.

April 7, 1887 Thursday
Jess and Cora came over. Jess harrowed for me again. I mended C.'s shoe
   and finished my seed planting on the timber culture.

April 8, 1887 Friday
Cora, Jess Emma came over. I hunted cattle most of the day. C. helped
   me milk the Indian cow.

April 9, 1887 Saturday
I went after the stray horses and met the man that owned them. I did not
   get my breakfast until 10 o'clock.

Memoranda

It has been cold most of the week. The ground froze most every night.

April 10, 1887 Sunday
Easter. A rainy morning and it snowed about 9 o'clock and it rained until 4 o'clock. In the evening I went over to see Cora and found her with the blues but I had them so I couldn't console her much.

April 11, 1887 Monday
I plowed all day. Cora came over to make mothers dress and stayed all night. There was something said that made me feel bad because I did not behave very good and it gave me the blues worse than ever.

April 12, 1887 Tuesday
I could not find the horses until eleven o'clock and found a young colt. It snowed in the eve.

April 13, 1887 Wednesday
Went to put in Mr. Bliss crop. Father and I went. I worked untill late then got supper and then went to bed but did not sleep good.

April 14, 1887 Thursday
Went to work early and Jess came by hunting horses but I did not speek to him.

April 15, 1887 Friday
Got up early and worked hard all day and did not get done untill 4 o'clock and then we started home and did not get home until half past ten.

April 16, 1887 Saturday
I went over to Jess's to see if he was going to move Cora's house and we moved it and C. helped us. Then we enjoyed a good visit in the "old maid's" shanty. Another windy day.

April 17, 1887 Sunday
Cora came over and we went up to the new house and we had a fine visit long to be remembered.

April 18, 1887 Monday
I went apiece of the way with Cora. She was sick and went home before breakfast. I went to J. after his saddle.

April 19, 1887 Tuesday
I ran horses in the morning. In the eav I nailed shingles on the new house.

April 20, 1887 Wednesday
I went to the Post Office and to see Mr. Corbaley and found Cora up there came home with her.

April 21, 1887 Thursday
I went to Jess's after shingle bolts and Cora came home with me and stayed all night.

April 22, 1887 Friday
I went to the mill. Cora went home as I went by. I got a letter from Nim.

April 23, 1887 Saturday
Jess came over and I went home with him and brought C.'s organ over to Father's.

April 24, 1887 Sunday
Cora came over and we all went up to the new house and heard some music for the last time for a while played by that hand. C. & J. had a visit in the eve but did not feel good.

April 25, 1887 Monday
I went after lumber for Smith and went by Jess's and Cora rode to the forks of the road with me and I told her and Jess and Emma good by.

April 26, 1887 Tuesday
I stayed at Mr. Barnhart's. I started from the Lake in the morning and stalled at Bungers and had to leave some of my lumber and stalled at the coulee and I had to unlode again.

April 27, 1887 Wednesday
I woked up early and started for Smiths once more and got there at eleven o'clock and met Norman and Smith coming to look for me. I stayed the rest of the day and night.

April 28, 1887 Thursday
I started home and went by L. Grandy's and Lambert's and got home by four o'clock.

April 29, 1887 Friday
I made some single trees and fixed my wagon and harness.

April 30, 1887 Saturday
I went to the mill and got another load of lumber and left it at the Lake and came home and made a toung for Father's wagon so I could use it for a trail.

Memoranda
Very windy Friday and Saturday.

May 1, 1887 Sunday
I helped Repaint catch some horses and rote to Cora and Rowell and some in my diary.

144

May 2, 1887 Monday
I started to the Lake to hitchup and got to Lamberts at six o'clock and stayed all night and Mr. Corble came and stayed all night to. He was hunting horses.

May 3, 1887 Tuesday
I got up with a bad cold and was nearly sick. I started out and got to Smith's about 3 o'clock and Mr. Bliss was there and wanted me to look for his horses the next day for they had got away.

May 4, 1887 Wednesday
I started to look for Bliss horses and he went to take teem to the mill. I found them on the had of rock island creek and I run her to fathers.

May 5, 1887 Thursday
I got up early and tried to catch Bragg and did not cach him for two hours. Then I went to the mill and Mr. Bliss helped me load up and I went to the coulee.

May 6, 1887 Friday
I got up early and did not see but one horse but soon found the rest and hitched up and started and got to Smith's between one and two o'clock. The boys was eating dinner.

May 7, 1887 Saturday
I started home and got to Lamberts at one o'clock and left at two and it rained on me all the way and I got home wet and hungry about dark

Memoranda
Cold and windy the most of the week and rain Saturday.

May 8, 1887 Sunday
Mr. Bliss was here in the morning. I wrote to Cora and to Nim and rote up in my diary. It was a cold and windy day and I thought I would rest.

May 9, 1887 Monday
I went to the mill after another load of lumber for Smith and it commenced to rain on me when I got half way. It rained all the rest of the day and most of the night and it snowed at the mill about 6 in. I stayed at the mill.

May 10, 1887 Tuesday
I started early and went to the coulee below the Sage flat and I write this by the lite of the camp fire and it is glong low. I went to stir the fire and burnt my finger.

May 11, 1887 Wednesday
I got up early and my horses was gon and I found them about a mile
from camp. I got to Smith about 9 o'clock in the morning and I
helped them.

May 12, 1887 Thursday
I got up early and started for the river to help some French out of a bad
fix they had broke ther wagon. We loaded up and got back to Smiths
after dark and stayed all night at Smiths.

May 13, 1887 Friday
We started this morning but not very early because we had to load ther
wagon again and went to the slide and we stalled with six horses and
had to unload and make to trips. We got to the top of the hill at
Lamberts.

May 14, 1887 Saturday
I got up early and Jim and fam was gon and I found them five miles from
camp. They was coming home right across the prairie and we started
at 9 o'clock and had a hot and dry trip. We got to the Lake at half
past one with some tiored horses and unloaded and I got home by six
o'clock.

May 15, 1887 Sunday
I wrote to Cora. I did not get up very early then shaved and went to
Nashess and Corbles and then to Okanogan to see if I could hear from C.

May 16, 1887 Monday
I started to the mill after another load of lumber and started from the
mill at 2 o'clock and camped on the parrie and at Bungers' so I staked
the horses and went to bed.

May 17, 1887 Tuesday
I got up early and started when the sun was half hour high and got along
all right and got to Smith's just before sun down and had to go to
Christesons after a retica

> *May 17, 1886 in her diary entry Cora says,*
> *"I drew Lewis' picture."*

Master Lewis: Onjons,

Badger, May 17th 1886.

May 18, 1887 Wednesday
I started home early came by Lamberts and bought 8 sacks of potatos and some blankets and the wedes so I had a load without a bed on my wagon.

May 19, 1887 Thursday
I started to Rowells and got to the mill and Cohorly Will had sawed his hand off and wanted me to go to the Doctorss with him so I rode hard all day to get ready.

May 20, 1887 Friday
I got up before it was light and started to the mill before five o'clock but it taken us till 10 o'clock to get by the Lake and we eat our dinner at Lamberts and then drove to Eddnes.

May 21, 1887 Saturday
I got up as soon as I could see good and Mrs. Wills got breakfast and we started 15 minutes before 5 o'clock. I drove 35 miles before dinner and we diest C hand and then started and drover to Duke St.

May 22, 1887 Sunday
I got up half past 2 and started once more for Ritzville to cach the trane at half past 7 and got there at half past six and had to hury to get Charlies things on the train and did not have time to eat my breakfast till after the trane left so I didn't get to go to the Folks as I expected to do so I stayed there all day and was lonesome.

May 23, 1887 Monday
I started home at eight. I eat my dinner at Durke Spring's and then drove on out on the hill about 10 milles from Echearts and camped for the night. I got my supper and went to bed. I saw Perpont and he told me where Gibs horses was.

May 24, 1887 Tuesday

I got up it was sun up. I got my breakfast and started at six and drove
down to the sink and eat my dinner at the sink and drove to Eddens
in the eve and camped.

May 25, 1887 Wednesday

I woke up it was sun up so I got my breakfast and started once more for
home and got to Lamberts for dinner and eat my dinner with him
and went by Okanogan and got the mail and got a letter from C. and
got home after all was in bed.

May 26, 1887 Thursday

I stayed part of the night at home once more but started to Spokane
this morning and eat my lunch at the sink once more and rode to
Echorton and stayed for the night.

May 27, 1887 Friday

I started to look for Gibs horses. I eat my dinner at the sheep camp and I
heard of the horses at Coolers and I rode the length of the creek and
mist them and herd of them 15 miles back.

May 28, 1887 Saturday

I went to Sprague on Saturday. I started for Spokane at one o'clock and
got to Spokane at sun up and I found several of the boys and men
that I knew from thongman and I stayed until train time and then I
went to Spangle and I rode with C. Lery to the flat and then walked
to W.

May 29, 1887 Sunday

I got my breakfast at Gimbles and went over to J. H. to see Cora and
found her sick. Nim went to the gate with me. Cora and I had a
plesent visit untill late bedtime and I stayed all n

May 30, 1887 Monday

I stayed most all day with Cora at J. Hays. She was sick then I went to see
Will and talked to him for a while then went to Waverly and went to
bed in M J stable.

May 31, 1887 Tuesday

I got my breakfast at Gimbles and Nim took me to Spangle to meet
the train. I went to the Falls on the cars and stayed all night ote the
tunnel had caved in and there was no train.

June 1, 1887 Wednesday

I got up at 2 o'clock and took the train for Sprague and got there at 4 o'clock. I got my breakfast and started to look for Gib's horses and rode all day and did not find them and I stayed all night at forks.

June 2, 1887 Thursday
I got up and started to hunt horses once more. I rode till noon and got my dinner at Poples Sheep ranch and started out once more. I had got no trace of then yet later than 10 days. I stayed all night at Cans.

June 3, 1887 Friday
I got up and started and Harington and I rode all day and I got to the city at noon and I went down to the creek and they had bin there 3 days before. I stayed at Mary Stossckst Co.

June 4, 1887 Saturday
I got a nother horse and started for Crab Creek and my new horse throwed me off and I woked up to the fact that I was left a foot on the prairie to stand and watch my horse run off across the prarie with my sadle and I was left to follow if I wanted to so I ran him in corell and caught him and it was raining so I did not hunt no more and I stayed at Mitcham's

June 5, 1887 Sunday
It cleared up once more and I started to look for the horses again and I went over to what is called Sears Valley and I heard they had bin there Friday but had left so I went back to Glosscocks.

June 6, 1887 Monday
I started out and I heard of them where they had bin Saturday at dark and I rode all day and did not hear of them any more so I stayed all night with a bachelor near Davenport.

June 7, 1887 Tuesday
I started down Crab Creek and went down to Bacon Ranch and I never saw a man that had ever heard of them so I stayed all night at Bacon and went out hunting for a short distance.

June 8, 1887 Wednesday
I started back to Meringlsle and I rode what is called Sorck Valley but did not hear of them so I got the store just before so I went up to Glosscocks.

June 9, 1887 Thursday
I found Tucker she has been put in Glosscocks pasture and the fellow said he wanted $5 for his trouble and he would bring them all in in two hours for $5 a piece so I found it was heading them in the hills

for the reward and I got too close to them and the had to turn them loose and a man came by and told me where they were and I found them after dark at Tembles in his lot. I started the horses and went to Hangton and stoped to write to C. and the boy that was watching the horses came in. I went to Glosscocks for Bragg and Tucker and I started at 1 o'clock for Popols and it was good time tied some of the horses. Sat. I started for Richesons Ranch and I started on Tucker and I turned Bragg loose and he folowed me for about 12 mile and then he turned back 7 miles. Then I rode him. I stayed at Richesons.

June 12, 1887 Sunday
A rainy morning but I started to Smith's as I had one of his horses and rained most all day. I got to Smith's at 4 o'clock and I found Norman there at work on the house. I stayed all night.

June 13, 1887 Monday
Another rainy morning and I stayed at Smiths till 4 o'clock and then it quit and I started home with the horses and I got home at dark and found them all well and Bliss and 2 strangers were there.

June 14, 1887 Tuesday
John and B taken the horses over the mounton as they went to look for some of the catle that was over there and I went to Corbles with Blackhawk and Nan was there and I stayed all night.

June 15, 1887 Wednesday
I helped the boys cach a wild horse and Corble rode it to hunt horses. I rote to Cora and Gip. I was at the store awhile and got some writing.

June 16, 1887 Thursday
I helped the boys start to Foster Creek and Nannie and I went home in the eve and there was a sedler stayed all night there.

June 17, 1887 Friday
I started to Rowells and went by Draff Bros and stayed all night with them. There was a man there with his leg broke.

June 18, 1887 Saturday
I started once more and went to the Ferry and crost and wint to the Soap Lake Ferry and the cable was broke and I had to get an Indian to cross me in a small boat. I got to Rawells about four o'clock and found him at home but he had his horse to start to look for some stock and he left me to tend supper and went off.

June 19, 1887 Sunday
I started home and I got to the Okanogan River and had to wate for
Corbley to come and cross me over the river and I stoped with the
Indians hour and 1/2 before I could cross and I crossed the Columbia
and I stayed at Parsons.

June 20, 1887 Monday
I started on and stoped at Downeys and got my dinner and got to the
Lake at five o'clock and I eat my supper at Barnharts and I got home
about dark.

June 21, 1887 Tuesday
I went to Corbles and got there at noon and I stayed there all night. The
boys got there at noon off the round up.

June 22, 1887 Wednesday
Was at Corbles, they went to the river on the round up so I wrote to
Cora and I got a letter from Cora and I was some lonesome.

June 23, 1887 Thursday
I milk for Mrs. Corbley, then went up to the mill and then went home in
the eve.

June 24, 1887 Friday
Norman and I went to the river at Wenatchee after some yearlings cattle
and stayed all night.

June 25, 1887 Saturday
We helped Corble round up and brand his cattle and found some of the
cattle and stayed all night again with Corble.

Memoranda
A very windy day Saturday.

June 26, 1887 Sunday
We started home with the cattle and came by Corbles and got home
about sun down and found Gip there.

June 27, 1887 Monday
Gip and I went after his horses and it took us most all day to find them.
We brought them home and [worked] the Fisk mar after supper and
went over to see Chorbley.

June 28, 1887 Tuesday
Nannie and I started to Spokane Falls and Nannie drove the bugy for
Mrs. Sehurer and we camped at Moses Coulee.

June 29, 1887 Wednesday
We started at half past six and eat out dinner at the 35 mile stake and went to with in 4 miles of Blind Spring and camped for the night.

June 30, 1887 Thursday
We got alate start this morning and Wheeler was half drunk all day. We eat dinner at the Bend of Wilson Creek and drove out on the prairie and camped south of the Butte.

July 1, 1887 Friday
I got up and got breakfast and had to wate an hour for Cultis Jim & the old Lady to get up. We stoped for noon at the Creek 2 ½ mi the other side of Cristle Spring. We camped at Mondows.

July 2, 1887 Saturday
I got up before sun up and went to see about the horses. We got to Deff Creek about ten o'clock and I stoped at Mr. Merimans and seen Cora and she looked very bad poorer than I ever saw her. We went on to the lake and left the wagon and 4 horses and came back in the bugy Merimans.

July 3, 1887 Sunday
We stayed untill after dinner at Mr. Mermans then we went to Spokane Cora, Nannie and I. Nannie stayed at Corables and C. stayed at Mrs. McKinneys and I found Nim and we stayed at the hotel.

July 4, 1887 Monday
We stayed until one o clock at the Falls then we went to Spangle and found Mr. Hays and Mr. Thayers folks and Nannie went home with Mr. Hayses in the back and Cora and I came in the buggy.

July 5, 1887 Tuesday
I stayed at J. Hayses and all day felt tiord. I didn't do any thing.

July 6, 1887 Wednesday
I was still Mr. Hays. I picked some berrys then I went to sleep then I road some.

July 7, 1887 Thursday
Nim came over and we went to Hughes and I didn't get back till late and Cora and I went buggy rideing and had a fine time one long to be remembered.

July 8, 1887 Friday
I picked some berrys for Mrs. Hays and my self and talked to Cora the rest of the day.

July 9, 1887 Saturday
I picked some more berries in the morning then Cora. Nannie, and I went to Mr. Tyres and spent the eve and Nannie stayed all night.

Memoranda
Some very warm weather.

July 10,1887 Sunday
Cora and Mr. Hayses girls went to S.S. with me and we went to get Nan and Nim came over and spent the eve with us.

July 11, 1887 Monday
We started for Medical Lake and got there in time to go to hear Mrs. Jones preach and she preached a good sermon and Nan and I had a boat ride and then stayed with Mr. Seburr.

July 12, 1887 Tuesday
We started for Spokane but it was late before I got my horses and we got there at 9 o clock and Nannie stayed at Corbles.

July 13, 1887 Wednesday
I got up and commenced trading as the bisness commenced and got through late in the eve and we had to stay all night again.

July 14, 1887 Thursday
We started for home and got to get out on the Medical Lake to get some horses and we stayed at the ranch till after dinner and went to Mr. Meriman and stayed the night.

July 15, 1887 Friday
We started and I put in a new horse and we eat dinner at Mandovia and then we went four miles the other side of Cotton wood and camped on Hawk Creek for the night.

July 16, 1887 Saturday
We started early and eat dinner on Wilson Creek and went to the bend of Wilson Creek and stayed for the night.

July 17, 1887 Sunday
Sunday morning, I hitched up a horse that had never bin worked before because she would not load and we eat dinner 4 miles west of blind springs and went to the Coulee and stalled on the hill.

July 18, 1887 Monday
We started at sun up and went to Moses Coulee for dinner and went to Weheren springs and stoped for the night.

July 19, 1887 Tuesday

We started home once more and got home at noon tiord and dusty unloaded some of my load in the eve then retired for the night.

July 20, 1887 Wednesday

I was sick most all night and all morning rote to Cora is all I done in the morning.

Yarns About Bears.

A bloody battle occured one day last week on the Longacre ranch northeast of town between the Titchueal Bros. threshing crew and a black bear. The pitchfork brigade soon surrounded, and after a desperate fight, slaughtered the monarch of the Cascades. The boys and the neighbors know from experience that bear steak is good.

On Wednesday last another bear came to inspect Sam Robins' steam thresher a few miles north of Waterville. Tom Clark shot and wounded him. The infuriated brute then made for the threshers with jaws and claws fully extended. The "pitchfork brigade" was ready for the assault, and Ed. Fitch, who was a little in advance of the others, with his strong arms split his head open with an axe.

Bears are very numerous around Badger mountain. Two were seen last Saturday evening—one said to be very large—in the Payne canyon on the east side of Badger by a boy hunting cows.

Last week while riding on the south side of Badger mountain Messrs. Album and Jennings came on to a black bear. The boys had no firearms, but determined to capture the brute with their lariats, and started in pursuit. Mr. Album made a cast which landed fairly over Bruin's head and brought him to a sudden halt. Jennings then threw his rope around the bear, and fastened the end to a tree. Album then pulled in the opposite direction, and Jennings killed the animal with a club.

July 21, 1887 Thursday

I went up to the P.O. early in order to mail some letters and stayed most all day and didn't get no letter and was disapointed. I got my supper at Mr. Wills.

July 22, 1887 Friday

S. B. Nash came early and stayed most all day. I stacked hay in the eve and Norman ran the machine.

July 23, 1887 Saturday

I dident do much of any thing in the morning and I went to Okanogan in the eve after the mail but was disapointed

Memoranda

We had some very warm weather & some rain Saturday eve.

July 24, 1887 Sunday

It is very windy. Gip came over after his horse to go and look after his horses. Mrs. Robins and Mrs. Stener came over. I read most all day and did not feel good and I wrote to Cora in the eve.

July 25, 1887 Monday

I staked hay till noon and it was so windy that we couldn't do any thing in the hay so I hitched up Black Hawk and worked him   he worked very well for the first time.

July 26, 1887 Tuesday

I staked hay all day but did not get done but got one stack most finished.

July 27, 1887 Wednesday

I went to the mill and to the P.O. but dident get any letter then I came back by Jameses and Robins and got home late.

July 28, 1887 Thursday

Norman and I worked on the new house all day.

July 29, 1887 Friday

We worked on the house again puting on the cornice it was a slow and hard job.

July 30, 1887 Saturday

We worked on the house again untill noon. Then we cleaned out the woll then worked on the house again untill night.

Memoranda

Very plasant wether most all week.

July 31, 1887 Sunday
I went up to the new house and read most of the morning then went to
Okanogan after the mail & got a letter from Cora.

August 1, 1887 Monday
Norman and I worked on the new house all day.

August 2, 1887 Tuesday
We worked on the house again. Mr. Bliss came by going to leave for the
round.

August 3, 1887 Wednesday
I worked on the house untill noon then went to the PO in the eve after
the mail and to see Nash and I got a letter from Cora.

August 4, 1887 Thursday
I worked on the house by my self all day as Norman had to run the
machine and I was nearly sick as I was sick most of the night.

August 5, 1887 Friday
I worked untill noon on the house by my self then Norman helped me.
In the eve I went over to Charlies.

August 6, 1887 Saturday
I and father went on the mountain after mill house logs. We got back at
4 O clock then I hitched up Black Hawk and drove him awhile.

Memoranda
It has bin windy most of the week and Saturday and Sunday very windy.

August 7, 1887 Sunday
I was lazy and did not get up very early. I shaved and read some. Gip
came over. Mr. Anderson came in the eve. Gip and I went to Cora
well after Mrs. Payne Pick I went down after it.

August 8, 1887 Monday
I caught Bird and trimed her feet then got ready and started to the Falls.
I started at 8 o clock. I eat my dinner at the lean stoke then went to
Moses Coulee and stoped for the night.

August 9, 1887 Tuesday
I started at 7 O & went to Grand Coulee hill for dinner then went to
Blind Springs and stoped for the night.

August 10, 1887 Wednesday
Got up and started once more and met the Mclean boys taking there
stock out to the bend. I eat my dinner on the hill east of the creek

then within 1 mile of Cherstle.

August 11, 1887 Thursday
It was a cool morning but I didn't injoy as I did one cool morning once
before along here I stoped for dinner at Mandonia & then went out
on the White bluff Pearrie and camped near the timber.

August 12, 1887 Friday
I got to Spokane about half past 9 o clock and found sevrel of my friends
there. I got my dinner at Corsons and my supper also and I slep in
the wagon.

August 13, 1887 Saturday
I was in the Falls all morning. Mr. Hays and Mr. Cobb came to the
wagon before I got up. I started for Waverly at 2 o clock and my horse
got lame and I stoped near Liberty and stayed all night.

August 14, 1887 Sunday
I started for Mr. Hays and I met Jason and all Ginble and sevrel others
that I knew and got to Mr. Hays at ½ past 10 and Cora and I went to
S.S. horse back and met sevrel that I knew.

August 15, 1887 Monday
I stayed at Mr. Hays till after noon then Jess and Emma and I went to
Waverly in the hack but I didn't get to see Nim as he was gon so we
went back to Hays burg and stayed over night.

August 16, 1887 Tuesday
This is Cora birthday and I am at Mr. Hays and Cora and Emma and
Edna and Momy and Claud and I went to Mr. Thayers and spent the
day and had a very plesant time and Cora weighed 130 lbs.

August 17, 1887 Wednesday
I stayed at Hayses all day and talked to C. most of the day she was sick
but she was some better in the eve.

August 18, 1887 Thursday
We started to Spokane that is Jess and Emma we eat our dinner at
Spangle then went to Spokane and oat there at 8 O clock.

August 19, 1887 Friday
We looked around to see what we could do and we rented a stable of Mr.
Murpy for $6 per month and had our horses shod.

August 20, 1887 Saturday
We fixted our wagons and went after lumber and Jess stalled and we
never got back till 6 O clock.

August 21, 1887 Sunday
I did not get up till late then went to the Methodist church then came
back and wrote to Mother and Cora then went to hear Mrs. Jones
preach.

August 22, 1887 Monday
We started to haul lumber. Jess stalled and I had to pull him out. We got
in late then we went after another load and it got dark on us and we
left our loads till morning.

August 23, 1887 Tuesday
We went after our wagon then wated till after dinner and then started
after another load and got in good time and Jess and I went down
Tochin after supper.

August 24, 1887 Wednesday
We started after another load & to try our luck again and we got along
fine all day and made two trips then went down again after supper.

August 25, 1887 Thursday
We went after another load of lumber and found the mill stoped so we
did not hall but one load then we looked around in the evening to see
what we could find.

August 26, 1887 Friday
We went to Darts mill after lumber and did not get back till six o'clock
& I found Cora there sick but her and I went to the shore in the eve
and had a pleasant time.

August 27, 1887 Saturday
I did not haul lumber. I stayed at home with Cora as she was nearly sick
and we went buggy rideing in the eve and had a very pleasant ride and
visit.

August 28, 1887 Sunday
Cora and I went to hear Mrs. James preach then we went to the
Arelington and spent a very pleasant time then we went for a walk
across the river and back to church.

August 29, 1887 Monday
Cora and I went downtown. Cora done some trading and then went to
dinner and then Cora went to Waverly and I went to the train with
her and I was lonely the rest of the eve.

August 30, 1887 Tuesday
Jess and I went to holl lumber and it rained on us the most of the day.

We got along fine & got home at five o'clock.

August 31, 1887 Wednesday
We went after another load and it rained on us again. We loaded with Lath and Jess's team nearly gave out and we never got home till after dark.

September 1, 1887 Thursday
It was a rainy day and we did not do anything only colect some money we had earned and looked for another better job.

September 2, 1887 Friday
We went after lumber again and I halled the largest load that I had halled over 10 hundred ft and we had to take it clear through town and up the hill and it was dark and rainy.

September 3, 1887 Saturday
Another rainy day we did not do nothing. in the eve I went to see Mr. Corble then to see Mr. Dort about a bill of lumber.

Memoranda
A very rainy week. It rained some every day this week.

September 4. 1887 Sunday
It was the latest that I had ever ate my breakfast. I went to hear Mr. Corble preach in the morning and Mrs. Jones in the eve & was lonesome all day.

September 5, 1887 Monday
Jess and I went after lumber and got along all right and got home at back at 3 o'clock.

September 6, 1887 Tuesday
We went after another load of lumber & did not get back till late and was tiard and hauled 14 hhd ft.

September 7, 1887 Wednesday
We halled lumber & got along fine & I went to the C & C mill after some feed after I got my load off & after supper I wrote to Cora.

September 8, 1887 Thursday
I went after lumber again and got back at 6 and had to go downtown to pay for some hay that I had bought for me & I bought a suit of clothes.

September 9, 1887 Friday
We went after lumber again today & I had to go to the top of the grade

on Hangman to unload & Emma gave me a letter from Cora.

September 10, 1887 Saturday
Hauled lumber again and got along fine. I went down town & bought some clothes & watch and did not get to bed till late.

September 11, 1887 Sunday
I got up late then went to hear Mrs. Jones preach then went downtown but did not find anybody I cared to see & was lonely and went to Ch to the Cong Ch.

September 12, 1887 Monday
We halled lumber out along the praire all day. Got a letter from Cora & one from Mother & answered Cora's.

September 13, 1887 Tuesday
We hauled lumber. Jess and I went downtown to the Octon but did not buy anything.

September 14, 1887 Wednesday
We halled lumber got along fine got back at five o' clock. Jess and I went down town after supper.

September 15, 1887 Thursday
We started after lumber and met Mr. Dort and he told us the mill was broke so we went back and I did not do anything. We went over and settled up with Dort.

September 16, 1887 Friday
We went after lumber again & had to wate for them to saw it & was late in getting home & found Gip there.

September 17, 1887 Saturday
We went to Demeses mill & had ahard trip & got home late & I was sick all day.

Memoranda
12 – 1064
13 – 1358
14 - 1866

September 18, 1887 Sunday
A rainy day & I was sick all day & went to bed for a while then got & wrote to Cora and Gip & I went to church & had to stand up because here was no seat.

September 19, 1887 Monday
We went to hall lumber again.

September 20, 1887 Tuesday
We halled lumber again & it was dark whin we got home & we had to get our own supper.

September 21, 1887 Wednesday
Halled lumber again & did not get home till dark.

September 22, 1887 Thursday
We went after lumber again & Jess horse gave out & we was in the night in unloding.

September 23, 1887 Friday
We went after lumber again & came back another road & got in late again & Jesses horse got very tiord before we got here.

September 24, 1887 Saturday
I went after lumber by myself as Jess did not go & got along fine & got back early & Gip and Emmg came from Waverly.

September 25, 1887 Sunday
I went to hear Mrs. Jones preach & the morning & then took astroll around town. We went to Catholic Church in the eve that is Jess, Emma, Edna and I.

September 26, 1887 Monday
I halled lumber again & got a very late start. It was half past seven when we got started to the mill & we never got back till very late.

September 27, 1887 Tuesday
Another late start & another time to middle in the night.

September 28, 1887 Wednesday
Another late start but we got back alittle earlyer by hurrying all day.

September 29, 1887 Thursday
We went after lumber & I was sick all day & a piece of lumber fell on me & hurt me & we did not get back till after dark then had to get our supper & I took some medsn & went to bed.

September 30, 1887 Friday
I went after lumber again & it rained all day & we had a hard day of it. We came back but did not unload & we had to get our supper again & did not get much.

October 1, 1887 Saturday

I went and unloaded my lumber & had the lock ------- then went and settled up with Demese for halling; and Emma and Jody came on the train.

October 2, 1887 Sunday

Joe & I got up & we found them eating. I went to hear Mrs. Jones again then Joe & I took a stroll down town and I went to hear Mrs. Jones again.

October 3, 1887 Monday

Jess and I went to saw mill and we halled two loads and I stalled with the last load & had unload part of it. Joe went with us in the eve.

October 4, 1887 Tuesday

We hall lumber in the morning & in the eve we stayed in town for we could not get any lumber till morning.

October 5, 1887 Wednesday

We went after lumber again & I stalled & Jess had to hook on & help me out. I wint back by my self and got along fine and I found Cora and Gip at.

October 6, 1887 Thursday

A rainy morning & I stayed in the Falls.

October 7, 1887 Friday

We went to Deweses mill after lumber. I stalled & Jess had to pull me out. I left my wagon on the other side of the river.

October 8, 1887 Saturday

I unloaded my lumber then Cora & I went down town & done some trading.

October 9, 1887 Sunday

I eat my breakfast with Cora & Joe & Emma. Cora & I & Edna went to me church then went to the Winsor hotel and spent a pleasant time then to hear Mrs. Jones.

October 10, 1887 Monday

Joe and I slept together & I got up and went to the train with him & C. & E. Then got my breakfast with Emma & went to hall lumber.

October 11, 1887 Tuesday

I got up and got my breakfast & went after lumber & came back & found Cora in bed & did not go back in the afternoon I stayed with Cora.

162

October 12, 1887 Wednesday
I went after lumber & when I came back at noon I found Cora in bed
sick and I stayed till one o'clock with her then went after another
load.

October 13, 1887 Thursday
I went after lumber once more & came back at noon & Mr. Robertson
came & took Cora to the Dr & I stayed & settled with Mr. Winpy.

October 14, 1887 Friday
A rainy day but I went after lumber but only halled one load & I went
with Cora to see Mrs. M. start to Walla Walla then went down town
with Cora to trade some.

October 15, 1887 Saturday
I went down town with Cora to finish her trading & her & Mr. Mayse's
folks started home at noon & I went to the mill after lumber & was in
the night getting back.

October 16, 1887 Sunday
It was late when I got up and I went to the resterant & got my breakfast
then went to S.S. at the hall then went to Y. M. C. A. & then took
astroll with Em and Mrs. M. then went to hear Mrs. Jones.

October 17, 1887 Monday
I went after lumber and had bad luck & stalled & had to unload & did
not get to town in time to unload so I got my supper and went to bed
tiard.

October 18, 1887 Tuesday
I unloaded my load & went down town to buy some hay and helped
unload it and then went down town and bought some pevursions &
then eat my supper.

October 19, 1887 Wednesday
I went after lumber and got along fine & got back early & went to see
Emma & went to the P O & to prayer meeting with her.

October 20, 1887 Thursday
I halled lumber again and got along nicely & got back early & went
down town awhile and then wrote to Cora and then to bed.

October 21, 1887 Friday
Went after lumber once more and Mage got sick & I had to doctor him
& was till after night getting back & found a strange teem in the
stable.

October 22, 1887 Saturday

I got up in the night and found one of my horses sick so I doctored him most of the day.

<h2 style="text-align:center">Memoranda</h2>

It is a very windy day.

October 23, 1887 Sunday

As I was eating my breakfast I heard the fire bell and wint to see the fire but was disipointed as there was no fire. I went to hear Mr. J. preach and then E. & I went to the Y. M. C. A. and then to the lecture.

October 24, 1887 Monday

I went after lumber & then went with Emma & Grandma to the lecture & then stayed all night at Grandmas & I got a letter from Cora.

October 25, 1887 Tuesday

I halled lumber again and went to the lecture again and went to Grandma's & stayed all night as it was a cold night.

October 26, 1887 Wednesday

I halled lumber from the Coulee mill & was late getting back & I had found them gon to the lecture so I went by myself. A snow day.

October 27, 1887 Thursday

A rainy day but I worked all day & got in late tiord & late. I went down town a little while and seen John Teyan.

October 28, 1887 Friday

I started to Waverly at ½ past 11 o'clock and my horses gave out and I did not get to Mr. Hayses till nine o'clock and found Cora anciously look for me.

October 29, 1887 Saturday

I stayed at Mr. Hays all day & packed up Cora's things & Cora & I went to Waverly & to Mr. Thayers.

<h2 style="text-align:center">Memoranda</h2>

A rainy week.

October 30, 1887 Sunday

I stayed at Mr. Hays all day & Nim & Will came over to see me.

October 31, 1887 Monday

We started for Spokane & we stoped near Mr. Stones for dinner then came over to the Falls about dark.

November 1, 1887 Tuesday
Cora and I fixed up our room and I went down town with Cora.

November 2, 1887 Wednesday
X - My fatal day. I helped Cora do some trading and fixed for my
wedding & at half past eight the fatal knot was tyed & I was a happy
boy.

November 3, 1887 Thursday
I did not do much. We went down to the train to meet Mrs. Hayes but
was disipointed as she did not come.

November 4, 1887 Friday
I went after lumber once more got along fine & found my wife looking
for me went I got home.

November 5, 1887 Saturday
I went after lumber again. I got along all right.

November 6, 1887 Sunday
Went to hear Mrs. Jones preach in the A M & in the eve went to hear her
again.

November 7, 1887 Monday
Cora went to Cheney & I went to hall lumber and I stalled & did not get
home till 11 o clock and was tiored and hungry & wet for it rained all
day.

This diary, written by Lewis Titchenal, was given by Lewis to his
son, Ray Titchenal. Ray in turn gave it to his son Richard Titchenal.
Richard's wife Gladys, after Richard's death, gave it to Vera Zachow.
Vera is the daughter of Margaret Titchenal Hansen who was Ray
Titchenal's oldest daughter. It is in Vera's possession at this time.

This freight wagon hauling goods to Manson is similar to the one driven by Lewis. (He drove the first freight wagon over the Indian trails from Spokane to Douglas in 1883. From Bessie's account of her father)

Lewis recorded his daily expenses.

1890 Tax Receipts
Washington Territory

The Titchenal family history was described by Cora Johnson Titchenal and her mother-in law, Mary Titchenal to Lindley M. Hull in the book "A History of Central Washington" published in 1929.

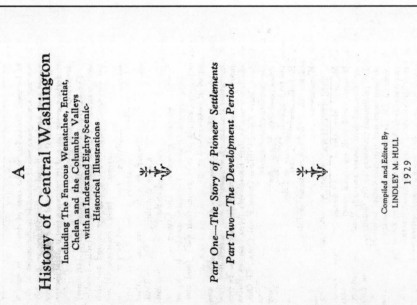

Titchenal Family History as Published in A History of Central Washington

In part it states:

"On April 1, 1882, Mr. and Mrs. David J. Titchenal left Bates County, Missouri, with well equipped emigrant traveling outfits and directed their course towards Washington Territory. The additional members of the family consisted of four stalwart sons and two daughters: Lewis H., Norman S., Nimrod D., John, Nancy and Phebe. Few families can trace their American ancestry to an earlier date than the Titchenals. Two Titchenal brothers left Alsace (now a province in France) and settled in Jamestown, Virginia, in the year 1620. The ancestors of those brothers belonged to the reigning house of Alsace when that small country was a principality in its own right. In the course of time the descendents of these two men settled in Illinois and in 1868, we find our subjects, D. J. Titchenal and wife removed to Missouri. Mrs. Titchenal before marriage was know as Miss Mary Moore. Her people bore a prominent and creditable part in the early history of Illinois. Her father was Major John Moore, and her grandfather was Col. Abel Moore, who fought in the Blackhawk War, and it was to his regiment that Chief Blackhawk actually surrendered, though historical credit naturally went to General William Henry Harrison, who directed the forces of the campaign. This same Col. Moore lost two sons in an Indian massacre.

The Titchenal family in their westward trek, crossed Kansas and Nebraska, following the old California trail as far as Laramie, Wyoming, which they reached June 1, and where they camped about ten days. At this place on the morning of June 7, there was eight inches of snow on the ground. At this time the Union Pacific Railroad Company was building the short line from Green River, Wyoming, to Portland, Oregon. The demand for men and teams for construction work was keen, and the Titchenal party was approached by a contractor, who said that he would furnish free transportation to Idaho, and pay $4.50 per day for man and team and $2.50 for single men, provided the emigrants would work thirty days. The offer was considered good, and as there were many other pilgrims westward bound, a sufficient number to make up a trainload was soon on the way. The horses and mules were loaded in box cars, while the wagons were placed on flat cars and the wheels taken off, which

V. R. Zachow

arrangements converted these vehicles into Pullman sleeping coaches of a novel kind. Ogden, Utah, was reached in the night time, and the stock was taken off to rest and feed. But when morning came evidence of sharp practice was discovered when the stockpens were found to be securely locked and pretty well surrounded with armed guards. The situation appeared to be serious for the contractor demanded a new agreement where by the emigrants should work sixty days instead of thirty, and mortgage their outfits as a guarantee of good faith. While discussion was going forward among the men as to best means of surmounting the difficulty, the women in considerable force repaired to the corrals for action. They ignored the armed guards and with effective implements they tore the hinges off the gates, which were thrown open and the horses and mules driven out upon the common. In a surprisingly short time the stock was rounded up, caught and harnessed to the wagons, which were quickly made ready to move. The sheriff's posse of 25 men, that had been called for, was too small in numbers to make headway against the determined emigrants. A parley followed in which the emigrants frankly admitted obligations for transportation received, and that they were ready to carry out their part of the agreement, but they did not propose to be robbed in such a high handed manner. The contractor saw the point and proposed new arrangements for transportation, and very soon a new trainload was on the way northward to Onida, Idaho, about 25 miles east of Pocatello, where they decamped and went to work. At the end of six weeks new trouble arose when it was learned that the contractor would not pay for work done. This was pretty serious but rather than incur the loss of time and expense in going into the courts, they loaded their outfits and moved on, taking the Old Oregon Trail via Boise, Idaho, Baker City, Oregon and Walla Walla, Washington. From there they went to Colfax where the men took work at freighting and logging, and again met with trouble in getting pay for their work, and much time was lost. From Colfax they moved their camp to Rockford, 25 miles south of Spokane, reaching the place eight months after leaving Missouri.

Rockford became their headquarters from which to make a survey of Eastern Washington. They leased a farm and the following spring put in a crop of wheat. At this time the elder Mr. Titchenal with the oldest son, Lewis, started out to explore the Big Bend country and look for a location. In a day or two they fell in with a Spokane party consisting of L. B. Nash, later a federal judge; O. H. Kimball, ex-paymaster of the N. P. Railroad, and Peter Bracken formerly with an Atlantic steamship line.

170

They were headed for Badger Mountain, distant from Spokane 175 miles. On getting to their destination they found themselves preceeded three days by Hector Patterson, Ole Ruud and Mr. Frazier and two others, Ferrin by name. Of the Nash and Titchenal party, only Kimball and Bracken located claims. Our subjects then returned to Spokane via Soap Lake, Crab Creek and Cottonwood or what is now Davenport. Lewis and Norman Titchenal now took a four-mule team and started for Badger Mountain, going via Spokane where they took on 3000 pounds of freight which included a barrel of whiskey. The freight was for the store of Nash, Kimball and Bracken. They reach Badger, June 8. Two days later the Titchenals located three claims in section 23 and 25, T. 24, R. 22. They then took their teams and began hauling logs for their store building 20 X 40 feet with 12-foot walls. This work was completed in July whereupon the boys returned to Rockford to help harvest their crop of wheat. Their machinery for this particular harvest was the old time cradle and the wooden handrake. With the crop secured they hauled another load of freight to Badger Mountain. They then returned to Rockford for the family. The road established by these trips across many miles of country was for a long time used as the general highway. Arriving at their new home, the men fell to and began the erection of log cabins on the several claims, also one large barn, all of which work was completed before winter. Enough wild hay was secured for the winter feed of stock. In common with many others they suffered heavy loss in stock during the hard winter of 1889-90. The snows that winter in this high country fell to a great depth, and remained on the ground 180 days, or six months.

Thus we find that the Titchenals were identified with the especially interesting history of this Badger Mountain settlement - the first west of Coulee City. Although this colony included a store, postoffice, and a blacksmith shop, it did not follow tradition and become a permanent town. Among the items of interest we find that R. S. Steiner, who later became a superior court judge, taught the first school, for which the cabin of Ole Ruud furnished shelter; that a school house built by donation on Douglas Creek, near the present town of Alstown, became the first official temple of learning in Douglas County; that in 1883, a Mr. Adams located a claim 2 ½ miles east of what is now the town of Douglas. He then "scripped" an additional forty acres, laid out a townsite and named it Okanogan. About this time Mr. Adams joined a movement to create a new county, which resulted in carving the counties of Lincoln, and Douglas from the county of Spokane that had reached from the eastern boundry of the Territory to the Columbia River. Douglas County as established was larger than some of the New England states. Desperate efforts were made to build up Okanogan, but its bone dry condition, so far as water was concerned caused much of its population to desert it for Douglas, which is believed to have started in 1885. For a time this town had the distinction of serving as county seat. According to reports the townsite of Waterville was within the land claim-secured by A. T. Green, who dug a well and at a depth of thirty feet found a strong flow of water. He then staked a government townsite which was accepted, and Waterville moved rapidly forward as a growing and important town, while Okanogan for the lack of water had as rapidly disappeared from the map.

Platt M. Corbaly was the first settler in Douglas County west of Coulee City, and he was the first man to bring in a family. In 1887, S.C. Robbins brought in the first threshing machine, which was hauled over the Ellensburg Mountain from Kittitas Valley.

All of the Titchenals moved away from this first settlement. Lewis developed a ranch on Warner Flat, near Cashmere, then called Mission, Washington, where he located in 1897. He was an effective worker for construction of the Highline ditch Canal and planted orchard and alfalfa there."

Lewis promoted the apples he grew. He demonstrated the use of the wooden apple box to the weights and measure committee of congress, therefore establishing the apple box as an accepted measure. The apple box replaced the round bushel baskets that would not stack in railroad cars for shipping. The square apple box made apple shipping possible.

Lewis later suggested that the old abandoned railroad bed going over Stevens Pass be turned into a farm to market highway to move their fruit to Seattle. His efforts helped establish the Stevens Pass highway.

Nim D. Titchenal had an orchard tract near Wenatchee and was the pastor of Church of God, Faith of Abraham in Wenatchee. Norman was established in Cashmere when John as well as their parents, David and Mary Titchenal, and sisters Nancy and Phebe moved there in 1902.

Lewis Hamilton Titchenal, son of David and Mary Titchenal
Born February 27, 1860 in Madison County, Illinois.

"It was just 50 years ago today [May of 1883] that I first arrived in this country, says L. H. Titchenal of Cashmere. "There were five of us in the party that came from Spokane and located in what is now called Titchenal canyon nine miles south of Waterville. This party consisted of my father, D. J. Titchenal, O. H. Kimball, Peter Bracken, L. B. Nash and myself. We built the first store in that part of the state which was called Bracken's store. I went up on the mountain, cut logs and hauled them down to build the store. I also hauled in freight from Spokane which was the nearest railroad at the time.

As near as I can recollect, there were only six or seven white men living in the vicinity of Wenatchee. These were: Phillip Miller, George Miller, Sam C. Miller, the Freer brothers and Dutch John Galler. I think that E. Messerly was also living there at the time, also Tallman Tripp came about that time. There were a large number of settlers who came in during that same year. In fact, it might be said that the settlement of the valley started at that time.

We got up a petition to cut off Douglas, Lincoln and Adams

counties from Spokane county which took in most of eastern Washington as far as Wenatchee, and thus started the new county governments.

The establishment of the Bracken store was quite an advertisement for this new county, and a great many settlers came in during that year.

L. B. Nash and W. E. Stevens brought a sawmill in the next year 1884. They located on Badger Mountain. This was before any one had any idea of raising fruit in the Wenatchee valley or raising wheat in the Big Bend. The principal business was raising horses, cattle and sheep. They ranged all over the central part of the state. We used to swim the cattle and horses across the Columbia river and drive them to Ellensburg where we loaded them on the Northern Pacific. Some stock was driven to Sprague or Ritzville to be shipped out.

All of the houses that had been built up to that time were of log and none of them had any floors except that provided by Mother Earth until Stevens' mill was built and commenced to saw lumber in the fall and winter of 1884 and 1885.

Platt Corbaley and his wife and daughter came into this country and located at the head of the Corbaley canyon in June of 1883. There were very few white women living in this part of the state at that time.

On Christmas Day in 1883 the first flag was raised by the citizens of this part of the state. It was run up to the top of a 75 foot flag pole at Bracken's store. This was a silk flag 10 feet long. Bracken had been a steward on a ship sailing between San Francisco and the Orient for 20 years, and he brought this flag with him. There were 75 men and boys at that flag raising which was practically all of the population of this part of the state.

All that I know who were at that flag raising and are still living are the three Titchenal boys, Howard Honner and Jimmy Melvin of Waterville.

The first school house in Douglas county was built the next year in 1884 on Douglas creek. It was built on government land and when somebody came along and took up that section we had to move the house off to another site, across the line."

Phebe Titchenal's Homesteader's Cabin

Here is what a homesteader's cabin looked like in the Waterville country 36 years ago. It belonged to Miss Phebe Titchenal, now Mrs. Clarence Wright. The place is located southeast of Waterville. Lying on the ground are Owen Minton, John Titchenal, and Will Sheehan. Mrs. D. J. Titchenal is shown standing, and her husband [David] is sitting in the doorway. Circa 1887 Courtesy the Waterville newspaper

By Kirby Billingsley

Waterville swarmed with visitors this afternoon to celebrate the 50th anniversary of the founding of this pioneer trading center of the fertile Big Bend wheat country.

For the big banquet in the Community hall tonight, arrangements first were made for 350 plates. Up to last night 520 had reserved seats and dozens more had applied.

To Waterville it was a day to honor the pioneers, the men who came here in the early days and toiled behind a one-bottom walking plow (often known as a "foot burned"), turned the first sod and sagebrush. It was a day to honor those who pulled up their covered wagons, unhitched

175

their horses and built homes of logs.

It was a day to honor those who had the vision and courage to stay, even after many of their neighbors quit and returned east following a hard winter or dry summer; to honor men who made their shoes from the skin of a cow's hind leg, which was done by fitting their heel into the hollow where the hock joint was and tying the toe.

And the women will not be forgotten. Wives who cooked and mended and cared for the sick, who made gardens, improvised windows of cloth, taught children, rendered lard, made their soap and "salted down a barrel" for the winter.

From Seattle, Spokane, Wenatchee, and Yakima, pioneers gathered for the unveiling at 5 o'clock this afternoon of a monument in the new Pioneer park near the center of town, which was dedicated by Governor Martin.

Designed by Clarence Mitchell, member of a pioneer family, four plates on the monument will commemorate four events of 50 years ago: Formation of the town of Waterville 50 years ago today; admission of Washington into the union in 1889; organization of the Masonic lodge at Waterville in 1889; and of the Odd Fellow lodge the same year. Later, an emblem of bronze will be made showing a pioneer family – man, woman and child.

The settlers cabin Lewis and Cora built as their first home was similar to Phebe's cabin. Cora talks about the cabin often. Settler's were required to live on their claims.

The newspaper article and photograph were published March 1939. It is not known which Waterville newspaper the article was clipped from.

1888
Cora Johnson Titchenal

This book has been in use for many years by the hands that have been resting for a long time.

It will now be used for a diary by Mrs. Cora Titchenal, who is living at father Titchenal's near the foot of Badger Mountain in Douglas Co. Wash. Ty. [Douglas County Washington Territory]

January 1, 1888 Sunday
A very windy day. The snow was about 16 inches deep and was drifting. J. Hoppy called. I played some on my organ and sang until my throat was sore and read some.

January 2, 1888 Monday
I helped some with the work and wrote a letter and a song ballad for Fannie Thayer. Mr. Bliss and Mr. S. Kunkle were there over night.

January 3, 1888 Tuesday
I wrote another letter and sewed a little. Gilmore was there to dinner.

January 4, 1888 Wednesday
I sewed some on my red dress that I spot in the rain at Spokane.

January 5, 1888 Thursday
I finished fixing my dress.

January 6, 1888 Friday
A very cold day and none of us did anything worth noting.

January 7, 1888 Saturday
Gilmore and Jesse and Mr. Bliss came and I darned Jesse's mittin, and did some mending.

January 8, 1888 Sunday
Another cold day. I felt bad all day, and read and sang.

January 9, 1888 Monday
I did not feel well so did not do much but write some letters.

January 10, 1888 Tuesday
I went with Lewis to Mr. Will's and we took dinner with Gilmore at the bachelor's hall and came home feeling better than usual.

January 11, 1888 Wednesday
Lewis went to Waterville and to Badger and did not get back until <u>late</u>. I

made Gilmore a night-cap. Jesse and J. Sullivan took dinner with us.

January 12, 1888 Thursday
Lewis was not well. I sewed and read some: in the evening we spelled some.

January 13, 1888 Friday
Lewis read nearly all day. I copied songs in my blank-book.

January 14, 1888 Saturday
Lewis continued his reading and I continued writing.

January 15, 1888 Sunday
Gilmore and Jim Owens were there. I wrote a letter and was lonesome and played some.

January 16, 1888 Monday
I commenced to make Lewis's shirt that his mother gave him Christmas, and the rest of them spent the day in reading.

January 17, 1888 Tuesday
I finished my boy's shirt while he read and in the evening we all read.

January 18, 1888 Wednesday
I was feeling bad all day and did nothing but read.

January 19, 1888 Thursday
Another miserable day with me and I read some.

January 20, 1888 Friday
A snowy day. I did not do much but write a letter and read some.

January 21, 1888 Saturday
I sewed a little.

January 22, 1888 Sunday
I read some and sang a little.

January 23, 1888 Monday
Mother and Nannie washed but I did not do anything. Gilmore was there.

January 24, 1888 Tuesday
I wrote some letters. Lewis weighed 165 and I 138.

January 25, 1888 Wednesday
Lewis went to the Lake. I did not feel well so I was in bed a part of the day and read some.

January 26, 1888 Thursday
I did not do anything.

January 27, 1888 Friday
I washed. Gilmore was there a while.

January 28, 1888 Saturday
I did not get up until late, but ironed some. It was a rainy day.

January 29, 1888 Sunday
I laid down to read some and went to sleep. In the evening we all read.

January 30, 1888 Monday
Lewis commenced work on our house. I sewed.

January 31, 1888 Tuesday
I went to Jesse's after some tools, found nobody at home: went up to Mr. Will's a few minutes. Then came back and went with Lewis to work on our house. I took the first horseback ride I had taken for three months.

"Lewis and I moved home to our little log cabin."

179

March 2, 1888 Friday
Lewis and I moved home to our little log cabin. The snow was about 3
inches deep and we moved in the sled. Norman came with us to do a
little carpenter work.

*This is the rocking chair and lamp that came with Cora from Missouri. These items
traveled in the covered wagon and are still in the family.*

March 3, 1888 Saturday
We were both buisy all day in putting things to rights and I was very tired
when the week ended.

March 4, 1888 Sunday
At home alone all day, but spent the day pleasantly in reading and
talking.

180

March 5, 1888 Monday

I did my house work and helped Lewis some. Phebe came and brought us some milk.

March 6, 1888 Tuesday

We went to Jesse's after some of my things, came back and stayed overnight at Fathers. Mr. Court, the preacher was there and we enjoyed some music. Mr. Miller and Mr. Andrews were there over night, too.

March 7, 1888 Wednesday

I was nearly sick: We moved some more of our things home and Lewis worked on our new house.

March 8, 1888 Thursday

I washed our cotton clothes and Lewis worked on the poarch.

March 9, 1888 Friday

I washed our flannel clothes and Lewis was buisy with his carpenter work.

March 10, 1888 Saturday

I mopped the floor and ironed some. Gilmore and Jesse came which was their first visit to us and Jesse's last one before going to Spokane Falls, to work.

March 11, 1888 Sunday

We spent the day at home alone.

March 12, 1888 Monday

I did my house work and wrote some letters. Lewis hung the doors to the new room.

March 13, 1888 Tuesday

I helped Lewis some about the house and wrote another letter.

March 14, 1888 Wednesday

I ironed some. Lewis took Norman's workbench and tools home and I went with him and we came home late.

March 15, 1888 Thursday

Lewis went to post some notices on the school-house, Phebe came over and brought me some letters then we walked over there and Lewis and I stayed there overnight.

March 16, 1888 Friday

I helped sew some on Mother's new dress. Lewis drove all the horses up and put the harness on "Grover". We stayed there again all night.

March 17, 1888 Saturday
Lewis went to the mill after his lumber: A windy evening and we came
home late.

March 18, 1888 Sunday
At home alone again.

March 19, 1888 Monday
A very windy day. Lewis began to rebuild his fence and the wind blew it
over again. I wrote a letter and shingled Lewis's hair.

March 20, 1888 Tuesday
Lewis built fence. Gip was here a while. I cleaned the yard some in the
evening.

March 21, 1888 Wednesday
I tacked the cloth on the walls in our new room. Mother and Phebe spent
the afternoon with me.

March 22, 1888 Thursday
I made my old carpet, and Lewis worked on his fence.

March 23, 1888 Friday
Lewis finished his fence went after his horses and killed a jack rabbit. I
washed off the new floor and sewed.

March 24, 1888 Saturday
Lewis went to his father's after a plow and some hay and I went with him
and we came home by moonlight.

March 25, 1888 Sunday
Lewis rode "Bragg" and I rode "Bell" and we went to the Lake to
preaching but we did not hear much of a sermon and came back and
took dinner with the "old folks" and spent the evening there. Mr. Ira
Moore was there in the evening.

March 26, 1888 Monday
I went to help Lewis catch his team to plow and the horse he was riding,
fell and hurt him so he could not work and he helped me put my
carpet down.

March 27, 1888 Tuesday
Lewis was some better and went after his father's wagon in the evening. I
wrote some letters. Mr. Kunkle called.

March 28, 1888 Wednesday
Lewis moved Mr. Kunkle's <u>house</u> and <u>furniture</u> down to the river and I
stayed at his father's overnight while he was gone.

March 29, 1888 Thursday
I sewed on Mother's quilt and Lewis came home sick.

March 30, 1888 Friday
Lewis plowed some in the afternoon and I cleaned the yard.

March 31, 1888 Saturday
The ground was white with snow. Lewis worked on his barn until dinner
and plowed in the afternoon.

DOUGLAS COUNTY, WASHINGTON TERRITORY.

Poll Tax Receipt for the Year 188

Received from ___ L. H. Titchenal ___

the sum of TWO DOLLARS in full for his COUNTY POLL TAX for the
year 188 ___

No. 48 ___ O. Redfield

County Assessor.

April 1, 1888, Easter Sunday
I read some and Lewis went after his horses; in the afternoon we went to
see Mrs. Will and her baby boy.

April 2, 1888 Monday
Lewis went to the school house to take a stove but the teacher did not go,
then he went after the horses and plowed. I milked the cow, did my
house-work and wrote a letter.

April 3, 1888 Tuesday
Lewis finished plowing the piece north of the house and sowed and
harrowed it.

April 4, 1888 Wednesday
A very windy day. I helped Lewis stake off the orchard and worked in the
house the rest of the day and Lewis plowed. In the evening Mr. Geo.
A. Harper from Iowa came and stoped with us awhile to look at the
country.

April 5, 1888 Thursday
Lewis plowed and I was busy with my house work and sewed some.
Phebe came.

April 6, 1888 Friday
I did a big washing but Mr. Harper carried the water for me.

April 7, 1888 Saturday
I mopped the kitchen floor and ironed some. And was very tired when
   night came.

April 8, 1888 Sunday
I was nearly sick but we all went over to father's and Mr. Harper stayed
   all night there. We came home late.

April 9, 1888 Monday
I went with Lewis to his father's after grain and we brought my organ and
   Mr. H. home with us. Lewis sowed the grain south of the house.

April 10, 1888 Tuesday
Mr. Harper helped Lewis set out our first fruit trees and they hauled a
   load of wood too. I did some mending.

April 11, 1888 Wednesday
Mr. Harper started for his home in Iowa. Lewis looked for the Nash
   mare. In the evening mother came and brought me some pie-plant
   roots and three new comers (Missourians) were here and I ironed
   some.

April 12, 1888 Thursday
Lewis looked again for the mare but did not find her. I sold my claim and
   did some mending.

April 15, 1888 Sunday
We were so lazy that Mother and father came over before we had
   breakfast but didn't stay long. I was nearly sick all day.

April 29, 1888 Sunday
We were at home all day. John and Phebe and the little Burges girls were
   to see us.

April 30, 1888 Monday
I helped Lewis plant tree seed on his timber claim.

May 1, 1888 Tuesday
We planted tree seeds again and in the evening we planted some corn.

May 2, 1888 Wednesday
Lewis plowed some and I washed my white clothes.

May 3, 1888 Thursday
A cloudy morning, but I finished my big washing. It rained some and

Lewis plowed, after the rain and I blacked the stove and cleaned the yard.

May 4, 1888 Friday
Mother was here in the morning and Phebe was here to dinner. Lewis plowed until in the afternoon then I went with him after the harrow.

May 5, 1888 Saturday
I cleaned both rooms of the house and in the afternoon helped Lewis plant more tree seeds and was very tired.

May 6, 1888 Sunday
After my house work was done I took a walk with Lewis in the orchard and came back and read myself to sleep. Then after a nice nap we went over to see Mother and the girls. Some drunken Indians were there. We came home late.

May 7, 1888 Monday
I was nearly sick all day and only did my house work and wrote some letters. Lewis planted some tree seeds and was running horses the rest of the day. Gilmore called and was nearly sick.

May 8, 1888 Tuesday
Lewis was trying to get "Grover" gentle and cleaned out his gun ready for the indians as they were drunk and causing some trouble. In the afternoon he went after some cows. I ironed and trimmed my old hat over. Mr. Dorn was here for supper. It was a very windy day.

May 9, 1888 Wednesday
I baked lightbread for Gilmore then got ready and went with Lewis and Nannie in their new hack to the city of Waterville. We came home by Badger and called to see Mrs. Corbaley.

May 10, 1888 Thursday
A very windy day. I helped Lewis re-plant some of his timber-culture. In the evening he went to his father's to attend to some horses, stayed late and I cried.

May 11, 1888 Friday
Lewis plowed: in the afternoon I was buisy with my housework and in the P. M. I commenced to paper the cabin.

May 12, 1888 Saturday
Lewis plowed. Phebe was here to dinner. I finished papering the cabin, washed the window and blacked the stove. Mr. Dorn was here to supper.

May 13, 1888 Sunday
Gilmore, Nannie, Lewis and I went to meeting at Waterville in the hack and came back to father's and spent the evening there. Mr. Ladd was there.

May 14, 1888 Monday
Lewis and his father went to Waterville. I stayed with Mother and the girls and sewed all day on a quilt and made me an apron.

May 15, 1888 Tuesday
After running horses for a long time Lewis finished his plowing and in the evening was breaking a wild horse. I was nearly sick all day.

May 16, 1888 Wednesday
Gilmore helped Lewis with his horse -Grover-. They hauled a load of logs for the stable. I was here alone most all day and did some writing.

May 17, 1888 Thursday
We made some more garden. Gilmore and John here to dinner and they hauled two load of stable logs.

May 18, 1888 Friday
Lewis went on the mountain after a load of logs and I stayed at his father's.

May 19, 1888 Saturday
Lewis fixed the spring and made a pair of bars and mended his harness while I finished papering the old cabin: in the evening we went to Okanogan to see Mr. Hoppe and took supper at Mr. Martin's.

May 20, 1888 Sunday
A cool day with some rain. I read quite a while.

Bessie Alice born Sept. 15, 1888   Joseph Ray born Dec. 31, 1889

Jesse Cole Johnson's Death
November 4, 1889

November 6, 1889   *Spokane Falls*

Dear friend Cora,

I write this morning to tell you that dear Jesse is at last freed from his suffering.

Yes, last Monday morning twenty minutes of ten his spirit took its upward flight and is now resting in the arms of his blessed redeemer. He has left a sure record that all was well with him. Oh; may we all be as ready and willing to go as he was. The funeral services were held in the Southern Methodist Church yesterday at 2:00, Rev. Parsons officiating.

Mrs. Hays, aunt and myself came on the train yesterday. Expect to go back today. Mrs. Hays will write you as soon as she gets home. All send love. Now Cora write to us and believe me to ever to be to you as of old.

Your true friend,
Sate Hays

PS The text yesterday you will find recorded in John 16th chapter and 33rd verse. The pieces sang were 'Safe in the Arms of Jesus' and 'The Sweet Bye and Bye'. He was buried in the Fairmount cemetery. It is a beautiful place and where his grave will be well cared for. The baby will be removed soon where she will rest beside him.

Cora's Speech

This speech is written on the back of a letter from
Wenatchee Reclamation District to L.H. Titchenal, dated
January 18, 1922. Since it was written in pencil, it may be
only a draft of Cora's speech; or it may be the notes she used to
memorize what she was going to say to a group of pioneers, or
perhaps a local historical society.

"I am no public speaker, but I do claim to be a pioneer. I believe
none of the other speakers have dated any further back than the year
1880. That is the year in which I begun pioneer life. My parents died
when I was quite young & in April 1879 – my only sister was married
& came west. My oldest brother & family & 2 other brothers – 1 older
& 1 younger than myself – started across the plains in wagons from near
Kansas City Mo.

There was another family started with us, making 4 wagons
altogether. Others joined later.

We were just 100 days on the road, arriving at my sister's on the 23rd
day of July. That was 35 miles S.E. of Spokane Falls— There was no city
of Spokane & no R.R. at that time. I made my home with my sister &
brother in law in a little log cabin on a homestead which they still own
– tho they live in the City of Spokane now – they built a better house
before winter.

My brother in law hauled his supplies from Walla Walla making
2 trips a year, getting enough each time to last 6 months. The
nearest schoolhouse was six miles, but that winter the people of the
neighborhood built a small school house on the bank of Hangman Creek
where we had a 3 months school.

After the R.R. came and the town of Cheney was built I attended
the Cheney Academy – which afterwards burnt down & one of the State
Normal Schools was built in the same place.

On the 4th of July 1882 the N.P.R.R. was completed as far west
as Cheney & I had the pleasure of riding on the excursion train from
Spokane to Cheney which was the first passenger train that had gone

over the road that far. On the 4th of July 1883 I attended the big ball that was given in the Echo Mill which was the first flour mill built at Spokane Falls. I have a copy of the first Dily [sic] paper that was printed there. I happened to have a friend who was setting type in the office & he gave me a copy which I kept. This same friend afterwards worked in the printing office for our fellow townsman, Mr. L.E. Kellogg when he printed the N.W. Tribune in Cheney.

> This information about the speech and the speech itself as well as the letters that Cora wrote were provided by Gilla Bachellerie, in an e-mail, before she was diagnosed with cancer and later passed away.
>
> Gilla was the daughter of Lois Jacobson and granddaughter of Bessie Titchenal Lawrence.

Gilla Bachellerie

James Hays and Sarah Alice Johnson

| James H. Hays | b. Aug. 27, 1847 | d. Nov 16, 1932 |
| Sarah Alice (Alice) | b. June 29, 1855 | d. Sept. 20, 1941 |

James and Sarah's Children

Mary Edna (Edna)	b. March 3, 1881	d. April 4, 1900
Cora Mamie (Mamie)	b. Aug. 16, 1882	d. Dec. 13, 1977
Claude McBride	b. Jan. 1, 1884	d. Jul. 31, 1952
Jesse Warner	b. Oct. 30, 1886	d. Jul. 17, 1949
Roy Washington	b. Feb. 22, 1890	d. Sept. 24, 1932

On April 2, 1879 Alice Johnson married James Hays in Bates County, Missouri. The next day they headed west, taking the Southern Pacific train to San Francisco. They took a steamboat to Portland, then came by boat to the Dalles, Oregon, arriving there the night the town burned. They bought a team and wagon to continue their trip to the Palouse country. James and Alice homesteaded on Hangman Creek near Waverly, Washington Territory, thirty-five miles southeast of where the City of Spokane is now located. Cora lived with them for a time.

The Hays Family
As dictated by James Hays, July 10, 1917

Nathaniel Hays (great-grandfather of James Hays) was born in South Carolina about 1750. He served in the Revolutionary Army seven years under General Green. The Colonel's name was Francis Marion. Nathaniel Hays was in about all of the principal battles of the Revolution.

William Hays (grand-father of James Hays) was born and raised in South Carolina. He migrated to Tennessee about 1800 (1805). He married Martha Hamilton in Tennessee in 1815 and then went to Missouri via St. Louis. No wagon road from St. Charles to where they settled in Saline County, Missouri. Made the trip by horseback and lived in the country about sixteen years before they had any white flour. Their clothing consisted of buckskin, cotton and wool manufactured by themselves. They made their own salt, from the Salt Springs located near Marshall, Missouri. The family of William Hays consisted of 11 children – 4 boys and 7 girls; namely, Thomas, James, William, McBride (father of James Hays), Charity, Mary, Frankie, Martha, Betsy, Sally, and one other girl.

McBride Hays (father of James Hays) was the youngest of the eleven children and was born in 1822, just after Missouri became a State. He was a big muscular man, weight about 220 pounds. His wife's name was Mary Johnson. She was born in New York and raised in Indiana. The family of McBride Hays consisted of William Burton, James, Martha (married Byrd) Mary Ann (married Levy), Lydia (married Lacy), Sally (married Baker).

James Hays was born August 27, 1847 near Slater, Missouri. He was educated in the common school and lived on a farm. He joined the Confederate Army in 1864. He was with Joe Shelby, Elliots Battalion, Company "H". He was the youngest member of the Company. He was in 3 or 4 bad scurmishes—Battle of West Fort, or K. C. Saw General Price and Marmaduke on the battlefield. Heard them give orders. The equipment at the time was not modern, but very good. Only a few brick-loading riffles—balance was in Cavalry. He furnished his own horse, which he sold to the Cavalry for $800.00. After the war, he returned to his father's farm, and went into partnership with a brother—then sold

191

out to him in 1879 and married Alice Johnson of Bates County, Missouri on April 2, 1879 and started for San Francisco April 3, 1879. About May 1, 1879 they went from San Francisco to Portland and from Portland to the Dalles by boat, passed around Locks on R. R. at that time. Stayed in the Dalles over night and the town burned up that night. Then they bought a wagon and team there and migrated to Washington Territory, finally locating near Waverly.

James Hays
History of Spokane County, Washington
By Rev. Jonathon Edwards 1900

James Hays, a pioneer of 1879, son of McBrill and Mary Hays, was born in Saline county Missouri, August 27, 1847. He was raised and educated there and spent the first thirty-one years of his life in that state, engaged, after reaching years of maturity, mostly in farming and stock raising. In 1864, however he joined the Confederate army and he served under General Price until the close of the war, being mustered out in Louisiana in 1865. In 1879 he came to that part of Stevens county which now constitutes Spokane county, locating finally on Hangman creek, midway between Fairfield and Waverly, where he now has a farm of about eight hundred acres, all of which is in an excellent state of cultivation. He raises wheat principally, but is also interested in stock raising. Mr. Hays is one of the most thrifty, progressive and successful farmers in his part of the county, but he always finds time to take an active interest in the political affairs of county and state. He was one of commissioners of this county in 1891 and 1892, and has held the office of school director in district No. 10 for the past 15 years. He was married in Bates county, Missouri, April 3, 1879, to Alice, daughter of William and Nancy Johnson, and they have had five children, namely: Mary Edna, born March 3, 1881, deceased April 4, 1900; Cora Mamie, born August 16, 1882; Claude McBride, born January 1, 1885; Jessie Warner, born October 31, 1886 and Roy W., born February 22, 1890.

The James Hays family home near Waverly was completed in 1904.

Dear Friend Bessie,   July 25, 1903

    I am over at Mr. Hays' playing Mamie this week.

    Tell Charlie that his picture is the dearest little thing. Mrs. Hays is so proud of it that she says she is going to have it enlarged. She thanks you very much for the others sent too.

    Jessie received a letter from Mamie and she was to leave Seattle Thur, for Portland. She is having such a nice time. I am so glad.

    Mrs. Hays is canning fruit this morning. She said tell your mama that she will write as soon as possible but there are so many to cook for and the fruit to care for that she cannot to-day.

    Tell Ray and Charlie that Roy is plowing with a Gang plow. He and Claude were working together, but Claude had to stop and work with the binder. So Roy is left in the field all a lone.

    Well Bessie I suppose I will have to stoop.

    Lovingly

    Lula Chaney   *Box 104 Waverly Wn*
    P.S. The new house is just grand.

Article published about James Hays

James Hays, Waverly,, Wa.

James Hays, who owns a well developed and highly cultivated farm of 800 acres three and a half miles from Fairfield, came across the plains by team from Salinas County, Missouri, and located on a government homestead of 160 acres, which has since been his home. His additional land has been acquired from his earnings on the original quarter section, and today $50,000 is a fair estimate of his total assets. He has placed improvements on his farm and has an excellent home. In 1903 he received for the produce marketed in excess of $8000. Mr. Hays has just completed a modern residence at the cost of $4500. He was county commissioner in 1901 and 1902. Mr. Hays has found this an exceptionally fine country for following agricultural pursuits, and has never been unable to find a market for his products. Big yields of a fine product and good markets have been the means of his exceptional success. He has a family of four children.

Jessie Hays, Lead team, Claude Hays 2nd team, _____ 3rd team
The James Hays family shown plowing their farm of 800 acres which is three and a half miles from Fairfield.

'Wheat farm at Waverly, Wash about 1912 - James Hays Sr. Ranch.
Aunt Alice Hays and Mame in buggy,
Roy Hays holding saddle horse, Jim Hays on drill.'

Hays and Thayer with their Header crew

August 23, 1887 Thrashing the grain, filling sacks of grain and stacking the straw

A. D. Thayer and James Hays,
Waverly, Washington.
Two pioneers in Spokane County
Washington Territory in 1880

Harvesting grain about 1912

Bessie Alice Titchenal   Cora Mamie Hays

Cousins, Bessie Titchenal and Mamie Hays wrote letters to each other after the
Titchenal Family moved to Mission (Cashmere)

Fairfield, Wash   *March 23 – 1903*
Miss Bessie Titchenal

    Dear Cousin,

    *There is so much sickness in and around Waverly they closed the school.
All of Mr. Nute Thayers children have the measles and a lady died in
Waverly a week ago with them. Another woman died last night with
something else and one of LW Davises boys died with scarlet fever one of
Mr. Abe Robinson's little boys also has the scarlet fever and we heard to-day
they have dyptheria and small pox there too.*
    *Papa is in Spokane on the jury he came home Sunday & I was sitting
on the side walk in the sun reading a book. He came up to me, told me to
hold my hand and then he gave me a gold watch and chain with a slide
with two pearls and two opals in it. It is just beautiful. I am so delighted
with it.*
    *Claude is building fence to-day. Jesse is plowing and Roy is poisoning
squirrels and has gone now to sew grass seed.*

We bought two iron beds and got matting for our bed room and the sitting room & are going to use the carpets we had for my bed room and front room and the floor in the boys room. Bath and dining room & kitchen are painted + halls. If the weather stays nice we will move the rest this week. When you come up you will be my room mate. Telephone I must answer. It was Lonnie.

It is five, thirty by my turnip so I must close & get supper. Answer soon.

From your cousin. Pretty.

The Hays children sledding at the Hays home in Waverly

Sarah Alice and James Hays, Mabel and Cora Titchenal and Mamie Hays

Mary Edna Hays oldest daughter of James and Alice Hays.
Born March 3, 1881
Died April 4, 1900 at The Protestant Sanitarium in Spokane, Washington

Roy Hays
age 14
Born February 22, 1904
by Elite Studio, Spokane

The wedding photo of
Roy and Gertrude Hays, Waverly,
Married Feb. 6, 1915
by Libby Art Studio

Cora Mamie Hays
Born August 16, 1882

Cora Mamie Hays Jones
and her daughter Jean

Claude McBride Hays,   Jesse Warner Hays
Born January 1, 1884   Born October 30, 1886

The Hays Family - Waverly
Back row - Ollie Oliver Hays, Jesse Hays, Rolla Jones, Cora Mamie Hays Jones, Roy
Hays, Gertrude Wetherman, Rita Wilson Hays, Claude Hays
Front row - James Hays, James Roy Hays II, Jean Jones, Alice Johnson Hays
Taken at the Hays Ranch, Waverly, Wash. circa 1918

From Cora's letters

"We sold out and moved to the Wenatchee Valley in April 1897, locating on Warner's Flat, two miles east of Cashmere [then Mission]. This was then Okanogan County with Conconully the county seat. We bought only sagebrush and sunflowers. We Leveled the ground and improved upon it, living there a little more than six years without any water to irrigate with.

Mr. Titchenal [Lewis] was elected president of the High Line Ditch and worked on it a great deal of the time with man and teams. It was only a small ditch at that time and very few were interested in it so it took a long time to build it. Everybody rejoiced when the water was turned on the land so we could grow fruit trees and alfalfa. Some of the land was very rough and rocky and to me it seemed unreasonable to think it could be made to produce the rich bearing orchards and lovely homes that are here now.

We planted our first fruit trees - just one acre - in the spring of 1902 thinking we would have water in the ditch that year to irrigate with but did not, so Bessie and Ray hauled water from the river in a barrel on a one horse sled to water the trees and keep them alive thro the hot summer and Mr. Titchenal cultivated the ground after coming home from working on the ditch. The next year we got the water on the land and set out more trees and planted alfalfa."

1898
Diary of Cora Johnson Titchenal

Sat. Jan. 1, 1898 Saturday
I came to Mission Nov. 6 and was here alone with the children until Jan. Lewis came from the Big Ben with supplies for the winter and a new stove.

Jan. 2, 1898 Sunday
Mr. Wilcox called. We had plenty of snow but were all enjoying ourselves better than we did the latter part of the previous year.

Jan. 3, 1898 Monday
Lewis went to Mission. I ironed some.

Jan. 4, 1898 Tuesday
Lewis went to Wenatchee after lumber to ceil the kitchen. He got seven boxes of apples. Mr. Wilcox went with him. They got back late.

Jan. 5, 1898 Wednesday
Lewis went to the timber after wood and hauled a log 57 ft. long with Barney and Mose. I finished ironing.

Jan. 6, 1898 Thursday
Lewis hauled wood. I sewed some. The children played in the house as it was too cold to play out.

Jan 7, 1898 Friday
Lewis hauled another load of wood.

Jan. 8, 1898 Saturday
Lewis hauled wood. We went to the literary at the school house on Brown's flat. Very few were there.

Jan. 9, 1898 Sunday
Mr. Hickey called. Lewis went over to Mission. Norman was gone to the Sound.

Jan. 10, 1898 Monday
Lewis was sick. Charlie was quite sick too.

Jan 11, 1898 Tuesday
Mr. Dresser came to work on the house so we had plenty of racket for a few days.

Jan. 12, 1898 Wednesday
Mr. Dresser and Lewis were ceiling the kitchen and we had to live in room at the same time, and had two stoves in it.

Jan. 13, 1898 Thursday
The thermometer was down to zero and the house not finished but they hammered all day.

Jan. 14, 1898 Friday
They put on the lumber and Mr. Dresser went home. I cleaned the house up a little but was not very well.

Jan. 15, 1898 Saturday
Lewis helped the Shotwell boys put up ice. I mopped the floor and done some more cleaning.

Jan. 16, 1898 Sunday
Lewis helped them cover up their ice. I did some reading and wrote a letter.

Jan. 17, 1898 Monday
Lewis went to Wenatchee after more lumber but did not get any. I sewed some.

Jan 18, 1898 Tuesday
Lewis took the cows up to Mr. Hickeys and did not get home till after midnight. It snowed all day.

Jan. 19, 1898 Wednesday
Lewis went to the timber after wood. I did the housework and sewed some.

Jan. 20, 1898 Thursday
Lewis went to help get out bridge timbers and hauled the first logs for the bridge to be built at Mission.

Jan. 21, 1898 Friday
Lewis helped cut bridge timbers again and hauled a log home for wood. Mrs. Warner and Taylor Hughes called.

Jan 22, 1898 Saturday
Mr. Burbank called. Lewis went with Mr. Hughes to help put ice at Mr. Warner's. I cleaned the kitchen.

Jan. 23, 1898 Sunday
We all went to Wenatchee to hear A. J. Eychaner preach and to H. Patterson's to dinner. Came home at night after meeting.

Jan. 24, 1898 Monday
Lewis went to haul bridge timber. I was sick all day with headache.

Jan. 25, 1898 Tuesday
Ray was real sick. Lewis cut bridge timbers. I did some mending and some baking. A cold day.

Jan. 26, 1898 Wednesday
Lewis worked in the timber again and got home late. I did some writing.

Jan. 27, 1898 Thursday
Lewis worked in the timber. I sewed some. Ray was better.

Jan. 28, 1898 Friday
I washed some. Lewis worked at home building a hay pen. Charlie helped him. The weather was much warmer.

Jan. 29, 1898 Saturday
I finished my washing and mopped the floor and churned. Lewis went after a load of hay across the river with Joe Shotwell.

Jan. 30, 1898 Sunday
Lewis went to Wenatchee to church with Mr. Warner's folks. I read some and wrote a letter to Alice Hays.

Jan. 31, 1898 Monday
Lewis forded the river and went after another load of hay. I ironed while I was waiting supper for him.

Feb. 1, 1898 Tuesday
Mr. Wilcox called. I wrote a letter. Lewis went after hay and got home late. I sewed some.

Feb. 2, 1898 Wednesday
Lewis went after hay again. Bessie and I put a quilt in the frames and partly "knotted" it.

Feb. 3, 1898 Thursday
Lewis finished hauling his hay and fodder. I finished my quilt and took it out of the frame.

Feb. 4, 1898 Friday
Warmer. Lewis went with Joe Shotwell to get a log for posts. I sewed some.

Feb. 5, 1898 Saturday
A thawing day. Lewis went to the timber came home late and wet. I cleaned up the house some.

Feb. 6, 1898 Sunday

We all went to Wenatchee to hear the last of the meetings there and a church was organized with a membership [of] 21. Came home after night.

Feb. 7, 1898 Monday

Warm. Lewis was at home all day. I was nearly sick and did not do much except the usual house work.

Feb. 8, 1898 Tuesday

We all went over to Mission after some of Norman's things and brought his organ home with us. Took dinner at Dresser's.

Feb. 9, 1898 Wednesday

Lewis cut up and salted the hogs. In the evening he went up to Shotwell's. I did some writing. Charlie was not well.

Feb. 10, 1898 Thursday

Lewis went to the Big Bend. The children and I stayed alone for a week. I cooked out the lard and done the feeding.

Feb. 11, 1898 Friday

I cooked out more lard and found plenty to do. In the evening I wrote to Nannie.

Feb. 12, 1898 Saturday

A nice day and the snow melted some. I had a headache.

Feb. 13, 1898 Sunday

A nice day but we were lonesome. In the evening I sang and played on the organ some. The Chinook wind blew very hard.

Feb. 14, 1898 Monday

I finished the lard. I had a very sore throat. In the evening Virgil Bryan and Joe Shotwell called and brought us the mail.

Feb. 15, 1898 Tuesday

I was sick all day and did not do much. In the evening Virgil came and helped me to put up the fence that the wind blew over.

Feb. 16, 1898 Wednesday

The Chinook ceased. The weather was colder. Bessie was sick and I still had a very sore throat.

Feb. 17, 1898 Thursday

I felt some better and cleaned up the house some. Lewis came home and brought me some chickens.

Feb. 18, 1898 Friday
It snowed nearly all day. I planted some tomato seeds in a pan. Lewis put some new rubber in the shoes he bought.

Feb. 19, 1898 Saturday
Lewis took his plow to the shop in Mission. In the evening it snowed hard.

Feb. 20, 1898 Sunday
The new snow soon melted. Lewis was at home all day. I had the sick headache and sore throat.

Feb 21, 1898 Monday
Lewis went and worked on the bridge logs. I sewed some. An Indian came to saw wood.

Feb. 22, 1898 Tuesday
Lewis worked at the bridge again. I cooked up the hogs heads. It snowed some. The Indians got drunk.

Feb. 23, 1898 Wednesday
A nice day and Lewis worked at the bridge timbers. Ray went up there and took Lewis his dinner.

Feb. 24, 1898 Thursday
Lewis went and helped finish hueing the bridge timbers. I melted snow to wash with but did not finish washing.

Feb. 25, 1898 Friday
A nice day. I finished a big washing. Lewis made posts. The children were out most of the day.

Feb. 26, 1898 Saturday
I cleaned the kitchen and baked Lewis a birthday cake. He finished his posts. Several Indians were here – two squaws. Lewis was home all day.

Feb. 27, 1898 Sunday
A nice day. Lewis hauled a barrel of water on the sled and went to Mission. The Indians finished sawing the wood and were here to dinner.

Feb. 28, 1898 Monday
A very warm day and the snow melted fast. Lewis went with a pack horse to work on the ditch to be gone all week. In the evening I did some writing.

March 1, 1898 Tuesday

Another warm day. The children played out doors all day. The Richardson boys called. Ray had to go after the cows.

March 2, 1898 Wednesday

A cloudy day. I began to smoke the meat and cleaned the yard a little. In the evening I wrote a letter.

March 3, 1898 Thursday

I made soap, smoked the meat and ironed besides the usual work. In the evening I wrote some more.

March 4, 1898 Friday

A very warm day. I did some mending. Mr. Belcher called and we had some music. I finished my letter to brother Henry.

March 5, 1898 Saturday

I smoked the meat, churned and cleaned the kitchen. Joe and Harvey Shotwell brought old Bell home. The children bathed.

March 6, 1898 Sunday

I looked for Lewis all day but he didn't come home until midnight. It was a nice day but we were lonesome.

March 7, 1898 Monday

A very windy day. Mr. Warned called. Lewis helped him to stake out the lines. In the evening he went to Mission.

March 8, 1898 Tuesday

Lewis dug post holes and burnt his posts. Mr. McMillen stayed overnight with us.

March 9, 1898 Wednesday

Mr. and Mrs. Trask called. Mr. and Mrs. Huff and Mrs. Steadman made us a nice visit.

March 10, 1898 Thursday

I sewed some. Lewis finished making the partition fence between us and Mr. W. The Chinook wind blew very hard at night.

March 11, 1898 Friday

A very windy day. Lewis and Virgil helped Mr. Hughes move his hen house up here. Lewis took his team and started for Badger Mountain and we were left alone.

March 12, 1898 Saturday

I smoked the meat again. The children went after the cows. I cut out a dress for Bessie and mended Ray's shoe.

Baker Hiatt & Co.
Wenatchee Wn.
1896

March 13, 1898 Sunday
A cold windy day. The children and I put the wheels on the buggy and went to Mr. Burbanks and brought our guineas home.

March 14, 1898   Monday
I was not very well. Bessie and I sewed carpet rags. Mr. Hanson went

with Ray to get the calf out of the ditch.

March 15, 1898 Tuesday
A cold morning. Mr. Holmes came and borrowed the garden drill and got some milk. I did some mending. In the evening I did some writing.

March 16, 1898 Wednesday
A squaw washed for me. Mr. Hanson hauled me a barrel of water. I cleaned the rooms upstairs.

March 17, 1898 Thursday
After doing up the work the children and I took the buggy and team and went to Wenatchee. Came home late and was cold.

March 18, 1898 Friday
I cleaned the kitchen. In the evening while I was writing a letter Lewis and Norman came from the Bend with seven horses and Mr. Bannock's well drill. They were tired and hungry.

March 19, 1898 Saturday
I ironed some. Lewis and Nim went to Mission and forded the river. I did some mending.

March 20, 1898 Sunday
A cold day with quite a hail storm. I played on the organ and sang till I was horse. We spent the evening in reading and talking.

March 21, 1898 Monday
Mr. Holmes called. Lewis and Nim went after the engine for the drill but did not get it.

March 22, 1898 Tuesday
Jake Shotwell and Hanson called. The boys went and got the engine and set the drill ready to dig us a well.

March 23, 1898 Wednesday
They loaded the engine and hauled water then went to the blacksmith shop.

March 24, 1898 Thursday
Mr. Butler came to work for us. He and Nim worked on the drill and Lewis started the plow. I done the usual house work. Set a hen.

March 25, 1898 Friday
Mr. Butler plowed and Lewis worked all day trying to get the engine to work but it failed to pump.

March 26, 1898 Saturday
They got the engine to work and drilled 13 ft. Norman came but was sick and coughed very hard. He stayed over night. I made Bessie an apron.

March 27, 1898 Sunday
The ground was white with snow but it soon melted away. Mr. Holmes called. Lewis and Nim went to Mission after the boat. I had a headache.

March 28, 1898 Monday
The boys worked with the well drill. Jake Shotwell and Mr. Wilcox were here. I did some mending.

March 29, 1989 Tuesday
Lewis sewed his grain. Nim went to Mission in the buggy. John Culbs called. Charlie fell and cut his face. I sewed some.

March 30, 1898 Wednesday
I mopped the floor and did the usual house work. Lewis finished sewing his grain. In the evening they drilled some on the well.

March 31, 1898 Thursday
The boys worked with the drill but the well filled in as fast as they drilled. Mr. Belcher was here to dinner. I wrote a letter and made me an apron.

April 1, 1898 Friday
Mr. Holmes called. Lewis and Nim went to Mission in the buggy.

April 2, 1898 Saturday
The day of the annual ditch election. Lewis was elected Pres. of the board of directors. Mr. Wilcox was here to dinner. Mr. McMillen was here over night.

April 3, 1898 Sunday
Jake Shotwell and wife spent the day here. Also Mr. White. It was a nice warm day. Nim went to the Big Bend.

April 4, 1898 Monday
Mr. Butler and Lewis plowed the garden and planted some potatoes. I was not very well but sewed some.

April 5, 1898 Tuesday
Lewis and the children planted potatoes. Mr. Butler quit work here. I washed.

April 6, 1898 Wednesday
Mr. McMillen began to work here. Lewis went to Mission and got a lot

of fruit trees.

April 8, 1898 Friday
Mr. McMillen set out fruit trees. Lewis went to Mission and got home late. I sewed some.

April 9, 1989 Saturday
Lewis plowed. Mr. McMillen finished putting out our orchard. Traded Dollie to Mr. Wilcox. I ironed.

April 10 Sunday
Easter Sunday. Burbank's called. A blue grouse came in the house and I caught it. In the evening Joe and Harvey called. Nim came from the Bend.

April 11, 1898 Monday
Lewis and Nim went to Mission to do some blacksmith work. I and the children went to Burbanks after some grape vines and hop roots. Mc. dug post holes.

April 12, 1898 Tuesday
They moved our fence from the long disputed corner. Mr. Hanson and Mr. Cane helped. I mopped the floor.

April 13, 1898 Wednesday
The boys worked at the well again but had poor success. In the evening Phebe and Eliza came from the Bend to make a visit.

April 14, 1898 Thursday
Lewis and Nim went to Mission and brought back the bedroom set that we traded Lindsey for. We set out some trees and rose bushes that mother sent us.

April 15, 1898 Friday
Lewis was sick. Nim and Norman worked on the well drill. Eliza and Phebe started home. Mr. McMillen plowed. I did the housework.

April 16, 1898 Saturday
Lewis and Bessie were both sick. The boys worked on the well drill. I cleaned the kitchen and done the usual house work.

April 17, 1898 Sunday
A very windy day. Harvey called. Mr. McMillen helped me put the meat away.

April 18, 1898 Monday
Lewis was not able to work so Norman helped him with the well. School

commenced.

April 19, 1898 Tuesday
Norman and Nim went to Mission. Mr. Mc. finished planting the
potatoes. Bessie was not well enough to go to school.

April 20, 1898 Wednesday
The boys worked at the well but had more bad luck. Lewis was no better
so Norman went to the Dr. and got some medicine.

April 21, 1898 Thursday
Mr. Dresser made us a visit. Norman and Nim worked at the well again.
Bessie and Ray went to school.

April 22, 1898 Friday
Lewis was some better and sat up some. McMillen broke the plow and
harrowed. I sewed some.

April 23, 1898 Saturday
I churned and mopped the floor. Norman went to Mission in the
afternoon and Lewis helped Nim with the well and they had more
bad luck.

April 24, 1898 Sunday
Harry Shotwell called and Lewis traded the buggy and harness to him.
Norman and Mr. Dresser were here and started to Alaska on the train.

April 25, 1898 Monday
Lewis and Nim worked with the well till noon and then quit it. Lewis
foxed the bed springs and we put up the new bed-stead.

April 26, 1898 Tuesday
Lewis and Nim took the engine to Mission. Bessie and Ray went to
school. Charlie and I were alone. I ironed some.

April 27, 1898 Wednesday
I washed Nim's clothes and he took the evening train for Spokane. We
were left alone. Lewis was not well.

April 28, 1898 Thursday
Lewis went to hunt the cows that had been gone since Monday and
found them at noon. Charlie and I rode Bell and went to see Mrs.
Warner and got some rose sprouts.

April 29, 1898 Friday
Bessie and Ray went to school. Mr. Holmes called. Lewis worked on his
plow. I did some mending. I watered the plants.

April 30, 1898 Saturday
I cleaned the kitchen did some baking and in evening the children and I put out 70 tomato plants. Lewis went to Mission.

May 1, 1898 Sunday
A nice warm day. Mr. McMillen was here to dinner. I did some writing and shingled Lewis's hair. The children bathed.

May 2, 1898 Monday
I did a big washing. Lewis traded wagons with Mr. Clonger. Then he went to Mission and worked on his plow the rest of the day.

May 3, 1898 Tuesday
Bessie and Ray went to school. Lewis plowed some. I was not very well and did some writing.

May 4, 1898 Wednesday
Lewis went to Mission to help them with the engine. Charles and I were alone all day.

May 5, 1898 Thursday
Lewis harrowed his corn ground. In the afternoon I walked down to the garden and set out tomato plants and watered them.

May 6, 1898 Friday
I cleaned out the front room and mopped the floor. In the afternoon I sewed some. Lewis worked in the field.

May 7, 1898 Saturday
We moved out the heating stove and I cleaned the kitchen.

May 8, 1898 Sunday
Mr. McMillen and Mr. Wilcox were here to dinner. I read some and wrote a letter. In the evening Lewis went to Mission and Mr. Hanson called to see him.

May 9, 1898 Monday
Lewis finished marking off his corn ground and went to Mr. Hayman's after seed corn. The children went to school.

May 10, 1898 Tuesday
Lewis commenced planting his corn.

May 11, 1898 Wednesday
I did the usual house work and in the evening Charlie and I went down to the garden and put out some more tomato plants.

May 12, 1898 Thursday
I molded five rolls of butter and in the evening Charlie and I went to Harvey's after some ice. I set the Guinea eggs.

May 13, 1898 Friday
A very warm day. I went to Wenatchee with Mr. Warner to do some trading. Lewis planted corn. I did the usual work in the evening we all went down to the garden and watered the plants.

May 15, 1898 Sunday
A warm day. Lewis took the calves out to the range. Harvey and Lora Shotwell called. I shingled Ray's and Charlie's hair.

May 16, 1898 Monday
In the afternoon we had a thunder shower and Mr. Hanson came in while it rained. Lewis made his wagon bed over. I sewed some.

May 17, 1898 Tuesday
Lewis finished his wagon and made a gate in the fence. He also helped me move the meat in the cellar. I sewed some and churned. Windy.

May 18, 1898 Wednesday
Another windy day. Lewis went to look for the horses and didn't find them till late. Charlie and I were alone. I sewed some.

May 19, 1898 Thursday
After Lewis brought the cows and horses we went to Mission after the lime to plaster the house with. We got home late cold and hungry.

May 20, 1898 Friday
I did a big washing and was very tired at night. Lewis was working at the house. The plasterer was here to dinner. Bessie and Ray went to school.

May 21, 1898 Saturday
A cloudy day with some rain. Lewis hauled 3 loads of sand. I cleaned the kitchen ironed and helped the kids to sprout potatoes.

May 22, 1898 Sunday
Lewis worked all day. I did the regular house work and wrote a letter.

May 23, 1898 Monday
Lewis hauled two loads of water and helped the plasterer to prepare the lime for plastering the house. I did some baking and some ironing.

May 24, 1898 Tuesday
I helped Lewis all day with the lime and was very tired at night. Bessie

and Ray went to school. Charlie helped us.

May 25, 1898 Wednesday
A warm day. I was about sick. Lewis finished putting on the kitchen ceiling, then went after the horses and hauled a load of water.

May 26, 1898 Thursday
Lewis got ready and went to the Big Ben. I was not well but worked all day at churning, baking bread and various other work.

May 27, 1898 Friday
Rainy and cool. Roy Dresser came after some tomato and cabbage plants. Bessie and Ray went to school. I and Charlie worked in the garden.

May 28, 1898 Saturday
Ben South came after some plants. Zeb Parish came after Lewis' saddle. Mr. White called to see Lewis. The children and I cleaned out upstairs.

May 29, 1898 Sunday
The children and I were alone all day. Hans came and borrowed the hoe and worked in his corn. I did some writing.

May 30, 1898 Monday
Decoration day. The children and I cleaned out the west room and in the afternoon we went down to Mr. Burbank's.

May 31, 1898 Tuesday
A squaw worked for me. Mr. Halferty came and began the plastering. Mr. Bachelor came with him to help. I had plenty to do as Lewis was gone.

June 1, 1898 Wednesday
The men worked on the house. The children went to school. In the afternoon I went to get Mr. Wilcox to haul a load of sand.

June 2, 1898 Thursday
I churned and did some baking and cleaned the kitchen. In the evening Lewis and Mr. Winniford came. Mr. Tibbets and Mr. Burbank called.

June 3, 1898 Friday
The men worked on the house and built the front flue. Lewis hauled a load of sand and a load of water and helped with the flue.

June 4, 1898 Saturday
I starched and ironed some clothes and did some baking. Lewis went to Mission. The men went home. Harvey called late.

June 5, 1898 Sunday
A very warm day. Hanse was here to dinner. In the afternoon I wrote a letter.

June 6, 1898 Monday
Lewis and I went to see the sick Indian. I wrote a note to the doctor for them. In the afternoon I did some sewing. Lewis went to Wenatchee.

June 7, 1898 Tuesday
Lewis went to Mission to send some thing to the ditch. I did some baking and ironed some. In the evening I worked in the garden.

June 9, 1898 Thursday
I did a big wash. Bessie and Ray went to school. Lewis irrigated the garden. A very warm day.

June 10, 1898 Friday
Lewis slacked and stained some more lime for the plaster. I churned, mopped the floor and did the usual house work.

June 11, 1898 Saturday
Cool and windy. Bessie and Ray cleaned the wheat out of the orchard. I ironed and did some mending. Lewis hauled water and slacked more lime.

June 12, 1898 Sunday
A warm day. We all went down to the garden and had new potatoes and peas for dinner. Mr. Winniford was here. Mr. Wilcox and Harvey called.

June 13, 1898 Monday
Mr. Halferty and Lewis worked on the house. The fruit tree agent called. I baked bread and did various kinds of work.

June 15, 1898 Wednesday
A rainy day. The men worked on the house. In the afternoon we had a very heavy rain. I sewed some.

June 16, 1898 Thursday
Mr. Halferty finished plastering the house. Lewis worked about the house. I worked in the garden until I was tired out.

June 17, 1898 Friday
Lewis worked in the house and in the evening went to Mission. I cleaned the house some and did the milking.

June 18, 1898 Saturday

Mr. Hickey came after some wheat. I did some baking, churned and cleaned the kitchen. Lewis worked the road. Ray and Bessie hunted horses all day.

June 19, 1898 Sunday

I did some writing. In the afternoon we all went to the Indian funeral. In the evening Mr. Hickey and Harvey called. Mr. Winniford went back to the ditch.

June 20, 1898 Monday

Lewis worked the road and turned the wagon over and hurt his foot. Our dog was killed. I did some writing and sewed some. Bessie and Ray went to school.

June 21, 1898 Tuesday

I did the milking and helped Lewis get ready to go to the ditch camp. In the afternoon I sewed some and cleaned the west room upstairs. Mr. McDougle called.

June 22, 1898 Wednesday

Lewis did not come home and I was uneasy about him and sick too. I walked down to Mr. Warner's after supper. Lewis came that night.

June 23, 1898 Thursday

Mr. Winniford came very early. He worked some on the house. Lewis went to Mission. I did some baking for the picnic dinner.

June 24, 1898 Friday

The children and I went to the school picnic and had a nice time. Mr. Winniford worked on the house. Lewis went to J. Shotwell's.

June 25, 1898 Saturday

I cleaned the kitchen and washed some of the windows. In the afternoon we all went to Mr. Warner's after water and mulberries. Then Lewis went to Mission.

June 26, 1898 Sunday

We killed a skunk. Harvey called. I went down to the garden. In the afternoon Mr. Cloninger and his daughter and Miss Blankenship called.

June 27, 1898 Monday

Lewis went to work on the ditch. Bessie and Ray went to school. Mr. Winniford went to Wenatchee. Charlie and I went to Mr. Wilcox's after gooseberries.

June 28, 1898 Tuesday

Mr. Winniford went to work for Mr. Horn. Bessie and Ray went to
school. Charlie and I were here alone. I sewed some and canned some
berries.

June 29, 1898 Wednesday

A lonesome day for Charlie and I as all the rest were gone. I sewed all
day.

June 30, 1898 Thursday

Alone again. I sewed – made Charlie a white waist. In the evening went
down to see Mrs. Warner and Virgil. He was hurt.

Patterns Cora used

July 1, 1898 Friday

A very warm day. I did a big washing and mopped the floor. Bessie
and Ray rode to school and back with Mr. Hickey who went to
Wenatchee.

July 2, 1898 Saturday

Mr. Warner sent me some raspberries. I did a big ironing, some mending
and some baking. Lewis came home late.

July 3, 1898 Sunday

I shingled three heads. Hanse called. I did some baking for the picnic
dinner and got ready to go.

July 4, 1898 Monday

We all went to Mission to celebrate the fourth. Went part way in the
wagon, crossed the river in the boat, walked to Mission and went the
rest of the way in Mr. Cloninger's hack.

July 5, 1898 Tuesday

I put things away and after dinner we went down after water. Lewis built
fence and I picked currents for Mr. Warner and myself.

July 6, 1898 Wednesday

Lewis worked on the fence again and in the evening went to see Mr. Hayman and Wilcox. Charlie and I went to the garden. The Indians were here. Mr. Hughes called.

July 7, 1898 Thursday

Lewis went to Wenatchee very early to see John and to get a cow and calf and came back in the evening. Mr. Hughes was here to supper. I sewed some.

July 8, 1898 Friday

The last day of school. I worked in the kitchen nearly all day. Mr. Hughes and Hanse were here to dinner. Harvey called. Lewis began to cut his hay.

July 9, 1898 Saturday

A very warm day. Lewis cut and raked hay. Mr. Hughes and Hanse were here again. I washed windows and cleaned the front room.

July 10, 1898 Sunday

Another warm day. I cleaned up the house some. In the evening I did some writing. Lewis and the children hauled a load of water.

July 11, 1898 Monday

Warmer than ever. They stacked Mr. Hanson's hay and were here to eat. Lewis cut hay. In the afternoon I sewed some.

July 12, 1898 Tuesday

They let Mr. Hanson's team run away. Begun to stack hay here. Lewis was still cutting. I swept the house all over and did the usual work.

July 13, 1898 Wednesday

Much cooler. The men worked in the haying. I went down to the garden after vegetables. Hr. Holms called. Lewis finished cutting.

July 14, 1898 Thursday

Mr. Hughes went to Wenatchee and Lewis and Hanse hauled hay. I did a big washing besides the other work.

July 15, 1898 Friday

I churned, cleaned the kitchen and did some mending. Mr. Hansen and Lewis finished the hay. Lewis worked in the house some.

July 16, 1898 Saturday

Cool and windy. Harvey went away. I ironed some and did some mending. Lewis worked in the house nearly all day. Ray went to Mission.

July 17, 1898 Sunday
Mr. McMillen was here to dinner. Lewis went to Mission. The children went after the cows and got some berries. I wrote a letter.

July 18, 1898 Monday
A windy day. Lewis helped Mr. Hughes on his house and I got dinner for his four men, went to the garden and baked light bread and got supper for the men.

July 19, 1898 Tuesday
Lewis helped Hughes and I got dinner for the men again. We went to the garden and got ripe tomatoes. I cleaned the west room.

July 20, 1898 Wednesday
I was sick all day. Lewis worked some on the house. The children hunted horses nearly all day.

July 21, 1898 Thursday
Lewis hauled water and watered the orchard. In the evening we all went down to Mr. Burbanks and got some fruit. Harvey called.

July 22, 1898 Friday
I mended grain sacks and helped Lewis get started for the bend after grain. The children and I were alone for a week.

July 23, 1898 Saturday
We cleaned up the yard some and went to the garden after vegetables besides the usual work.

July 24, 1897 Sunday
A lonesome day for us and we were alone till evening. Some Indians were here. I rested and read some.

July 25, 1898 Monday
A windy day. A squaw washed for me. I put things away and mopped the floor, milked the cows and got supper.

July 27, 1898 Wednesday
A very warm day. I was not well but finished making my striped shirt waist, besides doing the usual work and going to the garden.

July 28, 1898 Thursday
After doing up the morning work, the children and I went in Harvey's cart to a quilting at Mr. Jim Waythman's. Lewis and John came while we were gone.

July 29, 1898 Friday

A terrible hot day. Lewis and John went to Mission to work in the shop and get in the river too. I was sick all day.

Aug. 14, 1898 Sunday

We all went to Mr. Burbank's after some apricots and were there to dinner. Mrs. Sikes came home with us. Mr. S. came later. They were here to supper.

Aug. 16, 1898 Tuesday

My birthday. (Warm) I picked and packed 100 pounds of tomatoes and was tired out. Lewis went after his load of lumber that he left in the river Monday.

Aug. 17, 1898 Wednesday

Lewis hauled more lumber for his barn. Mr. Warner came and got my tomatoes and some melons. I cut out some sewing. Lewis got home late.

Aug. 18, 1898 Thursday

A cool morning. We went to the garden and got a load of melons. The children and I went to Mission with them and tomatoes. Lewis got home late.

Aug. 19, 1898 Friday

Lewis hauled 2 loads of lumber and forded the river. I canned some fruit and ironed and canned tomatoes.

Aug. 20, 1898 Saturday

Lewis hauled 2 more loads of lumber. I cleaned the kitchen.

Aug. 21, 1898 Sunday

A cool day. We all went up the river to Mr. Tibbit's place and forded the river. Stopped at Mission and at Mr. Hayman's and came home late.

Aug. 22, 1898 Monday

Cool and sprinkled rain. We went to the garden after tomatoes and I packed five boxes and sent to Mission. L. finished hauling lumber.

Aug. 23, 1898 Tuesday

Lewis cut some corn. I was almost sick but worked all day at various kinds of work. In the evening went to Burbank's after fruit.

Aug. 24, 1898 Wednesday

Lewis cut corn awhile and finished the bay window. I canned some fruit and in the evening went to the garden after some tomatoes and melons.

Aug. 25, 1898 Thursday
I packed the tomatoes and cleaned up the house. Mr. Burbank called to qualify me as school clerk. The children and I went to Mission.

Aug. 26, 1898 Friday
Lewis cut corn and I did a big washing and got supper for Mr. Stone and J. Bonwell who stayed overnight here. I was very tired.

Aug. 27, 1898 Saturday
I did some baking and fixed a lunch for the men. I washed the kitchen windows and mopped the floor. Bessie ironed some. We changed the curtains.

Aug. 28, 1898 Sunday
Lewis was sick. I rested and read some and did some writing. A windy evening.

Sept. 1, 1898 Thursday
A nice day. I fixed Lewis' clothes and he cut some corn. In the afternoon he went to Mission. The children and I went to Hayman's for plumbs.

Sept. 2, 1898 Friday
Cool and windy. We went to the garden and got tomatoes and melons. I helped Lewis to get ready and start to the Bend to harvest. I put up some tomatoes.

Sept. 3, 1898 Saturday
I ironed some and made tomato preserves and plumb butter, besides churning and doing the usual work.

Sept. 4, 1898 Sunday
A nice warm day. I had the headache after cleaning up the house. I laid down and rested and read some. Edna Burbank stayed overnight with us.

Sept. 5, 1898 Monday
Charlie Burbank stopped and eat melons with us. I made jelly and plumbutter.

Sept. 6, 1898 Tuesday
The children and I took the team and went to the garden. In the afternoon we went to Mission to take some tomatoes and got home late.

Sept. 7, 1898 Wednesday
Virgil called and Ray went with him to McDougle's. I canned plumbs and made jelly and had the sick headache too.

Sept. 8, 1898 Thursday

A warm day. I canned some more plumbs. In the P. M. a squaw came and brought me some peaches and some huckleberries.

Sept. 9, 1898 Friday

After doing up the morning work we went to Mr. Burbank's. I sewed for her and got some peaches.

Sept. 10, 1898 Saturday

Another warm day. I worked in the fruit, churned and cleaned the lamps. In the evening we went to the garden for melons and tomatoes.

Sept. 11, 1898 Sunday

Very warm in the morning but cool and windy in the evening. Harvey came and brought me his fruit jars. I did some writing.

Sept. 12, 1898 Monday

After doing up the usual morning work I sewed some on Edna Burbank's dress, then done up the evening chores.

Sept. 13, 1898 Tuesday

I finished Edna's dress and finished canning up what peaches I had.

Sept 23, 1898 Friday

I cleaned the doors and windows upstairs and the upper hall. Bessie and Ray cut some corn.

Sept. 24, 1898 Saturday

A nice warm day. Bessie and Ray churned. I carried a bucket of fresh water from the river. In the evening John was here awhile.

Sept. 25, 1898 Sunday

A lonesome day for us and I worked a part of the day. Virgil called and brought us a timber grouse. I read and rested some.

Sept. 26, 1898 Monday

Bessie and Ray hunted horses all day. I cut out some sewing and sewed some. In the evening I carried a bucket of water from the river.

Sept. 27, 1898 Tuesday

A terrible windy day. Bessie and Ray found the horses and we had to haul water and go to the garden.

Sept. 28, 1898 Wednesday

Mr. Hickey brought me some fruit cans and I fixed some tomatoes for canning. In the afternoon we went to Mr. Burbank's after peaches. It rained some.

Sept. 29, 1898 Thursday

A nice day but cool. Bessie and I canned peaches and tomatoes. I made some tomato catchup, besides the other work. John came by on his way home.

Sept. 30, 1898 Friday

A nice day. We canned tomatoes, silver prunes and peaches. In the evening the children were writing. I read some.

Oct. 1, 1898 Saturday

Bessie and I churned while Ray drove the cows away and brought the horses. After noon we went to Mission to the creamery and to see the new bridge. (Rainy)

Oct. 2, 1898 Sunday

A cool day. Harvey called. Lewis came home for a short visit but went back to the thrashing machine. The children went to the garden. I did some writing.

Oct. 3, 1898 Monday

Bessie and Ray started to school. I milked the cow and took old Bell and the calf to water, went to Mission, came back and got fruit at Hayman's and came home with the headache.

Oct. 7, 1898 Friday

Ray stayed out of school to get the horses and help me haul water. In the afternoon we went to Hayman's, came back and done up the work.

Oct. 8, 1898 Saturday

A nice day. After doing up the morning work we all went to Wenatchee to do some trading. Carrie Burbank went with us. We got home late.

Oct. 9, 1898 Sunday

We went to Wenatchee to hear Elder Corbaley preach, went to Mr. Frances's for dinner, crossed the Columbia river to the babtizing and then came home late.

Oct. 10, 1898 Monday

Bessie and Ray went to school. Charlie and I were here alone. I worked in the fruit all day. After school we took the hack and hauled a load of corn.

Oct. 11, 1898 Tuesday

Ray got the team and I worked with the fruit till afternoon, we went to the garden and picked some tomatoes, then went to Mission after windows and mail.

Oct. 12, 1898 Wednesday

I finished up the fruit. Bessie and Ray rode Mr. McMillen's pony to school. I was very tired when night came.

Oct. 13, 1898 Thursday

I cleaned up the house some and did the mending. Bessie and Ray went to school.

Oct. 14, 1898 Friday

A stormy morning. I did a big washing but did not have enough water to finish. Bessie and Ray went to the river after water.

Bessie Alice born Sept. 15, 1888   Joseph Ray born Dec. 31, 1889
Virginia born April 14, 1891 died April 19, 1891
Charles Arthur born May 14, 1894

Oct. 15, 1898 Saturday

I finished my washing and cleaned up the house. Bessie went after the horses and we hauled a barrel of water. Then I mopped the kitchen floor.

Oct. 16, 1898 Sunday

A cool windy day. After doing up the usual work I did some writing, baked some cookies and got dinner. Then we got the team and hauled some corn. Edna B. stayed here.

Oct. 17, 1898 Monday
The children went to school. Charlie and I were alone all day. I did some mending. After supper I was reading when Lewis came home from the Bend.

Oct. 18, 1898 Tuesday
Lewis made a hog pen then we chased pigs awhile and unloaded the wagon and hauled a load of corn. I got my organ home once more.

Oct. 19, 1898 Wednesday
Mr. Tibbits called. Lewis went to Mission after shingles. When he came back we unloaded the wagon and went to the garden. Then he hauled a load of water. I sewed.

Oct. 20, 1898 Thursday
I packed a big box of tomatoes and sent to the Bend by Lewis as he went back, then we were alone again. I cleaned up the house and canned some tomatoes.

Oct. 21, 1898 Friday
A nice day. Bessie and Ray went to school. I did the usual work and sewed some and helped the children with lessons.

Oct. 22, 1898 Saturday
Cool and windy. I made some melon preserves and ironed. After dinner we churned and were all about sick with bad colds.

Oct. 23, 1898 Sunday
Mr. Hanson came back. Norman and Mr. Halferty called. After dinner I did some writing and baked some cookies. Charlie Burbank stayed over night here.

Lewis began building their house in 1897.
The house is still there but not in a livable condition.

The Lewis Titchenal Family
and the Home Lewis Built in Mission

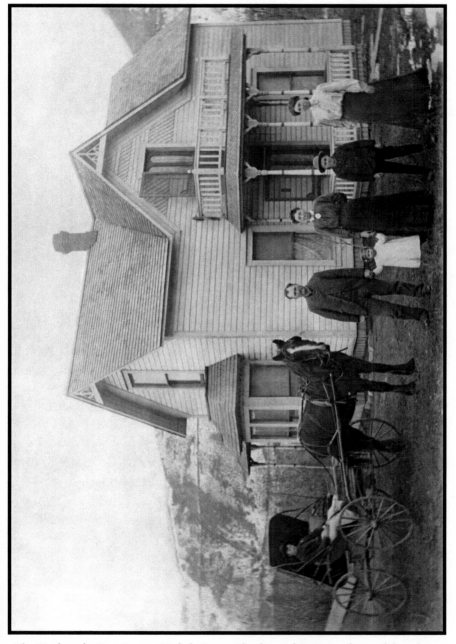

The Titchenals. Ray, Lewis, Mabel, Cora, Charlie and Bessie in front of their home in Mission (now Cashmere, Washington) Ray is in the buggy,   Circa 1905-

Ray Titchenal tells of his days as a school boy living near Mission, now Cashmere, in his book, "The Cowboy Packer." The following story is part of that book:

Ray Titchenal is the tall boy, fourth from left on the front row. Bessie, first on third row. Note Ray's "too small jacket." School was in Monitor, Washington

My mother used to take a team and wagon and ford the river to take cream to the creamery at Mission. We kids would knock the brake blocks out and put them in the wagon so they wouldn't float away. The team was used to the ford, and we didn't think of the danger if the river was deep.

We had to haul water from the river in two 52-gallon oak barrels. That was our water supply. We would pull the water sled up to the kitchen door, and mother would dip up a bucket of water and carry it into the house.

My sister, Bessie was a year and a half older than I. We started school at Monitor, both on the same horse, in Kittitas County. The Wenatchee River was the line between Kittitas and Okanogan County. We would go three months in Kittitas County, then the same kids and teacher would move across the river and go three months in Okanogan County. There wasn't enough kids in either county to hold school in two counties at once. Just a one-room school house, and one teacher taught from the first grade up to eighth.

In 1900 mother and we kids, [Bess, Charlie and I] took a team and hack and drove to my uncle's place the other side of Spokane. I did most of the driving, but mother was sitting beside me so I felt safe. We met a streetcar on the Monroe Street bridge and the horses spooked and crowded into the rail and broke the clip off the singletree. Mother held the team and I took a halter rope, tied it up so we could get off the bridge and get going again.

My uncle Jim Hays was farming two sections of wheat at Waverly. They were farming with horses. It took 32 horses to pull the combine. They had two big barns and lots of work horses.

In 1901 and 1902 the farmers used to work on the Highline ditch and take ditch stock for pay. This work was all done with horses. I drove a team on a slip scraper when I was only 12 years old. I was a big kid and thought I was quite a teamster – but I guess I was.

Cover of Ray's book Cowboy Packer.
Illustrated by Randy Titchenal, Ray's grandson.

Lewis and Cora were still building their house when Washington Territory sent volunteers to war in the Philippines. The following letter from Cousin J.E.N. is written in Manila, Philippine Islands on Feb. 25, 1899 when the Americans were fighting the Spanish-American War. He was writing to his cousin, Norman Titchenal, the brother of Lewis Titchenal. It is addressed to Mr. N. S. Titchenal, Mission, Wash. USA. The town of Mission was renamed Cashmere.

I was struck by the fact that this letter from Manila in 1899 might have been written by one of our troops fighting in wars any place in the world.

Manila, Philipine, Island
Feb 25 – 99

Cousin, Norman,

Your most welcome letter was received yesterday. I was just thinking of writing to you.

I suppose that you have heard of the fun that we have been having, I don't think that it will last much longer as the insurgants wont last much longer if they keep killing them at the rate they have so far and I am getting anxious to get done with them as I want to come home, I have all of this country that I want. I don't think that all of the islands are worth the ammunition they used in getting them.

They are not fighting much now as they have taken all of the ground that the troops now here can hold, but they will start up business again as soon as more troops get here.

It is just as hard to hold the lines as it is to run them back, if there had of been troops enough they could have had them whipped before now.

They can't stand fire and all that the Americans have to do is to stand and give them a heavy fire a few minutes then charge then and they will run just as long as they are ran after.

It always makes us feel cool when I get a letter from hom and they tell me how cold it is there. The hottest day of summer there would be considered a cool day here.

The most trouble they have is with the sharpshooters they get into town some way and shoot out of the houses. They are not good enough shots to get the man that they shoot at but the spent ball is apt to hit some body else.

I tell you, that the sharpshooters made it unplesant living in town for three of four days after the war broke out here the town was full of them and they use smoakless powder and you couldn't tell where they were but now they have burned most all of the Bamboo houses in town and they have no place to hide and are not so bad.

I was on gard at quarters part of the time and I came nearer getting shot there than I did at the front. I was on post and they were shooting at me and the sentry next to me from both sides and we couldn't tell where they were and I tell you that I felt in first class running trim but they routed them out from one side and couldn't find the others for several days but he got too brave and climbed up a tree and a man from my company saw him and made a good man out of him.

We have moved out of Manila and are quartered at present at Santa Ana, but cant tell how long we will stay.

During the hottest of the first battle my company was stationed as sharpshooters and since that we haven't done much only to chase insurgant sharpshooters and gard haad quarters our regimental head quarters are here

I am making quit a collection of native countribands of war. I have most every thing but a mauser rifle and the first chance I get I am going to get one.

I have a silver inlayed machete (or a dirk) but it was in a house that was burned and the temper was taken out of it and I don't know wheather it can be tempered or not and want you to tell me if it can be, it is worth

$6 or $7 if a good temper can be put in it.

We are having fine grub now. When this place was taken it was done in a hurry and the natives were all lucky to get out alive and the country is full of hogs and chickens and the gardens are at their best so we just have all kinds of good things to eat and bananas are ripe and the house that we are quartered in is in a banano grove.

I don't think that this country will amount to much or not soon at least it would be all right if a man had lots of money but a poor man has no business here at all the natives will work for what they can get.

I am getting sick of this country there isn't a thing here to see or no place to go and nothing to do but go on gard abut four or five times a week and that even gets old.

Co. F. hasn't lost a man or had one wounded so far.

Do you know Tom Hamelton he is a brother to John Brooks' wife he is here with the Wyomings he saw my name in the roster and came up to see who I was and told me who he was and that is all that I know about him. He is stationed close to us now but he is on one side of the river and I am on the other and we are not allowed to cross the river.

I will send you a picture of the trenches that part of the Wash. regiment charged the next time I write they haven't got them done yet or I would send it now

The insergants are very poor shots. They had two Krupp guns trained on blockhouse No. 11 and they wanted to hit No. 11 the first thing and the first shot they fired went about 35 feet above the house and the next shot tore the corner off of a Convent about 200 yds. to the left of the blockhouse and nobody knows where the third shot did go three shots was all that they got to shoot as the Americans got their gunners as fast as they would come out so they got tired of artilary in a short time and Co. H. captured the guns.

Well I will close for this time as I cant think of any thing interesting to write.

I guess that you know more about the way the things are going than I do. There is 25 miles of skirmish line and all kinds of reports come in and we cant believe any of them.

I was just finishing a long letter to the Waterville paper when the war started and I don't know wheather I will write another or not.

Answer as soon as you get this and tell me all that you know as I am very anxious to here from the U. S.

From your cousin J. E. N.

The Cousin J.E.N. signature on the letter presented an identification challenge since there was no name on the letter and it had been mailed in an envelope with J.E.N.'s commanding officer's name as the return address. The initials were unfamiliar to present day Titchenal family members. Since the letter had been written to "Cousin" Norman the writer had to be a relative who was apparently well known to Norman.

The identity of J.E.N. is based on the collective research by: Professor David Lindeblad at Wenatchee Valley College, Omak Campus; and Mark O'English, University Archivist who searched the manuscript archives and special collections in the Terrell Library at W.S.U. The conclusion of this research is that Cousin J. E. N. is John E. Norton. John E. Norton is listed under Co. F in the Spanish American War archives for Washington Territory. His connection to Waterville is his letter: "I was just finishing a long letter to the Waterville paper when the war started and I don't know wheather I will write another or not."

Additional support for the relationship of the Norton family to the Titchenal family follows:

David J. Titchenal's obituary lists under survivors: "A nephew, William Norton of Waterville." He is presumed to be related to John E. Norton.

In her Dec. 23, 1886 letter Cora writes of seeing Mr. Norton. In a diary entry she states: "Mr. Norton's folks moved to Lewis' house."

In his 1887 diary Lewis states on March 12, "Worked till noon and John and John Norton brought the horses and we all went home."

The High Line Ditch

[After moving] to the Wenatchee valley in April, 1897, locating on Warner's Flat, two miles east of Cashmere (then Mission.) This was then Okanogan county, with Conconully the county seat. There was nothing on the place. We bought only sagebrush and sun flowers (and rocks.) We leveled the ground and improved it, living there a little more than six years without any water to irrigate with, though it rained there more then it has of recent years, and we raised good corn and wheat hay, also some garden. Mr. Titchenal was elected president of the high line ditch and worked a great deal of the time on that with men and teams. Everybody rejoiced when the water was turned in on the land, so we could set out fruit trees and raise alfalfa. (From Cora's letter to the Editor October 9, 1925)

From 1898 to 1903 he was boss of the construction work on the Highline canal. (12/2/41 newspaper article nameing L. H. Titchenal as a pioneer and naming his early development activities.)

The Highline ditch is mentioned in two Lewis Titchenal obituaries.
The Wenatchee Daily World Oct. 18, 1951
"Lewis Titchenal planted his own orchard and operated it for many years. He also was instrumental in the construction of Highland canal.

Cashmere Record, 10/18/51
"Part of the credit for the construction of the Highline canal goes to him."[Lewis Titchenal]

> This letter is written to Bessie from Cora July 23, 1902. It may
> have been that Bessie was staying at Badger Mountain with her
> grandmother but it does not say....

Mission, Wash.   *July 23, 1902*
Dear Bessie

I will send you a letter from Mamie. I opened it because I thought there might be one with it for me & was anxious to hear from Alice. But she did not write.

We have all missed you since you went away but hope you are having a nice time.

I thought perhaps I could get away for a few days and come up after you but there seems to be no chance for me to leave now so you needn't expect me to come.

Norman is talking of going up there to take a man to look at the ranch. He has been helping with the hay. They finished cutting it Sunday & some of the ditch crew came down & helped stack & the cook came & helped me get dinner. There was nine men here counting Ray. But the cook had to go back & get supper at camp so that left me alone & just as supper was over Mr. Hickey & his girl & Joel Treadwell & his girl came & stayed till nearly 10 o'clock. It has been terrible warm here ever since you left. The thermometer went up to 100 Sunday but has not been so warm since. I wish you had your light dress.

Friday Evening

We have done a big washing to-day & Alice has been here this afternoon. Norman & Ray got a man to help them & they finished putting the hay in yesterday. Norman said his man had got out of the notion going to the Bend now so he is going to Wenatchee tomorrow to work for Nim. He went over to the Butler place to-day.

Mr. Thurman came over Wednesday evening & took another treatment yesterday morning. Roy stayed all day.

Your Papa stays at the ditch camp.

I have 4 gallons of Raspberries to can to-morrow. I got some cherries too at McFarland's.

Puss has adopted little "Teddie" so he is alright now.

Saturday Morning

Papa is going to Wenatchee to-day. If you don't come home soon I want you to write. I would like to go up there but can not leave home now

                                Mamma

Cousins, Bessie Titchenal and Mamie Hays

Cora Titchenal and daughter,, Mabel, age 4 years. Mabel was born October 3, 1903

Norman Titchenal, standing, brother of Lewis, with his friend Frank Dorn.
The men purchased the saw mill at Chiwaukum, Washington
from Henry Middleton in 1902.

Badge Mt. Lodge No 57 F. & A. M. Received from Bro. Norman S. Titchenal
the sum of Six Dollars, being amount of Dues from July 1, 1903 to January 1, 1905
A. B. Dorsey Secretary

A History of Wenatchee
"The Apple Capital of the World"

By John A. Gellatly

The following excerpt from the History of Wenatchee is printed here with permission.

...Along about 1902 the valley had become populated [to] a point where it seemed that some means by which the growing traffic between Wenatchee and Cashmere could be taken care of more rapidly than by horse-drawn vehicles. A group of local citizens headed by Hyman Harris, A. J. Linville of Wenatchee, L. H. Titchenal and others of Cashmere conceived the notion that a street car service between the two points would be financially feasible and would supply a badly needed facility. They formed a corporation known as the Red Apple Street Car Company, and after selling a limited amount of stock to local people, bought a part of the right-of-way and began the construction of a grade for the purpose of lying ties and rails. The work did not proceed very far from Cashmere where they had started the undertaking when, for two or three reasons, the work had to stop after spending a few thousand dollars. The first reason which slowed down the effort was the need for more capital; the second was that automobiles were coming into use and a condition developed whereby it seemed more practical to run a stage line by using Model T. Fords and later to use large cars which could carry a greater number of Passengers. It was not long until the street car program died a natural death...

~~~~~~~~~~~~~~~~~~~~~~~~~~~~~~~~

August 15, 1904　　　　　　　　　　　　　**Wenatchee Daily World**
"Make Dirt Fly on Summit Next Week"

F.W. Easley of Chelan will start actual construction on the Chelan county portion of the Cascade Scenic Highway. A party got off at Cascade tunnel and walked up the switchback yesterday to estimate cost of developing the road over the hump. In the party were John A. Gellatly, Lester Gellatly, Fred A. Warren, Matt Hickey, F.W. Easley, Mr. and Mrs. Tom Henry of Dryden; W.H. Mills, L.H. Titchenal, and Will Paton of Cashmere. The switchback bed is still intake. Easley believes he can finish five miles from the summit this year, leaving only 11 miles from Merritt next year. Every auto owner in the district will be asked to contribute funds.

Fairy Johnson

The following letter from Fairybelle is on three sheets of stationery from Chico Hot Springs Hotel, Wm. E. Knowles, Prop'r. Chico, Mont., which proclaims "a cure for rheumatism, stomach troubles and all skin and blood diseases." A box in the upper left hand corner contains an analysis by Prof. F. W. Clark, chief chem.. U. S. Geo. Survey, listing the "solid contents" of the minerals found in the "Plunge and private baths. Rates reasonable" The hand written return address is 61 Battery St., Seattle, Wash.

It is addressed to Bessie Titchenal, Cashmere, Chelan Co., Wash.

April 14th 1905

Dear Cousin Bessie:

I rec'd your ever welcome letter a few day ago. Was very glad to hear from you.

No! I had not forgotten the Vale of Cashmere, or the people in it but I was to busy to write.

I am glad the basket social was a success, and hope you had a good time. I am also glad to hear that you have organized Sunday School in Cashmere.

(They were talking some about it when I was there.) I hope that you can continue it, all the time.

I did not know where Frank Patterson was, or his phone number either.

243

If I had I would have called him up.

I hope you do not get caught, when you and Ethel go down to pull up Frank's Tomatoes. A Be ware of Dog sign on the fense.

I hope you had a good time when the girls and boys were up from Wenatchee.

And how glad I am to know that Maude Patterson is so much better. Poor girl has had a hard time.

I guess people are glad on the flat that Homes are gone. Especially George. And Titchenal's.

How I would like to see dear little Mabel, even if she does get into mischief. (she is just like her sister.) Give a big hug and kiss to her for Mama and I both. Yes, Bessie I would get her some of "Old Vicks Handcuffs" I think it would help her.

I am glad you had a good time Sunday, and you will have a good time again soon. wonder why every body is so afraid of the grade. (I never was Oh! no!)

Bessie I guess your wish is coming true. Do you remember what it was? You said you wished some one would move on the flat that had about 16 kids.

I am glad that Cashmere is burning. Also that they have a jail for the bad folks.

I wish I were there to ride "Jennie" and take some of the hate and foxiness out of her. But would take Marion to do that.

All the folks send their regards to you. (Ted included.) says "Hello Bessie".

Mama is well, but tired to death. She is nursing an old man from Montana nearer dead than Mrs. Sommerville was. I am well too. Mrs. McFarl is better but not well yet.

Mama over see's her too.

With love from both to all. Write soon to your loving cousin.

Fairy Johnson

~~~~~~

Cashmere, Aug. 3," 1906.

Dear Bessie:

I received your letters alright & suppose your camp has livened a little since the crowd got there. I hope the peaches tasted good to you. I told Norman not to eat any of them for he had his share before he started. How is Susie's eye?

I will send a letter that came for her. I so not think they can finish the hay to-morrow as we could not get hands enough. Mr. Hughes & C. Clark helped yesterday & Clark to-day. George Coleman has been working here all week. He went with Ray to the pasture Sunday & got his little sorrel horse again. It seems quite gentle now.

Guy was here Tuesday to get Ray to go camping with them, but he can not go. There is too much to do for him to leave now. Frank came back Monday & went camping up to the tunnel. I have not been to town or seen Ethel since you left. I have been working at the fruit as I could. There should have been more shipped to-day but I could not get it ready alone & do the other work. The peaches are better now but not such a good price. I will try to send you some. The rest are all buisy in the hay. Mabel eats enough peaches for you & her too. She often says she is going to Seattee to see Tessie. She has been pretty good. How did Nannie & Skeels finally settle Did Phebe & Letha meet them?

Now about you going to Spokane you know I told you if you went over there it would take all the money we could spare you now. I would rather send you more money now & have you get your stay out while you are there as you were not satisfied without going over there. I did not think about you going to Seattle this summer when I wrote to Alice that you would come out there. I have not written to Alice & you will have to beg their pardon for disappointing them as they have been expecting you for a month. I am sorry you cannot go both places but you will have to make the best of this trip do you for a while at least.

As for me going camping. There is no use to count on any thing of the kind when there is no one to do the work here or see after things. I would love very much to be there for a while but cannot go this summer. I would have to watch Mabel all the time or put a picket rope on her & stake her out if I was in camp.

I want you to write to Fairy, too. I will have to stop now & get supper & hope you will not feel disappointed about what I have written but stay & have a good time while there if you want to. You wanted my opinion, this is what I think best. Write often. I do not have much time to write.

The weather is cooler now but is dreadful smokey.
I hope the camping will do all of you good.

Your loving

Mother

Bessie Titchenal, graduation 1908

Bessie Titchenal, daughter of Lewis and Cora Titchenal, born September 15, 1888 at the homestead at Badger Mountain, Washington Territory, was the first and only graduate of Cashmere High School in 1908.

*Nancy Moore Titchenal, sister of Lewis Titchenal, was born January 19, 1870.
She and William Skeels were married August 15, 1896 in Wenatchee, Washington.
Nancy died December 28,1930.*

*Phebe Ellen, sister of LewisTitchenal was born June 26, 1874 in Johnstown, MO.
Phebe and Clarence Wright were married Dec. 26, 1905 in Cashmere, WA.
Phebe died June 21, 1958. Clarence died July 25, 1915 in Buckley, WA.*

October 16, 1908 Wenatchee Daily World

Too Many Apple Varieties

N. D. Titchenal of Cashmere says that the people of the valley are making a mistake in planting too many varieties of apples. "If we would confine our attention to the growing of but two varieties, I am sure that we would secure a better price generally, and at the same time increase the reputation of the valley as a fruit growing district."

~~~~~~

Seattle Wash
Nov 16, 08

Dear Mother [Mary Titchenal]

I will write you a line to day to let you know how I am gitting along. I haven't found any thing to do yet but I saw Frank Dorn here and he wants me to come to the tunnel he says I can make more thare than I can here so I think I will go tomorrow evening and look it over and see what thare is for me thare   it is a ruff place but that wont hurt me as I can take care of my self I think

I got Phebes letter yesterday and was a glad to know that she got home all right.

The old man White is here for a few days he has another invention but I am not going to invest in it I have more than I can handle just now and told him to sell my share if he could find a buyer I will try to find something to do until spring and it is no use to stay here for I could not save any thing thare is to many places to go and to much to see for a body to save money here

Well I will close for this time and go out and walk around a while as the sun is shining and that is so seldom I don't like to miss it so good by

From your loveing son

Norman

1909   **Unkown newspaper**

1909 Seattle Apple Exhibit

President Taft admired the Chelan County prize winning display at the Alaska-Youkon-Seattle Exposition in 1909. The summer long display was maintained with cold storage apples from the previous year.

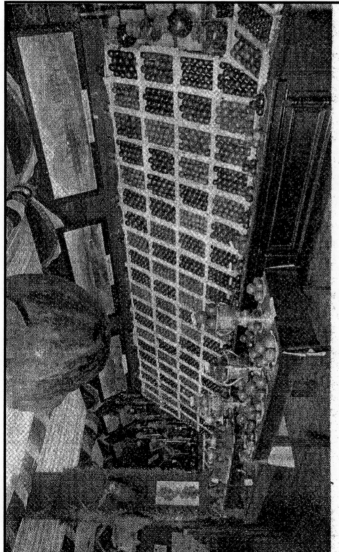

PICTORIAL PAST: 1909 EXHIBIT

President Taft admired the prize-winning Chelan County display at the Alaska-Yukon-Pacific Exposition in Seattle in 1909. Arranged by David Gellatly Sr., then secretary of the Wenatchee Commercial Club, it won many first-place cups in various apple varieties. The all-summer display featured apples kept in cold storage from the season before. A 4½-foot-high plaster of paris Spitzenburg apple formed a ceiling centerpiece.

Friday, January 14, 1910   The Cashmere Valley Record

Wenatchee and Cashmere Apples Win Best Prizes at Denver

Denver Apple Show, 1910
Elsworth France & Lewis Titchenal

Ellsworth France and L. H. Titchenal are winners of 14 prizes at the Colorada Apple exposition. Denver Apple Show, January 3, 1910.

A report from Denver, Colorado, says that Ellsworth France of Wenatchee and L.H. Titchenal of Cashmere are winners of 14 prizes at the Colorado Apple exposition. Judges today awarded France nine first prizes and Titchenal two firsts, and one second and two third prizes, the exhibitors taking $550 cash and added premiums worth $250 more.

The exhibits of France and Titchenal were the same apples which won a dozen prizes at the National Apple show at Spokane in November, aggregating $1400, making a total winning of the two exhibitions on 65 boxes of $2300.

Congratulations are being showered upon the two Washington exhibitors, whose fruit won on superior quality, color, pack, uniformity, condition and size.

Detailed winnings: France – First on 10 boxes White Winter Pearmains, fancy pack; first on 10 boxes Arkansas Blacks, commercial pack; first on five boxes Arkansas Blacks, Commercial; first on Arkansas Blacks, fancy pack; first on each single box of Pearmains, Oregon Red,

Continued from previous page
Winter Grimes, Golden and Winesap; first on best plate of Arkansas Blacks

Titchenal – First on five boxes of Rome Beauties, commercial pack; first on single box Rome Beauty, commercial pack; second on five boxes Rome Beauty, fancy pack; third on 10 boxes Winesap, commercial pack.

The Cashmere Valley Record

Friday, January 14, 1910   **Cashmere, Washington**
L.H. Titchenal of Cashmere and Ellsworth France of Wenatchee won 14 cash prizes between them at the Colorado apple exposition. Their apples earned the two exhibitors $550 plus premiums worth $250.00

1910   **Unknown Newspaper**

Demonstrating the apple box to congressional committee

L.H. Titchenal, of Cashmere, has been indefatigable in his efforts to maintain the high standard of Wenatchee valley fruits. He, with Ellsworth France, made a very successful exhibit last winter at the Denver National Apple show and afterwards he was selected as one of the men to go from this state to present the claims of the Washington growers against the Lafean bill. Mr. Titchenal is himself a very successful grower and has one of the best improved places in the Wenatchee valley.

Titchenal, in his fight before the committee, took up the box matter in a practical way and packed apples to show what would be the best result of a change in the size of the box. Mr. Titchenal left on March 5 and went direct to Washington, where he found the congressional committee in session on the 11th.

The growers of north central Washington owe a personal obligation to him for the time spent by him in this work. This was done at a great personal sacrifice owing to the fact that his own orchard at the time of his absence was in need of his attention.

Mr. Titchenal crossed the plains in 1882, driving a four mule team from Bates county, Missouri, to Wenatchee. His party was 8 months and 10 days on the road. He has crossed the Rockies three times by team and horseback, his first trip being at the age of 15. He lived 14 years in Douglas county and has been in the Wenatchee valley for 13 years.

March 31, 1911   Wenatchee Daily World

L. H. Titchenal President of Horticultural Association

L. H. Titchenal, president of the Chelan County Horticultural Association, and "Apple King" Mike Horan are working to establish the Wenatchee Apple District which would serve as a general selling agency.

~~~~~~

April, 1910   Cashmere Valley Record

Will Survey State Road

Louis H. Titchenal was in receipt of the following letter from State Highway Commissioner Snow, regarding the state road which is to traverse the Wenatchee valley. It is as follows:

"Replying to your letter of April 14, relating to the state road along the Wenatchee river, I will say that the last legislature established State Road No. 7, between Seattle and the Idaho line. This road will pass through Cle Elum; thence by the way of Swauk and Peshastin creeks to the Wenatchee valley; thence down the Wenatchee river following as near as possible the present established road to the city of Wenatchee.

"Regarding right of way, no state road will be laid out with less than 60 feet width of right of way, and you can so state this matter to the people along the line. The only changes that will be made in the location of the present traveled road will be at such points as we may find that the grades are too steep. You will see, therefore, that in a general way the state road will follow the present thoroughfare between the mouth of Peshastin creek and Wenatchee.

"I am glad to know that you have been appointed good roads commissioner and I appreciate the effort you are making to educate the people in the right direction in the road business. I cannot say when the survey of this land will be made, but probably during the present year.

Yours very truly,

JOSEPH M. SNOW

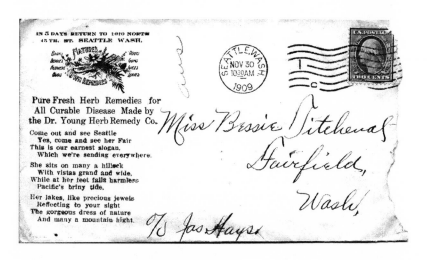

Dr. Young Herb Remedy Co. Laboratory   1010 North 45th, St.

Seattle, Wash. Nov. 30, 1909

Miss Bessie Titchenal.
   Fairfield, Wash.

My dear friend: Yours of Nov. 23rd received. Was glad to hear from you and you will excuse me I know for not having answered your card. You wish to know about the cider. Dr. said to tell you that he had never had any personal experience with but that ginger has been used at the rate of one pound ginger to about 15 gallons cider. In fact his mother says she has used it many times. Just stir the ginger into the cider.

Now about the "Bullion" It is an extract of beans, barley & oats and it requires a special apparatus and a long process to make it. But I'll tell you what I'll do. We sell it at $1.00 per pint usually, but I will let you have our gallon for $4.00 and let you send no apples for it. I don't know of a place you could buy it and we keep it on hand all the time.

Say Bessie, will you be at home soon? We have a great many people who wish us to get them apples, and we could sell them about 50 boxes if we had them, do you suppose we could get them?

How is your health now? I have often thought about your hand has that gotten all right? Dr has been very poorly he had quite a serious nervous break down this fall but is better now. H works too hard.

          Your Friend,
            Mrs. M. G. Young

Paradise, Mont.
Nov. 22, 1910

Dear Bessie:

The people in Spokane gave us a great send off so guess they were glad to get rid of us. The band played & They marched us around till I was almost give out then lined us up in front of the train & had our picture taken. I would like to get some of them but did not find out who was to send to for them. Perhaps Norman can tell you & you can send for one. I think the picture of our booth is just fine & we can keep it as a reminder of the hard work we did there. But you know we have to have such times in life to break the monotony of every day life, & bring our efforts to notice, whether they are appreciated or not. You will have many things to do in life that are unpleasant but so long as we are doing good we should be willing to sacrifice our own pleasure sometimes to help others.

Tuesday Morning:
We are going through a very pretty level country in Montana – the Yellowstone valley. It is quite large & has ditches thro' it. I think it is timothy meadows & there are big herds of cattle & sheep in sight. The hills further back are covered with snow & the wind is blowing hard. The Yellow Stone river is not very large & is a smooth stream as the country is level. We passed some beautiful scenery yesterday in Idaho & crossed the Penderiel (pronounced Pon-de-ray) Lake. It is grand. We came over the mountains last night so the streams are running toward the east. The ground was covered with snow this morning when we first looked out but the sun is shining now & no snow here. I see a few old log cabins which mark pioneer days but there are some nice residences. They set the time one hour ahead last night.
There are six other women in our crowd & we are getting acquainted & having a fine time. I took my first meal in the dining car last night. Everything is very nice.

I want you to write me & tell me how you get along. I want the chicken house cleaned out & some clean nests fixed for the hens. They ought to be laying now. Charlie said he would see to them but he must not neglect them. I suppose you will have plenty of milk & butter to sell since the Jersey's calf died. I hope Ray did not neglect her. I promised milk to Mrs. Drake when we had it to share. You will have to keep account of it. I hope you will get along alright.

I wish you all a happy Thanksgiving.

Love to all from Mama

~~~~~~

Battle Creek, Mich,
Dec. 10, 1910

My Dear Bessie:

This is quite a pretty place & has beautiful residences & lots of big maple trees. I know it is nice in summer.

It is not so cold here as it was in Chicago but there is about 4 or 5 inches of snow & they are going in sleighs. There was such a cold wind in Chicago & thermometer went down nearly to zero but it moderated yesterday & snowed there last night so all the country we saw to-day was covered with snow.

We passed some very pretty places & saw a few orchards but they do not look like the orchards in Wash. Neither does the fruit here look like it does there. We passed a window this evening that was filled with pretty apples so we stopped & read on a card "These apples were grown at Ellensburg Wash. & took first prize at National Apple show in Spokane." They looked good to us. Apples from our Show in Chicago were displayed in many windows & stores there. We went out to Mr. Burke's & had a nice visit.

We never heard from any of the folks that we asked to meet us at the apple show. I don't think we will tarry around in that cold country very long as it is about time for wild geese to go south.

Since you are all getting along so well at home & every one urges me to go on, suppose I will not think about going home soon. So you must get along the best you can. I hope the weather will not be very cold. You can use stone jars to put the milk in as you can heat them & the milk will not freeze before the cream rises. You can take one of them boxes that was in the South room, with a curtain over, & set it there by the cupboard to put some of the milk & butter in & it will not get so cold as in the pantry or milk cupboard & if the weather gets very cold you can cover it up. Papa said he did not care if you sell the stung apples just so the inspector did not get after them. I told Ray he could sort out some of them in the shed & take to Harris in

Wenatchee. He said he would buy them & there was no use in letting them all freeze if you can do anything with them. I expect to make more apple-butter as it would keep good & always ready for use. The cider barrel should be put in the shed & covered up so it will not freeze so hard or it will be ruined.

We only expect to be here a week then will be in Chicago one day. We will go to Kansas City, Mo. from here. Papa mailed the things to you from Chicago. I hope the silk suits you. I saw so many nice things I wanted & could not get I bought me a nice set of furs for $20.00 I have needed them too, will let you have the muff when I get home.

Hope you are all well & getting along alright.

Give my regard to all who inquire about us & accept love & best wishes to all from your Mother.

Ribbons: Spokan First Prise 4th National Apple Show, Aberdeen Good Roads Feb. 1910, Pioneers Delegate, Territorial Pioneed Associaton

Titchenals in California
January, 1911 photo taken in California

Picture taken on a trip out from Los Angeles in an electric excursion car in January, 1911. Lewis and Cora Titchenal and Emma Johnson in the crowd Front row from left: Emma Johnson, Cora and Lewis Titchenal.

*Los Angeles
Jan 17, 1911*

Dear Bessie:

You may think I am having a good time and forgotten to write but I have been sick since we arrived here. Yesterday was the first time that I have been able to go out at all. We took a street car went down in the city. Emma & Fairy went with us & showed us some of the pretty places. We went through the "Hamburger" – one of the largest Dry Goods stores in the west. It is 8 storied high & on the top of the building is a roof garden from which we could see all over the city & the surrounding country, It was a beautiful, clear day & we could see a long ways – near us everything looks green & the flowers are in bloom but we could see snow-covered mountains in the

257

distance. *Fairy wore a lawn waist without any wrap.*

I received all your letters & was glad to hear from you.

This is the day that the Horticultural meeting begins at Prosser but Papa will not be there. I think we will be home before they have the convention at Sacramento.

We will stop off in Portland one day.

Did Charlie do anything with the winter pears? They will not keep much longer. I see by the paper that there has been a cold spell in the Northwest so guess you are getting your share. I hope it will snow for the sake of the fruit. I will expect another letter here.

Lovingly

Mama

~~~~~~

Los Angeles, Cal.
Feb. 4, 1911

Dear Bessie:-

We received your letter with the one you forwarded from Sacramento. Glad you sent it. Papa signed it and sent it on to the committee so I guess they will meet us in great style if we get there. The heavy rains recently have caused great damage on the R.R. in this country but hope that we will get through alright.

Emma intends to go as far as Santa Barbara with us. We expect to go up there the 11th & in to San Francisco the next day & spend a couple of days then to Sacramento by the 15th.

We may stop in Portland 1 day so you can tell about where we will be if you want to write.

Papa says he does not care to let the type-writer go out but you can do as you think best. He said he thought it was broken as you have never written to us on it & he can't read your writing. He sent Mabel a post card.

I wish we were there to attend the meetings but hope they will have good success. I have often thought of our little band there and wonder how you were all getting along. Papa is eating oranges.

Love to all
Mama

Sacramento, California
Feb. 15, 1911

Dear Bessie:

We reached this city at 12:45 to-day. I headed for the P.O. where we found two letters from you. You may be sure we were glad to hear from home & to know that all was O.K.

We went to Santa Barbara on Sunday as it rained so hard Saturday & by waiting Joe & Emma could go with us. It was a nice day & it was a beautiful ride along the beach. We left Los Angeles at 8:15 arriving in Santa Barbara at 11:45. Poor Fairy had to stay home & said she would be so lonely after we were gone she did not know how she could stand it. I felt sorry for her. I hope you have written to her. She had received your card & expected a letter. She gave me her picture.

We left there at 6:45 Monday night & arrived in San Francisco at 9 o'clock Tuesday morning. After getting our breakfast we visited several places of interest. We had to cross the San Francisco bay to Oakland in a large steam boat last night between 9 & 10 o'clock. It was full moon & a beautiful night on the water. The light in the city looked so pretty as we looked back.

We then had to ride 4 miles on the train before reaching Oakland then we got off & stayed over night there so we could see the country between there and this city. When we landed here a committee man met us at the train giving us directions where to go & had a room engaged for us. They have arranged a large programme & we will have a big time.

I do not know yet how long we will be here but will go on as soon as we can. I guess we will go back by Seattle. Will write again. I wish Mabel meet us there.

Love to all.

Mama.

Lewis and Cora Visit
Joseph and Emma in California

Emma, Joe and their daughter Fairybelle standing in front of their beautiful California home. It was their American Dream.

One year and four days after the death of her husband Jesse, Emma married his younger brother Joseph Rodney Johnson. Their daughter, Fairybelle, was born Nov. 13, 1891 in Portland, Oregon.

Cora's brothers, Jesse Cole and Joseph Rodney Johnson came to Washington Territory with Cora on the 1880 wagon.

Jesse Cole Johnson was born July 30, 1860. He married Emma Cecil Griggs on March 4, 1883 in Altona, Bates County Missouri. Jesse and Emma had a daughter named Nettie who was born in Spokane, Washington but hers was a short life.

Jesse died Nov. 4, 1889 in Spokane, Washington. He was struck by lightening while working on a utility pole. Nettie's grave was moved to be beside her father.

Joseph Rodney Johnson, Fairybelle and Emma circa 1911

In the February 15 letter Cora wrote to her daughter Bessie, she and Lewis were visiting Joseph, Emma and Fairybelle who were living in a beautiful home in Los Angeles, California. Emma passed away on March 4, 1912 in Los Angeles, California. Joseph died ten years later.

Lewis Titchenal was among the three delegates chosen to attend the Dry Farming conference in Colorado, This article was published Tuesday, October 4, 2011 in the 100 Years Ago section.

October 4, 1911   Wenatchee Daily World
Three Delegates Attend Dry Farming Conference
Area delegates named to represent the state at the International Dry Farming Congress Oct. 16-20 in Colorado Springs are John Mernor and E. F. Gaines, both of Lakeside and L. H. Titchenal of Cashmere

Nov. 1911   Unknown Newspaper
Club Committees Are Named by President
L. H. Titchenal Makes Report of Cashmere Exhibit at National Apple Show

The first meeting of the commercial club since the election of officers occurred Monday night and was marked with a large attendance. President Casebeer named the following standing committees for the coming year:

Finance – J. C. Lilly, J. F. Sugrue, R. J. Graham.

Membership – F. T. Spiller, R. J. Graham, J. F. Casebeer.

Press and Printing – J. F. Sugrue, F. T. Spiller, J. C. Lilly.

House – Dr. W. G. Parker, J. L. Padfield, Harry Wiker, C. E. Lewis, A. J. Mills.

Transportation and Marketing – L. H. Titchenal, C. A. Huston, J. H. Sprague, C. B. Clark, H. J. Olive.

Various reports of the apple show were given by those who had charge of the excellent showing made in Spokane. L. H. Titchenal who went with the Cashmere district exhibit and in this class won the blue ribbon and $100 in money as a prize, gave a very interesting report saying that Cashmere apples had no worthy competition at all and that every prize there could have been taken had our fruit been entered in the various exhibits. Aside from winning $100 he sold some $90 worth of apples after exhibiting them and shipped on consignment 29 boxes yet to hear from. Mr. Titchenal's expenses, amounted to $171.87, and after this is paid he will have $17.87 to return to the club in addition to the proceeds of the 29 boxes yet to come. The sum of $125.00 advanced by the club as expenses to Mr. Titchenal will be returned intact.

November 22, 1911   Wenatchee Daily World

Chelan Exhibitors At Spokane

Wright, Simmons, Titchenal and Platter Already Have Apples at Big Show

H. S. Simmons, R. P. Wright, L. H. Titchenal and Joe Platter have exhibits at the National Apple Show and will have them in shape when the show opens next week. The Spokesman-Review in yesterday's paper had the following to say regarding these exhibits from Chelan county:

Six of the big carload displays had arrived by yesterday noon and most of these were in place, only the decorative features remaining to make them complete. H. S. Simmons from Wenatchee, R. P. Wright of Chelan, Rosenhaupt and sons of Spokane, Coeur d'Alene, Idaho, fruit growers and the Spokane valley each had their carload display on hand. The Keystone Fruit company of Entiat had one of its three cars in.

Apples by Boat, Wagon and Rail

R. P. Wright, of Wrightville fruit farms on Lake Chelan who wired as soon as he heard the show was to be held: "I'll be with you." is on the ground with a car of Rome Beauties. Mr. Wright is an enthusiast and one of the regular exhibitors at the fair.

To get his apples to Spokane he ships them down the Chelan lake by boat 13 miles, hauls them by wagon then, at Wenatchee, transfers them to the railroad. With all this handicap in shipping facilities one carload was not enough for Mr. Wright so he brought along 50 extra boxes of varieties to be used in box and plate displays. His carload is entered for all prizes – quality, pack and decorations. In 1908 Mr. Wright led in the highest number of scores of any nation, state, county, district or individual.

"This is the best car I ever had" said Mr. Wright. "It's a prize-winner, I believe. Say, I wouldn't miss this show for anything. From the standpoint of education you can't beat it. It is helping the apple business in every way."

Mr. Wright has a sign above his apples. "The land that never fails." Mr. Wright is such a regular exhibitor that it was suggested the sign should read: "The man who never fails."

H. S. Simmons of Wenatchee has his car nearly in place. It comprises Winesaps, Ben Davis, Mammoth Black Twigs, Rome Beauties and Spitzenbergs. Mr. Simmons is another regular exhibitor. Last year was the only show he has missed and that was because he was sick.

"Why this apple show is a help to everything in the northwest," said Mr. Simmons. "It is one of the greatest advertisers the industy has. It helps the grower, not only to grow better and more valuable apples, but helps him to market them better. Do you know that I have learned more at the apple show than ever before in my life and I have been in the apple business 25 years."

L. H. Titchenal has charge of a car of 16 varieties sent by the Cashmere commercial club.

Never Misses a Show

"Haven't missed a show yet," said Mr. Titchenal. "This will make 40 days' apple showing in Spokane for me. We have a fine display and are entered in the contest for irrigated apples. Winesaps are the chief variety of our display."

~~~~~~

Dec. 2, 1911   Cashmere Valley Record

Cashmere at Show
L. H. Titchenal Expressed Himself Well Pleased

Spokane, Dec. 2 – "Yes Sir, we're coming again," said L. H. Titchenal, who had charge of the Cashmere display. "The apple show has been a big success and we'll be here next year with a better display than ever. Cashmere feels proud. We go back with the first prize for irrigated display, with three first prizes on plate displays and another first prize on plate displays and another first prize on single box display and some seconds. In addition we sold 10 boxes of apples to James J. Hill for $10 a box, and that helps. He took two boxes of Spitzenbergs, four of Winesaps, two of White Winter Pairmans, one of Arkansas blacks and the tenth was that box of freak apples that look like Spitzenbergs, but really are Delicious.

Wenatchee Daily World
Wenatchee Valley Automobile club formed

The Wenatchee Valley Automobile club formed its permanent organization last evening with L.H. Titchenal, Cashmere president: Claude Thornhill, Wenatchee, vice president; O.W. Ernst, Wenatchee, secretary, and J.C. Lilly, Cashmere, treasurer. These, with John A. Gellatly, make up the board of directors. The club has employed Henry Adams with a team and wagon to spend the summer in working on the roads of the valley, taking out rocks, working out bumps and filling holes.

> The Titchenal oral history says that Lewis owned one of the first automobiles in the valley. He owned a Stevens Duryea.

Stevens Pass
Gateway to Seattle

By Joann Roe
Page 118-119 (IN PART) Reprinted here with permission.

In the boom environment, a fledgling industry that would eventually support the area-tourism-was born. Tourism depended on convenient transportation, and the automobile was rapidly becoming a practical means of traveling from the population centers west of the Cascades into the mountains.....

In 1911, L. H. Titchenal of Cashmere first envisioned the road as a wagon road (although he said auto enthusiasts were interested in a road over the pass, too) because there already was a road as far as Merritt. Only ten more miles to connect the road to the switchbacks would be required, at a cost he estimated at $15,000. The idea caught fire. Some, including Chelan County engineer Fred M. Berry at first, negated the idea of a Stevens Pass route, favoring improvement of the Blewett-Snoqualmie Pass road. After a trip over the switchback route with Will White, engineer of the highway commission, Berry estimated that about forty-five miles of road would have to be built – all the way from Merritt to Index – at a cost to the three counties involved (King, Snohomish, and Chelan) of a

265

least $200,000. He then threw his support behind the Steven Pass route, although he pointed out the advantages of connecting Leavenworth with Ellensburg via Blewett. Wenatchee booster Percy Schebe favored the switchback route to Tye, saying that only twelve miles of new road would have to be built to connect with an existing road (his "road" was a "trail," though.) Newspapers tossed around the figure of $1,000 a mile for forty-five miles. Berry, the professional engineer, proved more correct in the long run, but he too was low in his cost estimates.

In May 1912, residents between the Snohomish County line and Scenic organized a Good Roads Club to promote a cross-Cascades highway. The group, under Millard Fillmore Smith of Berlin, secured an appropriation from King County for work as far as Skykomish. Two months later, a booster group called the Scenic Highway Association was formed in Everett, with George Startup of Startup as president, L. H. Titchenal of Cashmere as vice president, and W. W. Baird of Everett as secretary-treasurer. Trustees came from eastern and western Washington. A group of decorated automobiles entered a Seattle parade during July to promote the road.

On a bright Sunday, July 28, 1912, boosters from the east side took the train to Cascade Tunnel, then hiked along the switchbacks to meet the west-siders west of Tye. Engineer Berry made the hike and announced that the switchback route was feasible. He reported that the switchback grades were in astonishingly good condition, considering their age and Pass route to compare its possibilities with that of Stevens Pass. Two weeks later another party was in Stevens Pass to view matters firsthand, this group composed mostly of Seattle and Everett residents but also including reporters from the Everett Herald, the Seattle Post-Intelligencer, and the Seattle times.

During the 1920s the Titchenals experienced financial difficulties. They continued efforts to sell apples while trying other ventures to earn the needed capital to maintain the orchard business.

Nov. 10 , 1922, Norman wrote to L. H. Titchenal about the mining interests and people that would be coming to Seattle to talk about mining. Norman had been in Alaska's gold rush and was interested in buying and selling mining stock.

Son, Charlie traveled throughout Washington trying to establish markets for their apples, only to discover that shipping costs made expanding their market unprofitable.

His brother John wrote to relatives living in Alton, Illinois to ask for their help in selling the Cashmere apple crop, but no additional apples were needed.

Lewis went to Seattle to buy and sell mining stock with his friend, "Doc." He believed this venture would earn needed funds.

Lewis and Cora sold most of their orchard, at a loss, during this financial crisis. The following letters are from that time.

Seattle Wn
Nov. 10 – 22

L. H. Titchenal and all.

Will write again but have nothing yet to tell only just happenings. Nelson Rhodes will be here the 15th and wired Collins to be here on that date. Poindexter has a date with him today and Cap't Hawley phoned him last night and made an appointment for tomorrow. Capt Hawley was at one time partiner of Tom Cole and they owned all the copper in the Mich peninsula. Collins has gone to see Jacobs today he wants to send Collins to Chicago. Peabody will tell next week wheather he will take the M and M or not. John Reece got back back from Sitka yesterday and wrote he would be at the office to-day. He had gone to Alaska to look at a nickel deposit… The Everrett people did not have him go to this week as there was some snow at Silverton. He has heard nothing from McGreogor if he don't get buisy he will have to get some one else to make the report for him as… Collins says it will only take 15 minutes when he sees Nelson Rhodes to have a job and go south. Can't tell what he will do but he thinks he will go to work for the English Co: and go south. He told us last week he got a letter from Lloyd George telling him he wanted to keep in touch with him. Lloyd George was Sec of the London Development Co. but had resigned and he and King Albert of Belgum and Eremitage and some more had formed a new co and quit the old co. and the new co was incorporated for 600,000,000 lbs

sterling so this is the line up now He was very curious to know why Capt
Hawley was here… and it may be for his Uncle Tom. Cole
Phebe is here she look like she felt better since having her teeth out…
We got the apples a few min ago. Tuttlle was supposed to bring the car
this week but has not arrived so far.
If you can stir up McGreoger so he will get buisy.

This is all so far
From Norman

Phone Main 5945

Hotel Seward
Zbinden Bros., Proprietors
Arctic Club Building
Seattle, Dec. 18, 1922

My Dear wife and famly

I received your letter Saturday morning and it gave me the Blues but I
don't know what to do with Charlie He wants to do some thing else than
take care of what he has got so I guess I had btter sell out what I have in the
ranch and let him do as he pleases if we have a nother chance it is hard for
me to write where there is so much noise since I have no room of my owe
We are quite Buisy and have lots to do only the snow bothers so much
the ice is so bad you cannot get around only down it has rained all day
and I think the ice is gon it is down town any way Now I don't know if
I can get home for Christmas or not will if I can but am afraid I can not
so do not worry After the freize it will not do any good and will do you
harm if has done me some as I could not work to any atavantage but will
do better from now on We have lots of things to deal in but the money
comes in slow in this business Dr. bought another mine last week for a man
from san frensico but Do not know when he will pay any commission to
us these men with lots of money do not hurry for the other fellow the mine
was on this side and they payed cash for it it was arsnic mine it is on the
road to Montecrists. We have a bunch of men that wants land in Mexico
they come to se us to day and this same man that bought the mine wants
in to go and look at a in Birlish lol as soon as the weather will permit and
some smelter people wants him to go and look over the Granby smelter: see
if you can Get Ray to pay that esesment on the Place $9.00 if not let me
know and I will try & send it over this is horable ink but I guess you can see

268

that well I will close as I will Be late now I am still staying at Drs yet as I cannot aford to stay any where else were I have to pay Room rent so Good Night

With Love
    L H Titchenal

~~~~~~

Tacoma, Wash.
Dec. 28, 1922

Dear Mother,

I have been intending writing for several days but can't seem to get at it it seems as there is always someone here in the office and is hard to think with a lot of people jabberin around.

Doc has left and going back to Cashmere things went pretty good till Christmas but haven't done much since but guess it will be all right again after New Years as everybody is trying to clean up pretty well this week and stock up again next week we handle wholesale only store & Fruit stand and been doing as good as could be expected building up a new business. I made a trip to Centralia and Chalis yesterday but the freight is to high to work that far away so don't think I will go outside any more.

Saw Uncle Henry Christmas day and we had Christmas Dinner together he is looking good said he was feeling fine working study at the mill they made Barrels Kegs & Buckets there

Did papa go home Christmas I saw him a few minutes when I came over but haven't been to Seattle since as. Have hade to stay pretty close here I have been keeping all the books since Doc left and have to work early & late to keep things moving

Did you get the things I sent Ralphs clothes, gloves nightgown & underclothes I will bring him some more when I come over if I can

I sent Mary Francis some dress goods &Harold a towl & wash rad set

Well wright and let me know how everything is Will try and be back in about 2 weeks will have to stay till the rest of the apples are disposed of.

Hoping you are all well will have to close as I got to go over the books and Less is waiting

With Love
            Chas
Address   White House Fruit Co.
        38 & G. St.
        Tacoma, Wash.

Envelope for the registered letter containing $10 to pay water tax

HOTEL SEWARD
Zbinden Bros., Proprietors
Arctic Club Building

Dec 29/22

My Dear Wife and family,
I recevaid your wour. letter this moining[.] I sent the money to pay the water tax and guess it will get there in time and well send you some also[.] we have been very buisy but I haven't gotten holt of any money yet but have signed some papers that aught to bring in some some time but thay do not have to go to work till March 1[one] so may not get any from that source soon and bought another on this side of the mountain but you cant tell how soon they will come through with the money but I expected Roy to give that to you but will send some any way[.] there is lots of people looking for good mines but mines are surce and hard to find and when you find a man that thinks he has one he thinks he has the world but we find some that will do some business[.] there is one coming to see Dr. to morrow that has been trying to find him for a year: I haven't hard from Charly since he went to Tacoma so don't now anything about him[.] did the aples all spoil that was in the garage or what be came of them.[?] I stay here at Dr. and it is hard for me to find time to write for the busning a round till they are all in bed so that is where they are now[.] You spoke of your presents[.] Alethe gave me a shirt and Wilma gave ma[me a] little knife fob for my watch chain that what I got and I did not give any body any thing[.] I was going to go over

and some cool people came and wented me to stay so I had to stay and we
have not closed it yet and may not but they thought sure we close before now
    I went to see Charly and see if I can get him to go over and look after his
apples.
    How is the weather over there [.]it is raing most of the time here since
it turned warm[.] there don't seam to be many people here from over there
this winter: they had a turkey here for dinner no body here only miling
any more than are here most of the time[.] they all got some thing from
each other but from no one els as I know of. I do not know when I can
get home but think I am going to make some money this season so I can
stay home or take my family with me one or the other[.] I am sending you
$10.00 in this letter[.] it is time for to get some from Okanogan but am
afraid we will be disipionted again the way the apples are selling but mosly
they way mining is looking up we will make is[it] all right[.] Copper went
from 13 ½ to 17 cts per pound to day and mining[.] We are very buisy[.]
I do not know just what Dr is doing about the Kaba mine [.] I know
what he is trying to but do not know how well he is succeeding [.] I mean
Douglas is in Spokane broke as usull[.] John Reese got a letter this week
from him[.] I think maby we will get it after while as I know he cannot
keep it much longer[.] Will I will close as it is late and I have to get down
towen earler to morrow as I have to meet some mining men by apointment
so Good night and a happy New Year

    Loving   Lewis

<hr>

Phone Main 5945

HOTEL SEWARD
Zbinden Bros., Proprietors
Arctic Club Building

SEATTLE Jan 24 – 23

    My Dear Wife and famly I will write you to night as I am at the Hotel
and by my self so I can [.] Phebe and the boys came over yesterday so I gave
them my room and come here. M G Has something the matter with his
head ears and throat and I am not shure that some of the rest tsent in the
same for especially the head[.] Aletha phoned for her mother to come as the
baby is sick he was porty to day but is better to night only has a cold to

much Bacon and potatoes and she thinks she cannot live if her mother is not here to care for and the baby: I sould have written befor this but it is hard for me to write as there is some body in the office all of the time full most of the time as there is three more people in the office bsids us and no place at the house much but I guess this is enough excuses we have been doing will better than I expected and hope to have some money soon but not shure before the first of March[.] Dr. gets some quite often but it takes lots to keep him going as Wehe and David and Wain and they phoned for Nannie to come to night. How is the weather over there it is raining here again it was colder for 2 days but commenced to rain to day at noon it has rained more this winter than I ever saw before I haven't seen anybody from over there till to night for a long time Park long came part way up the elevator as I come up to night and I only had time to say a few words to him. We have about closed up all of the deals. We had only the Kooba and I do not know if we can do much with it at present and we still have the coal mine on our hands. Yet as there is nobody much looking for coal at present but quite a few that wants gold & silver & copper mines[.] the bording House has promised to take the stock that we had to sell so we have no more stock to sell so want to get hold of some miner to sell not stock[.] we have some in vew but not sined up yet[.] we sold the arsnic and the Grafite Just closing them up so do not know just how long I will be here there are some people wants us to salt lake and some more to northen Cal to look at some mines so I do not know which we will do as I haven't seen any of ther money yet and not going till they dig it up. How is Charlie getting along with the apples and is it cold enough to freese them again.

Hope he will get them all out right away[.] hope you are getting alond all right I would have come over if I could and have speared the money was coming any way and Dr said he couldent spare me right then you do not know how bad I wont to see you and am coming over the first chance I get

I want to talk to Phebe and see if she wont go over there and live with Mother sh could and would be better off in every respect but do not no if I can get her to or not there is no boy there now to bother hers now and Mother neades her if only for a companion she [Phebe] does not look Natiral with her teeth out and she looks old and wears a wig and I think her hair is quite gray if you could see it she looks older than Nannie does. Well I will close for this time wth best wishes and much love from

Lewis by by

Ray Titchenal and Vera Alexander 1908

Back of photo reads: Vera Alexander and Ray Titchenal taken at the Alexander home Sept. 27, 1908 Pioneer Ave. Cashmere, Washington
Joseph Ray Titchenal married Vera Alexander June 5, 1912 in Cashemere, Wa.

1912 Ray and Vera

Titchenal Four Generations

Mary Titchenal, her son Lewis, granddaughter Bessie holding great-granddaughter Lois. Circa 1915

May 4, 1917   **Unknown Newspaper**

MRS. RAY TITCHENAL DIES YESTERDAY

Had Been Seriously Ill for Two Weeks –
Leaves a Husband and Three Small Children

Cashmere, Wash., May 4, Mrs. Ray Titchenal passed away yesterday morning after a brave struggle for the past two weeks, when life hung by a thread. Vera, as she was known by everyone, leaves to mourn her, a husband, three small children, parents, three sisters and two brothers. The funeral will take place this afternoon at the Church of God, with interment in the Cashmere cemetery.

Vera Alexander Titchenal was born Dec. 30, 1892 in Denver, Co. She was the daughter of Issac Everett and Ella Rissler Alexander. Ray and Vera were married June 5, 1912 in Cashmere, Washington. Their oldest daughter, Margaret was born Feb. 13, 1913 in Cashmere and her sister Bernice was born June 28, 1915. Twins Jay and Pearl were born March 21, 1917. Pearl did not survive. Jay was cared for by Vera's mother, Mrs. Ella Alexander. Jay was extremely small and delicate. Following Vera's death, Margaret and Bernice lived with Ray's parents, Cora and Lewis Titchenal. Later Bernice lived with Vera's sister Effie until Ray re-married Eunice Thurston, Jan. 7, 1920 in Cashmere, Washington.

Bernice and Margaret Titchenal in front of the Ray Titchenal residence in Cashmere, Wash. May, 1917. Bernice and Jay were born here. Their mother died here on the second day of May 1917. Back of photo reads, "their mother died here on the 6th of May, 1917." Death records indicate she passed away on May 2, 1917.

275

February 1920   Cashmere Valley Record
Mrs. Hazel Whisnand Titchenal
The funeral of Mrs. Whiznand Titchenal will occur at the home of the Wenatchee Undertaking company, Sunday afternoon at 2 o'clock, Rev E. E. Beaty of the Presbyterian Church officiating.

Deceased was born March 22, 1896, in Page, North Dakota, and came to Wenatchee with her parents in 1905. She attended grade and high school in Wenatchee and in 1915 was married to Charles Titchenal. They had three children, two who still survive, Charles Ralph and Mary Frances and a little baby born last Monday who only lived a few hours. The mother and baby will be buried together in the same casket.

Deceased has been a member of the Presbyterian church of Wenatchee for the past eight years. Besides her husband and two children she is survived by parents Mr. and Mrs. Whisnand of Napa, Idaho, three sisters, Mrs. Harold May of Wenatchee, Miss Zellen and Fern of Nampa, also five brothers, Charles and Milo of this city and Charles and Merrill and Robert of Nampa.

Her passing was peaceful and beautiful. Knowing that she had not long to remain she called her family to her one by one, talked to them and kissed them good-bye.

Mabel Naomi Titchenal Werner and her son Harold Lewis in Wenatchee about 1930. Mabel married Edgar Orren Werner July 18, 1928.

January 15, 1932   Unknown Newspaper

Mabel Werner

Mabel Titchenal Werner was born in Cashmere, Washington, October 3, 1903. Youngest daughter of L. H, and Cora Johnson Titchenal. She graduated from Cashmere High School in the class of 1923. The following September she united with the Church of God, and was baptized by Elder N. D. Titchenal September 2. Married to Edgar O. Werner, July 18, 1928. Mother of two children: Harold, who is left to mourn her loss, and baby Sybil, who passed away as the age of eight months, on December 30, 1931.

After several weeks of lingering illness, she passed away at the Cascade Sanitarium at Leavenworth, Washington, January 15, 1932, She leaves to mourn her loss, her husband, son, step daughter [Sylvia Marie Werner]; her parents, two brothers, Ray and Charles Titchenal; one sister, Bessie A. Lawrence; three uncles, Norman and John Titchenal of Cashmere, Washington, Elder N. D. Titchenal of Wenatchee; eight nephews, six nieces, two aunts, Phebe Wright of Seattle, Washington, Alice Hays of Spokane, Washington, many other relatives and a host of friends.

The following lines were written

In Memorium

By M. C. Lawrence.

The sun was slowly creeping
On the mountain in the west,
When calling to her bedside
Came the Messenger of rest.

The loving nurse watched him
Lay his pale cold hand
Upon dear Mabel's brow,
And saw her weary, aching head
In sweet submission bow.

But Jesus stood beside us,
And his Radiant garment shone
As he said in pitying accents,

I leave you not alone.

Ed, Harold, daughter, Mother,
Father, Sister and brothers,
Mabel awaits On that strand
Where the sun of heavenly glory
Shines in splendor o'er the land.

Oh! Those blessed words of Jesus,
How they ease our aching breast,
When we watch our loved ones
Leave us
For the land of glorious rest.-

Written by one she ever called "Aunt Nelia"

The following letter was written November 26, 1922 to Cora
Johnson Titchenal from her brother Henry Johnson concerning
the death of their youngest brother, Joseph Johnson. Cora lived
in Cashmere, Washington at the time, Henry was in Tacoma,
Washington and Joseph's family was in Los Angeles, California.

Tacoma, Wash., 11 – 1922

My Dear Sister & Family

*Yes I got your letters and was greatly surprised to hear of Poore Joes
Death especiely the way it happened. We read of those things every day but
don't realize what it means until it comes home to us. I have been thinking
for some time that is wouldn't be long until some of the family would be
called by Death but didnt think it would be the youngest of the family and
to think we had seen so little of him*

*I have always thought that I would go down thare sometime but it is too
late now have they got the money to give him a Decent Burrial did they
write anything about that*

*If he had of Died a natural Death it wouldn't have been so bad but to
think that he was murdered by one hornery fool lad it too bad what is the
jundmen of our day coming to any way.*

*Write & tell me all of the particulars as soon as Jim haer of them I didt
see any-thing of William if he called at the Hotel they didn't tell me – havnt
seen Richard for some time don't know whare he is living I went out to see
them whorl thy ware working on the Rivver but thy had moved the day-
before in some road work – Thy made a bad Job of their logging contract. I
let them have money to move back on – and they ware sued for wages but I
think they had money due them from the logging company.*

*Yes I am working most of the time average about five days pr week
including break down in the mill and Holidays.*

*Have gotten fairly good health for a man of Three Score and nine
Eat plain food and work hard – I don't touch moon shine*

*Yours Truly
With Love & best wishes to all*

Your Brother Henry

> This letter from Alice Hays was written to her sister Cora Titchenal concerning the death of their brother Joseph.

Spokane Wash   *12/25/22*

My dear sister,

How much I wish we could be together today for a good visit and rest. Claud and family are spending Hmas week with Rita's Mother.
Jim and I are alone this eve but there has been eleven differnt ones here today! Did not do any serving except grefine juice cake and nuts. Jesse wrote us they could not come until later in the season James Jr only had today vacation and they wrote for us to come to the farm for Hmas but Jim thought we had better stay home and continue the treatments.
Professor was here yesterday and made us a visit. Did Jim lots of good to have him come he requested me to write you and tell you not to worry one minute about paying him he is very much interested in your case and says the most important thing is for you to take your treatments regular.
Seems more of a task at the beginning than after you practice them then the hope of getting well and enjoying life afterwards and being able to do for those that are so dependent on us.
Professor told one Roy Thurman was getting along fine he says the greatest trouble is when they recover they get slack in their work before the cause is removed then the trouble returns I have talked with people that have had wonderful results from his treatments.
I for one am so grateful for the relief I ve had from that terriable stomach trouble.
Clint Lambert died of cancer he has suffered for four years. Mr Malen Tetus died of cancer also he was operated on and seemed to go so quickly afterwards. Mr Chaney of Waverly passed away Nim was persanly acquainted with them. Tell him Grandpa Walker has gone to the great beyond.
Mr. and Mrs. A. D. are in the city for the winter they are spending Hmas with Fannie and family Emma Thayer Lane and husbane are spending the winger in Cal

Tuesday

My dear sister,' There are so many many things I want to say to you that I wanted Hmas day to write that was the only thing I planed for yesterday company came while I was writing and was too late to finish. I am expecting Jean to-day she had a big part in an entertainment Friday before Hmas the folks wanted the home a part of the time holidays. You remember the goods Jesse sent her past Hmas she brought that thanksgiving made her a new pretty dress. I ripped cleaned and pressed my blue skirt and Jeans felt that she could no mor combined them made one piece trimed in buttons I had looked like new. She bought shoes rubbers stocking but could not get a new coat. I intended to do the sewing but she had to be fitted while she was here and the very day she came I had the misfortune to split the ball of my right thumb had a serious time came near having blood poisan could not use a pen for a long time. Mayme is having a serious time with her eyes I am trying to get her up here for treatments

I was called to the phone did not tell you I had to get a friend to make Jeans dress. She had out-grown until she said she was almost stripped.

Jim don't get along as well as when he can take exercise out-doors but he is faithful to his treatments. We received many Hmas greetings we did not buy any presents not even for the children.

Cora I tried so hard to keep cheerful and hide a part of my trouble but when your letter came telling me of our dear brothers terrible death my grief was almost unbearable. I often think of what Nim said to me after Ednas death he said when we grieve for the dead we grieve the spirit for it was his will that they go to a better home Our grief seems so sacred. Jesse as young as he was when Edna was taken said Mama we will try not to scatter gloom he has been such a comfort and pleasure.

Cora I have so much wanted to write you before now but I wanted so much to be with you seemed nothing took the place of you and Thanksgiving time and Happy Hmas for so many when my heart was so sad.

I am going to try to write to the boys. I haven't said all I wanted to but will ask you to be true to yourself in the way of taking care of yourself. The Professor said you must learn a little selfishness With much love for you and yours. Am always glad to hear from you

Your sister

TUESDAY, FEBRUARY 20, 1923   *LOS ANGE*

SONG GENIUSES ON RADIO BILL

Soprano and Mezzo Lead Bill; Marion Warde Will Present Pupils in Varied Numbers

SPARKLING Radio Entertainers. Left, above, Gladys Schatzkey (Paralta photo); below, Ruth May Shaffner, In center, Elvira Tanzi (Farnum Jr. photo). Right top to bottom, Fairybelle Creager (Empire photo); Charlotte Vermont, (Feder photo); and Margaret Fisher Monson (Witzel photo).

Features of the splendid program to be broadcast from The Examiner studio this evening are:

Ruth May Shaffner, soprano and Margaret Fisher Monson, mezzo soprano, courtesy of Sid Grauman.

Marion Warde of the Marion Warde Dramatic School, who will offer her pupils and teachers in a varied program of great interest.

Walter Farnum

Margaret Fern Melrose, teacher of voice in the Marion Warde School and herself widely known for her beautiful voice, will sing operatic selections. Walter Farnum, teacher of dialects and character actor of prominence, will sing character songs. Miss Alvira Tanzi, whose sweet voice has charmed radio audiences on other occasions, will sing ballads.

Alma Garvin, 10-year-old soprano, who is already a favorite with radio audiences, will be heard again in two popular numbers.

Miss Gladys Schatzkey, beautiful and talented dramatic artist, whose clever work in recital has called forth much favorable comment, will read two numbers and Miss Fairybelle Creager, popular member of the Marion Warde Players, will delight listeners-in with some of her inimitable darky numbers. Miss Phyllis Rae Garrison, pianiste and organist of note, will be accompanist of the evening.

Two vocalists of high attainment and great popularity are Ruth May Shaffner, soprano, and Margaret Fisher Monson, mezzo - soprano, who will offer a series of duets this evening. These artists appeared yesterday at Grauman's Million Dollar Theater at the Sunday morning concert and received applause

Phyllis Rae Garrison
—De Vorkin photo

which amounted to an ovation in recognition of their brilliant renditions

They will present this evening Kreisler's "Old Refrain," Beetho

ven's "Mine,'

Coll
Cha
Exa
deligl
tomol

Colleen Moore

snappy, chatty little talk on "Are Moving Picture Actors People?" Miss Moore has some humorous and original ideas on this subject, for she believes that not alone are they "people," but among the very "best people" in the world.

Fairybelle carried on the family singing tradition learned from her father Joseph.

This is the letter written by Fairybelle Creager from 5903 Holmes Ave., Los Angeles, Calif. telling of her father, Joseph Johnson's, murder at the hands of two thugs using black-jacks to beat him to death on Tuesday night, November 14, 1922. She is writing to her Aunt Cora in Cashmere, Wash., who was her father's older sister.

Dec. 30th 1926

My dear Aunt Cora,

After all this time (four years) I am writing a few lines, please do not feel hard toward me, for all this neglect, but what little time I have to myself any more is measured into seconds and I for one am about the poorest correspondent that California holds, so do not avail myself of a few spare seconds to write one I owe letters too. My dear Daddy put off writing to those he loved and talked of most, and died without letting you know how much he really enjoyed hearing from you and Uncle Gilmore. He seemed to talk mostly of you two, and we were planning so on a trip up north some time real soon. It just doesnot seem possiable he has been gone these four long years – for long and lonely they certainly have been for me. I still and always will miss him so very much – and so do my boys and Barbara- they remember him so distinctly, and how they loved him and he seemed so proud of them.

Our home has never been the same happy place, he was always so full of life and made our home so jolly at all times. Bronson is a quiet person to be around – not talkative, never sings – and is no hand to care about amusement, other than the radio and his reading – so our home life is so changed since Daddy is gone – as he always was singing talking and joking with me, and playing with the children, just the life of our home – and he was so well and seemed to planning so much for the future. Was just completing a fifteen day vacation, had spent most of the time fixing up the little house on the place next door to us, he had bought just the year before and it was the first evening he had been away, went away about 5:30 P.M. as he wanted to stop in town at the Bank, (which is open from 6 to 8 PM each day for the convenience of working men) and then went on to Hollywood which is about 12 miles northwest from where we are living, to see Billy Louder – a old time friend of his. Dad left their home about 8:30 P.M. – started home his watch stopped at 10:06 P.M. which would be just about the time it would take to make the trip home.

I waited up for him until 11:30 as Bronson was working at night, and

Daddy slept in his house next door – and I felt safer when I knew he was there, but I never heard a sound nor sensed anything wrong just supposed he was staying later than usual, and when my boy awakened me at 2 A.M. asking me if "Johnsie" was home. I noticed the time and supposed of course he was – and next morning Bronson came home at 6:30 A.M., noticed a small crowd of people about 50 yards from our house never thought much about it, as the street car junction is right there. Lots of people are always changing cars there. At 7:30 – a neighbor lady came to my door, asking for Dad – and just as I started over to call him, she stopped me, and showed me his watch and card wallet that had been picked up in the right-a-way – some thirty feet from where Daddy was found lying – unconscious – and terriably beaten. At first he was thought dead – but in moving him to identify him – signs of life manifested itself. Bronson and I got out to him just as some men were lifting him onto a cot – so we brought him into our house until the ambulance came and we took him to the hospital where we had the best of care for him – a special nurse – two good Doctor's. After a thorough examination, and six X-Rays made which showed he had a complete valt and base skull fracture – not a body bruise only on his hands where he had fought back. There were seven wounds on his head – three fatal at one blow. both the doctor's – the Coroner and Undertaker said it certainly was the work of Thugs with a black-jack – and two of them, as the blows were at such an angle – also foot prints were such that indicated there were two – his pockets were all turned and two badly torn, his watch chain was broken and because of his watch and wallet, being found so far from where he lay, I am inclined to believe it must have been thrown there by Daddy – proably infuriating the Thugs so, is why he was so unmercifully beaten. He lived four days without regaining consciousness – and how we hoped he could tell us – and how I longed for him to get well. I spent most every minute with him, hoping against hope he would rally and know I was with him, and he could tell me, but he passed on his journey.

Sunday morning November 19th 1922 – at 2:15.A.M. it was Tuesday night the 14th of Nov. he was way-layed and killed, just the day after Barbara Adeline was 10 years old and my 30th birthday. We had such an enjoyable dinner and evening on Monday, Nov. 13th, 1922 – and it was then Daddy made known so many plans, and it seemed so nice to realize things would be easier and brighter for him in the near future. He never cared about marrying again, and as the years passed did not seem to grow a bit older. I sometimes felt he grew younger with the years, as my babies grew up. He seemed to enjoy my boys so, and always planned about them. Daddy was very effectionate with the children and made over them a great deal, while their own Daddy is not demonstrative at all with any of them.

They certainly miss all of that as well as the jolly times together. My oldest boy, "Buddy" – (Bronson Jr.) really grieved himself ill – after Johnsie was gone. We had always called him "Johnsie's shadow" – and it was so lonely for him, he seemed lost.

We never did find any witnesses, so never really knew what happened to fulfill Dad's own wish. We had him cremated and placed in an urn beside Mother's at Rosedale Cemetery here – and I am supposed to take both to Spokane and have them buried beside Uncle Jessie in Fairmont Cemetery. I had hoped to do so long before now, but seven months after Daddy was gone, my baby girl Betty Josephine came – and I have not only been kept busy with my family but I was 18 months getting all Daddy's business settled, titles changed ect. but my health has not been so good. I have not been the same since this last baby – been so enamic, and do not gain even to my normal weight.

My family are all well and strong youngsters going to school doing splendidly – so it is hard to leave them, and I cannot take them all with me on such a long trip and during summer vacation we could drive up – but Bronson can only get two weeks off, and I would not care to drive over strange roads with the children alone – so I have been compelled to put it off these four years. I feel so guilty each time I think of my promise to Daddy to do this for him. I hope I can some time real soon.

Barbara was 14 years old, Nov. 13th last on Jan. 31st she enters her 3rd or Junior year in High School. With all her college credits which means a 95% average. She wants to be a teacher in High School of either mathamatics or language, she is 5 ft 6 inches tall – weighs 110 lbs. has dark brown hair (bobbed) has features very much like my mother, is quite a sensiable steady girl – a real companion, serious beyond her years in school and music she plays real well on the piano, has taken two years from a very capable instructor, after a fair start I could give her.

Bronson Jr. or Buddy was 11 years old last August. Is 5 ft. tall and very thin like his father in looks, light wavy hair – blue eyes, but like my Daddy in disposition, has a sweet voice for singing and loves to sing. He is in the 6th grade – and doing fair, but such a sensitive, nervious youngster and rather timid among strangers, has been the cause of his not progressing more rapidly at school. He is the only one of my family who appears delicate. I am hoping these next 2 or 3 years make a change in him for the better.

William or Billy will be 10 years old the 28th of this coming May. Is quite a husky for his age, is 5 ft tall weighs 90 lbs. has a round full face very much like Daddy's boy pictures he has dark brown real curly hair blue eyes, and a sunny disposition, a real lively youngster – in for all the sports, football – base-ball – ect. He is in the 5th grade. School work seems easy for him.

Then little Fairybelle – who was Johnsies "baby-girl", is a very fair skinned, blond hair, bobbed, rather a sensitive nervious girl of 7 years, last Oct. 18th, is 4 ft. 2 inches tall weighs 65 lbs. She has been taking piano lessons since April – does nicely and is completeing her B class or first part of the second grade in school.

Now for our Baby – whom Barbara named for you and her grandfather – Betty Joe, we call her, as Josephine seemed rather long for a baby. She has long black curls (I do not intend to bob them either.) dark almost violet eyes, fair complexion such a happy disposition. When tiny she was always smiling even thru her tears. She was three years old in July last, not quite 40 inched tall, weight, 38 lbs. just as active and alert as she can be – has always talked very plain – and thinks her whole family is just for her service. Of course being four years younger than Fairybelle, naturally she is certainly spoilt and coming into our home so soon after our great sorrow – we all look on her as our little ray of sunshine. She looks so much like the Johnson's that she was certainly rightfully named. Barbara asked several months before, if she might select the baby's name. had a boy arrived it would have been given Daddy's full name. I will send you snaps – as well as photo's of all the children. I just had the two little girls photo's taken before Xmas, have not them home yet because of the holiday rush.

I started to write a few lines and here it is all of these – and well on to mid-night – but I felt I must start this year right, and my first resolution was not to neglect my loved ones, and I sincerely hope, this letter and the others to follow will redeem me with you, for all these years of unintentional neglect.

I would love to hear from you, and about yourself and family, also the other kin-folk. I used to hear from Buford often, but it has been so long now. I do not know where he is.

Bronson has a good position and is in fair health – his mother and sister's live in town. his sister's teach in our city school. All are real well. I could write you more about our town – climate and our home but can do that another time – as it is real late now.

Worlds of love to you, dear Aunt, and hope you are well and will write me soon.

Believe me as ever Your loving niece.

Fairybelle J. Creager.
5903 Holmes Ave.
Los Angeles, Calif.

Family Sunday
Johnson Family Gathering

June 5, 1926
Back row: Mabel Titchenal, Henry Johnson, Lewis and Cora Titchenal,
Rolla and Mayme Jones, Jean Jones, Bessie and Will Lawrence,
Middle: Margaret and Bernice Titchenal, Mary Lawrence,
Sitting: Lois, Gordon and Burton Lawrence

October 9, 1925   Cashmere, Wash

Editor Daily World,

In your issue of October 1 you have asked the question, "How many people who were in North Central Washington in 1882 are still living here?" You stated that you would like to hear from them, so I thought I would answer for one, though I can date back two years prior to that. I came to Washington territory in July, 1880, and have made my home continually in this country since. I crossed the plains in a wagon, starting from Bates county, Missouri, on the 15th day of April, 1880, driving the team a good share of the way myself. My parents having died a few years before, I came with my eldest brother and his family, J. M. Johnson, now living on Badger mountain. Also two other brothers who passed away years ago.

We landed at Hangman creek, 35 miles southeast of where the city of Spokane now is, though there was no city or railroad in that part of the country at that time. The first few years after coming west I lived with my sister and brother-in-law, Mr. and Mrs. James Hays, who had taken a homestead on Hangman creek in 1879, and are now living in Spokane. Mr. Hays hauled all his supplies from Walla Walla, a distance of about 175 miles.

After the Northern Pacific railroad was built in 1882, I attended school at the Cheney academy, which afterwards burned down and the normal school buildings now occupy the same grounds.

In March, 1886, I went to Douglas County and took up a homestead nine miles southeast of the present town of Waterville, though there was no town there then. The land was not on the market, so I could file on my claim so I gave it up and went back to Spokane the same summer. Spokane was quite a city by this time, as it made a very rapid growth after the country settled up. I happened to have a friend who was working in the Spokane Chronicle office when they began to print their

287

daily paper and he gave me a copy of one of the first daily Chronicles published, which is dated Vol. I, No. 4, Spokane Falls, Washington Territory, June 16, 1883"

I still have the little four-page sheet, which is 13x18 inches in size – quite different from the one printed today, thus showing the development of the country. I rode on the first passenger train that went from Spokane to Cheney on the 4th of July, 1881, and which was as far west as the railroad was finished at that time.

On November 2, 1887 I was married in Spokane to L. H. Titchenal, who had a homestead in the Big Bend country. We did not go on a honeymoon trip in an automobile, but loaded our household necessities and food supplies in a four-horse freight wagon and started for the homestead, a distance of 165 miles, camping out on the way as the country was [not developed]

The D. J. Titchenal family had taken up homesteads at the foot of Badger mountain in 1883, which was then a fine grazing country, and were raising cattle and horses.

All went well with us until the deep snow and long winter came in 1889 and 1890, when nearly all the stock in the country died of starvation and continuous cold, which was known as the "hard winter." All the grain, hay, flour and vegetables in the country were used by the time the snow had gone and people had to go into Davenport country for seed grain. We went to Spokane for a load of supplies. Mr. Titchenal drove the first freight wagon over the Indian trails to Badger mountain in May, 1883. He went each summer to the harvest field to work, bringing home a supply of provisions until the country was more developed and people raised grain in that part of the country, which was more prolific then than it has been of late years. L. H. and N. S. Titchenal owned and operated the first threshing machine in that part of the Big Bend.

We sold out and moved to the Wenatchee valley in April, 1897, locating on Warner's Flat, two miles east of Cashmere (then Mission.) This was then Okanogan county, with Conconully the county seat. There was nothing on the place. We bought only sagebrush and sun flowers (and rocks.) We leveled the ground and improved it, living there a little more than six years without any water to irrigate with, though it rained there more then than it has of recent years, and we raised good corn and wheat hay, also some garden. Mr. Titchenal was elected president of the high line ditch and worked a great deal of the time on that with men and teams. Everybody rejoiced when the water was turned in, on the land, so we could set out fruit trees and raise alfalfa.

Some of the land was very rough and rocky, and to me it seemed unreasonable to think it could be made to produce the rich bearing orchards and lovely homes that are here now. You know the rest, as you have seen the development of the country with its electricity and everybody riding in automobiles on paved roads. I have been a pioneer in more than one country, but never saw such rapid development as there has been in the Wenatchee valley. Our children and grandchildren who are living in this fast age, having all the advantages of graded schools, telephones and electricity, will never realize what we pioneers had to experience, and the hardships we endured and some may never think of it, perhaps, unless their attention is called to it in this history. I doubt if any of them would venture to ford the Wenatchee river as I did before the bridges were built. There were only three bridges across the river one near the mouth of the river where the steel bridge is now, one at Monitor & at Leavenworth. I had large, trusty horses & have driven across the river many times when the water ran into the hack-bed.

Some may never think of it, perhaps, unless their attention is called to it by an old settler in this way.

I could write a small volume telling my experiences, but fear I have already intruded upon your time and patience, so will close, hoping to hear from more of the old settlers.

Mrs. L. H. Titchenal

1911   Wenatchee Daily World
TITCHENAL FAMILY, PIONEER OF THIS REGION
Pioneer Dies   Sincerely Mourned

D. J. Titchenal, Who Passed Away in Cashmere Thursday Night, Settled in Waterville 28 Years Ago.
EIGHTY-FOUR YEARS NEARLY ROUNDED OUT
End Came From Infirmities of Advanced Age – Two Daughters and Four Sons Survive to Mourn Their Loss.

Cashmere, July 1, 1911 - In the passing of D. J. Titchenal, who died at his residence in Cashmere Thursday night, one of the oldest pioneers of the Vale of Cashmere and of North Central....

Mr. Titchenal, who was born in Virginia eight-four years ago next November, came to Washington in 1882 settling at Waterville in the following year. Nineteen years of successful farming followed, when in 1902, he moved with his large family to Cashmere, where they have since lived.

Surviving Mr. Titchenal are an elder sister, Mrs. Julia A Johns, who resides in Oregon; a younger sister, Mrs. Melissa Williams, of Cashmere; two brothers in Albany, Ill., and a brother in Kansas City. His surviving children are Mrs. Phoebe Wright and Mrs. Nancy Wehe, both of Cashmere; L. H., N. S., and John Titchenal of Cashmere and N. D. of Wenatchee. A nephew, William Norton, resides at Waterville.

A long and useful life has been closed with the death of Mr. Titchenal. The end was the natural result of the infirmities of his advanced age and had been expected for the week preceding his demise. His mourners are many and sincere, in Cashmere and in Wenatchee.

The funeral was held at 2 o'clock this afternoon from the Church of God in Cashmere, the Rev. A. L. Corbaley of Waterville, conducting the services. Interment was in the Cashmere cemetery

~~~~~~

January1929   Cashmere Valley Record

Interesting Pioneer Passes Away; Had Reached Age 94

Mrs. Mary Titchenal and Husband Came West In Covered Wagon

Mrs. Mary Titchenal, age 94, passed away in Seattle Tuesday, January 29, after a lingering illness. Her daughter, Mrs. Phebe Wright, and sons, N. D. and John Titchenal, have been watching by her bedside for three weeks.

Mary Moore Titchenal was born in Madison county, Illinois, Oct. 31, 1834; she was married to David J. Titchenal Dec. 4, 1856. To this union seven children were born, all of whom are living except Dan, the oldest son who died at the age of seven.

In 1867 the family moved from Illinios to Missouri. Owing to Mrs. Titchenal's poor health they started west in the spring of 1875, going with wagon and team to Colorado where they remained one year. Having regained her health they returned to Missouri but getting the "western fever" again they started across the plains again in April, 1882. This time they landed in Spokane county, Washington, where they remained one year, then moved into the Big Bend country near the present site of Waterville. At that time there was no settlement in that part of the country.

In May, 1883, Mr. Titchenal and sons, Lewis and Norman, took up homesteads of 160 acres each and built log cabins on their claims at the mouth of what is known as Titchenal canyon nine miles south of Waterville. During that summer a few families and several bachelors came into the country.

A log house was built at the foot of Badger Mountain that was used for a store building by Messrs Kimble and Bracken, the supplies being hauled with the freight teams from Spokane. On Christmas day they raised the United States flag at the store where several had gathered for celebration.

On March 4, 1884, Mrs. Titchenal gave an inauguration dinner when Grover Cleveland first took his seat in the White House as president of the United States. She invited everyone in the country and there probably are a few people in the country who remember her hospitality to travelers and strangers as well as to her friends.

In 1887 they built a large house which was known as the "half-way house" on the road between Ellensburg and Coulee City where the stage and travelers passed, often stopping for meals. She never turned anyone away hungry and was always equal to the occasion.

In November, 1902, they left the old homestead and moved to Cashmere where Mr. Titchenal died in June, 1911. Since that time Mrs. Titchenal has made her home with her children and was quite active until about four years ago when she went to Seattle to live with her daughter, Dr. Nancy T. Wehe.

She is survived by four sons, L. H. of Cashmere, N. S. now in Phoenix, Ariz., and Mrs. Phebe Wright of Seattle. Also ten grandchildren, besides other relatives. She was a charter member of the Church of God that was organized in Waterville in 1892 and has been a devoted member ever since.

The body was shipped to Cashmere Wednesday. The funeral will be held in the Church of God on Friday at 2 o'clock. The Kuelbs Undertaking Co. is in charge and interment will be in the Cashmere cemetery.

John Titchenal of Seattle and N. D. Titchenal of Wenatchee, accompanied the body of their mother here from Seattle.

David Titchenal Family
David and Mary Titchenal with five of their six adult children

Standing: Nancy Moore, Lewis Hamilton, Nimrod David, John David, Phebe Ellen
Seated: David Jackson and Mary

Waterville Empire Press

Thursday, January 1, 1931   Waterville, Douglas County, Washington

BADGER MOUNTAIN PIONEER IS BURIED IN WENATCHEE

Mrs. Wehe, Member of Famous Titchenal Family, Was A Pioneer Resident, of the Old Cottonwood Settlement on Badger Mountain

Many pioneers of this section attended the funeral services held Wednesday afternoon at Jones and Jones Wenatchee for Mrs. N. T. Wehe, formerly Nancy Titchenal, pioneer of North Central Washington who died Sunday night. A.L. Corbaley, also a pioneer of this district preached the funeral sermon.

According to the history of North Central Washington edited by the late L. M. Hull, Miss Nancy Titchenal left Bates county Missouri with her family for Washington territory on April 1, 1882. The family in its western trek, crossed the Kansas and Nebraska trail and followed the old California trail as far as Laramie, Wyoming, which they reached on June 1.

At this time the Union Pacific rail road was building a short line from Green River, Wyoming, to Portland, Oregon and demand for men and team was keen. The Titchenals were approached by a contractor who said he would furnish free transportation to Idaho and pay good wages if the men would agree to work 30 days. After reaching Ogden, Utah, the horses and mules were locked up and an armed guard placed over them by the contractor who then demanded a new agreement whereby the men would work 60 days instead of 30, and mortgage their outfits as a guarantee of good faith.

While the men discussed the situation the women stormed the corral in force, ignoring the armed guards, broke off the locks and freed the stock, the train proceeding on its way.

The Titchenals first stopped at Colfax, later moving to Rockford, 25 miles south of Spokane.

The next spring the elder Titchenal and his oldest son, Lewis, visited the Big Ben country in search of a location. Their party was preceded to Badger Mountain by only three days by Hector Patterson, Ole Ruud and three others. Lewis and Norman Titchenal returned with 3,000 pounds of freight and located three claims at Badger Mountain. They then returned to Rockford and after following the wheat harvest, brought the rest of the family, including Nancy, to Badger.

The little Badger settlement, the first west of Davenport, then Cottonwood, did not become a permanent town. R. S. Steiner, later superior court judge, was the first school teacher, the session being held in Ole Ruud's cabin.

The Titchenal family moved to Cashmere in 1902, and Mrs. Wehe has lived there and in Seattle and Wenatchee since that time.

She was a licensed sanipractor, having made care and treatment of the human body her life study and work.

Few families can trace their American ancestry to an earlier date than the Titchenals. Two brothers left Alsace, now a French province, and settled in Jamestown, Virginia, in 1620. The ancestors of these brothers belonged to the reining family of Alsace when it was an independent principality. Later the descents of these two men settled in Illinois and in 1868 D. J. Titchenal, the father of Mrs. Wehe moved to Missouri. –

May 13, 1933   Wenatchee Daily World

Death takes John Titchenal, Pioneer

John Titchenal, 61, of Cashmere died Saturday evening at a local hospital after a year's illness. He was born January 1, 1872 in Bates county, Missouri. He came to Washington territory with his parents in 1882 , arriving in Rockford, Spokane county, in the month of November. There the family spent the winter, moving to Badger mountain in covered wagons in the month of September 1883.

The old homestead was located 10 miles southeast of the present town of Waterville. Mr. Titchenal spent his life in Douglas and Chelan counties. He witnessed the entire development of central Washington. The first settlers came to Badger Mountain in the summer of 1883, the Titchenal family being among the first to arrive.

He will be buried beside his father, mother and oldest sister, Nancy in the Cashmere cemetery. He is survived by three brothers, L. H. and N. S. Titchenal of Cashmere and N. D. of Wenatchee, one sister, Mrs. Phoebe Wright of Seattle, five nephews and three nieces.

Funeral services will be held in the Jones and Jones chapel Tuesday at 4 p. m. daylight saving time. His brothers, three nephews; Ray and Charles Titchenal and Wayne Skeels will be pallbearers.

September 26, 1941   Unknown Newspaper
Last Rites Held for Mrs. Alice Hays, Wednesday

Waverly, Wash., Sept. 26 – Mrs. Alice Hays, 86, one of Waverly's oldest resident matrons, passed away at the Sacred Heart hospital, Spokane, Saturday, Sept. 20, 1941, after a two week's illness, following a fall that broke her hip. She had lived in this community for 62 years.

Sara Alice Johnson was born at Lexington, Saline county, Missouri, June 29, 1855, and moved to Bates county soon after the Civil war, where she grew to womanhood. On April 2, 1879, she married James Hays and the following day started on their honeymoon in search of a homestead.

There was no railroad at that time across the country except the Southern Pacific, so they went by train to San Francisco. From there they took a steamer to Portland, Oregon, where they bought a wagon, team and harness, which they shipped by boat to the Dalles, Oregon, driving from there to Walla Walla, Washington. Here Mrs. Hays stayed with Mrs. J. M. Covington, while Mr. Hays and Mr. Covington came to the Palouse country and Mr. Hays to a 160 acre homestead, two miles north of what is now Waverly. In a few weeks he was joined by Mrs. Hays. When they took this place there were no improvements except a log cabin and a rail pen around a spring, surrounded by rolling hills covered with bunch grass. Of the people who were here when they came, only William Goff and Frank Elvy still live here. As the country improved the Hays' bought more land and made many improvements and it is still known as the Hays ranch.

It was here that she raised her family of five, and experienced the hardships of pioneer life. The next year her mother passed away in the east and a sister, Miss Cora Johnson, now Mrs. Cora Titchenal, came to make her home with them, and was among Waverly's first school teachers. Mrs. Hays was very much attached to her home and family, and was never happier than when she was doing something for them and for her many friends.

Her gracious manner and hospitality have endeared her to all who knew her and her patience through her long suffering was an example to all.

Five children were born to them, their oldest child, Edna, died in 1898 [1900]. Mr. Hays spent his last days on the homestead, and passed away in November, 1932. A son, Roy, passed away in September of the same year, and Mrs. Hays has resided there with his widow, Gertrude and a grandson, James Hays, II, since then to the time of her death.

She is survived by one daughter, Mrs. Mamie Jones of Bellingham; two sons, Claude M. Hays of Amask, Alberta, Canada; Jesse W. Hays of Idaho Falls, Idaho; seven grand-children; four great-grandchildren; one sister, Mrs. Cora Titchenal, Cashmere; many nieces and nephews; and a host of friends. Mrs. Hays was a member of the Spokane County Pioneer Society and a member of the Christian church, and also a member of the W. C. T. U. at Waverly for many years.

Services were held at the Presbyterian church at Fairfield, Wednesday, Sept. 24 at 2 p. m. with the Rev. H. A. Van Winkle, Central Christian church, Spokane and the Rev. C. C. Saunders of the Presbyterian church, Fairfield, officiating. Cremation followed.

~~~~~~

May 15, 1942   Wenatchee Daily World
Mrs. Titchenal of Cashmere Passes

Cashmere – Mrs. L. H. Titchenal, 76-year-old pioneer of Cashmere and of the central Washington region, died at her home here last night after a short illness.

Betty Cora Johnson was born at Lexington, Saline county, Missouri, Aug 16, 1865, and moved to Bates county when five years old. When 14 she came west with a covered wagon train to her sister's homestead, located 30 miles southeast of the present city of Spokane. She arrived July 23, 1880, after a 100-day trip, on which she drove a team, camping nights along the way.

She made her home with her sister, Mrs. James Hays and attended the first school in Waverly district, finishing her education at the Cheney academy, and later she taught school.

In 1887 she married Lewis H. Titchenal at Spokane Falls, Washington Territory. They had five children, Bessie, Ray, Virginia, Charlie and Mabel. They established a home near Badger Mountain, about nine miles from the present city of Waterville, and in 1897 moved to Warner Flats, two miles east of Cashmere, then Old Mission. Mrs. Titchenal had lived in the valley 45 years and was a charter member of the Cashmere Church of God.

Surviving are her husband, Lewis; one daughter, Mrs. Will Lawrence; two sons, Ray and Charlie; 15 grandchildren and 9 great grandchildren.

Services were held Tuesday from the Kuelbs Funeral Home, with Rev. Lyle Ranken officiating. During the services Mrs. Anderson Drake and Mrs. Charles Lapp sang "What a Friend We Have In Jesus" and

"No Night There", with Mrs. Isaac Davis at the organ. Pallbearers were Herbert France, Isaac Davis, Harry Brockelbank of Wenatchee; Alvie France of Peshastin; Anderson Drake and Glen Huffman. Interment was in Cashmere cemetery.

~~~~~~

May 20, 1942   Wenatchee, Wn.

The Church Letter
Church of God   Faith of Abraham

PASSES--- Sister Cora Titchenal passed away Friday evening, May 15 at 11:30 p.m. at her home in Cashmere after a 25 day illness. She was 76 years old, and leaves her husband, Bro. Louis Titchenal, 3 children, 16 grandchildren and 9 great grandchildren. The funeral will be held Tuesday May 19 at 2 p.m. at Cashmere, and Pastor Lyle Rankin will preach the funeral service. She greatly desired, at the last, to live to see her grandson, Ralph, who was hurrying from Washington D. C. arrive, and be happily married. He and his bride-to-be, Miss Adeline Dormeir of Cashmere, had set their wedding date, which was to have been in June, two weeks ahead because of his Grandmother's serious illness, but faulty stage connections delayed him six hours and he arrived just three minutes after she passed away. Since the wedding invitations were out, and the relatives gathered around, the wedding was held as planned Sunday evening at 8 p.m. Ralph and his bride will leave Wednesday for Washington D.C. where he is employed, by way of San Francisco where they will visit his sister, Mary Francis.

Among those expected for the funeral, from out of town, are Bro. Norman Titchenal of Seattle, Mrs. Chas Titchenal from near Spokane, and Margaret Hansen of Enumclaw.

~~~~~~

1942   **Wedding of Ralph Titchenal   Unkown Newspaper**

Miss Dormaier, Mr. Titchenal Marry Sunday

Mr. and Mrs. B. E. Dormaier of Cashmere announce the marriage of their daughter, Adeline to Mr. Ralph Titchenal of Washington, D. C., son of Mr. Charles Titchenal of Cashmere, Sunday evening in the Cashmere Presbyterian church. The bride-elect attended the Wenatchee Business college and is affiliated with Alpha Iota sorority.

Mr. Titchenal is the grandson of Mr. and Mrs. L. H. Titchenal, pioneers of the Cashmere valley. He also attended Wenatchee Business college and is at present employed at the senate house by Homer T. Bone in Washington D. C.

November 8, 1947   Cashmere Valley Record

Titchenal Was Pioneer of Mission

Lived In Washington 65 Years and Came to Mission in 1892; Was Expert Mechanic; 50 Years a Mason

Norman S. Titchenal, one of Cashmere's oldest pioneers, passed away in a Wenatchee hospital following an extended illness Saturday evening at the age of 84 years.

Mr. Titchenal was born February 25, 1863, in Illinois, where he grew to manhood and came to the territory of Washington 65 years ago settling at Rockford where he lived until 1885 when he moved to Waterville and took up a homestead. He moved to Cashmere in 1892 when it was still Old Mission and operated a blacksmith shop here, later partaking in the Klondike gold rush and then returning to take up ranching here.

He was united in marriage to Susan Thurman in 1905 and following her death in 1908 married Mrs. Julia France in 1911. The second Mrs. Titchenal passed away in 1921. Mr. Titchenal was a charter member of Mission Lodge 158 F. & A. M. of Cashmere, a charter member of the Waterville Church of God and the Church of God of Cashmere.

He is survived by two brothers, Louis of Cashmere and Nim of Vancouver, Wn., and one sister, Mrs. Phebe Wright of Seattle; two step-children, Alva France of Peshastin and Earl France of Seattle, one sister, Mrs. Nancy Wehe and one brother, John, and one step-son, LeRoy Thurman, preceded him in death.

Funeral services for Mr. Titchenal were held Wednesday afternoon at 2 from the Kuelbs & Braun Funeral chapel with Lyle Rankin officiating. Interment took place in the Cashmere cemetery with Masonic rites conducted by Mission lodge at the grave. He had been a member of the Masonic fraternity for over 50 years.

Expert Mechanic

It has often been said that the pioneer blacksmith could do anything except jewelry work, but Mr. Titchenal was also an expert watch and clock repair man. In fact he could fix any piece of machinery which was brought to his shop and was always busy with such work as long as his eyesight permitted. He had a shop at the Cascade tunnel when the Great Northern built through the mountains, where he made, sharpened and repaired tools for the workers.

He was also a carpenter and cabinet maker. He and his brother, Lewis, made the furniture, the windows and doors for their three-story pioneer house on Badger mountain near Waterville. They also made the shakes which covered the roof, and he made the pulpit and the tables and seats for the Cashmere Church of God.

His many activities included being in the real estate business with F. T. Spiller, was early day marshal and deputy sheriff, rancher and property owner in various areas around Cashmere. He was positive as to what was right and wrong and did what was right as he saw it. He was an ardent reader of the Bible and greatly interested in the fulfillment of the prophecies.

Several years ago cataracts formed on his eyes. Last year he had one removed and this year had that eye itself removed. Later in June he had the other cataract removed which operation was a success and the eyesight restored. However he fell from the hospital bed breaking his left leg, which was weak from a previous break, and had caused him to use crutches for years. The shock of all this combined with his long bed confinement was more than he could survive.

~~~~~~

March 27, 1949   Restitution Herald
Nimrod David Titchenal
Word has been received of the death of Nimrod David Titchenal at his home in Seattle, Wash., March 27, 1949.

The Titchenals moved from Alton, Ill., by covered wagon, in 1882 to Washington Territory. "Nim" later moved to Wenatchee where, on August 14, 1902, he married Miss Myrtle Patterson, who survives him. They had no children but reared a niece, Wilma Skeels Eberhart, who made her home with them.

Mr. Titchenal spent some forty years in Wenatchee, where he was pastor of the Church of God for thirty-five years.

Besides his widow, Myrtle, he leaves nieces and nephews; an older brother, Lewis Titchenal of Cashmere; and a younger sister, Mrs. Phebe Wright of Seattle.

Mr. Titchenal was born, January 20, 1865, near Alton, Ill., and died March 27, 1949, in Seattle, Wash. He was laid to rest in the Renton Cemetery to await the call of the great Life Giver.

October 18, 1951   Wenatchee Daily World

Lewis Titchenal, 91, NCW
Resident Since 1886, Dies

Lewis Titchenal, one of the valley's oldest pioneers, died at his home in Cashmere Sunday at the age of 91 [October 14, 1951]. He had been in ill health for some time.

The Titchenal family has lived in Washington state since 1883, when Mr. Titchenal accompanied his parents, the late Mr. and Mrs. David J. Titchenal, and his brothers and sisters from Missouri to the state of Washington by covered wagon. Lewis Titchenal was born on February 27, 1860, at Alton, Illinois.

The family settled at Rockford; and on November 2, 1886 [1887] Mr. Titchenal was married to Betty Cora Johnson at Spokane Falls. Following their marriage, they came to Waterville, settling on a homestead where they lived until 1897, the year they came to Cashmere, then known as "Old Mission." Lewis Titchenal planted his own orchard and operated it for many years. He also was instrumental in the construction of Highland canal. Mr. Titchenal was a member of the Church of God, Faith of Abraham.

Surviving are one daughter, Mrs. Will Lawrence of Cashmere; two sons, Ray Titchenal of Leavenworth and Charles Titchenal of Cashmere; 14 grandchildren; 19 great grandchildren and one sister, Mrs. Phebe Wright of Seattle.

Funeral services will be held Wednesday at 2 p. m. from the Kuelbs and Braun funeral chapel in Cashmere with Lyle H. Rankin officiating, assisted by Gary France. Burial will take place in the Cashmere cemetery.

Family Tree for Lewis and Cora Titchenal

Lewis Hamilton Titchenal		b. 2/27/1860
Married Bettie Cora Johnson	11/2/1887	
Bettie Cora Johnson		b. 8/16/1865

Children

Bessie Alice Titchenal		b. 9/15/1888
Married Will Edmund Lawrence	9/4/1912	
Lois Willola		b. 8/26/1914
Mary Cora		b. 5/23/1916
Gordon Ogden		b. 3/14/1918
Burton David		b. 2/3/1920
Joseph Ray Titchenal		b. 12/31/1889
Married 1st Vera Lucille Alexander	6/5/1912	
Margaret Arlouine		b. 2/13/1913
Married William S. Hansen	6/12/1938	
William Forest		b. 5/16/1939
Vera Rae		b. 7/13/1944
Bernice Ora		b. 6/28/1915
Married 1st Benton Merle Alley	8/3/1935	
Kathleen Rae		b. 1/31/1938
Nancy Madge		b. 11/30/1941
Married 2nd Oscar C. Esarey	3/18/1950	
Pearl		b. 3/21/1917
Jay Eugene		b. 3/21/1917
Married 2nd Eunice Anne Thurston	1/7/1920	
Glen Thurston		b. 10/24/1920
Married Ruth Elizabeth Millar	11/18/1944	
John Glen		b. 10/16/1946
Teresa Marie		b. 11/24/1947
Lewis Ray		b. 11/19/1948
Christina Rose		b. 9/8/1951
Patrick Scott		b. 10/16/1954
Roberta Ann		b. 3/9/1957
William Anthony		b. 3/11/1960
James Allen		b. 11/9/1962

Eula Betty   b. 4/1/1922

Richard Leon   b. 1/10/1930
Married Gladys K. Ellis   9/20/1956

Gerald Fredrick   b. 11/30/1931
Married 1st Mary Ann Theresa Stevens 1/7/1955
    Catherine Ann   b. 11/27/1955
    Joseph S.   b. 7/5/1957
    Jeanne Marie   b. 9/16/1959
    Andrew Jay   b. 3/22/1963
    Mary Beth   b. 11/6/1964
Married 2nd Marilyn Misner   2/1/2006

Robert Lee   b. 8/11/1934
Married Shirley Jean Benedict   8/7/1954
    Randle Lee   b. 3/27/1956
    Steven Allen   b. 11/24/1961

Charles Arthur Titchenal   b. 5/14/1894
Married 1st Mary Hazel Whiznand   11/24/1915
    Charles Ralph   b. 4/15/1916
    Mary Frances   b.1/19/1918
Married 2nd Louise Schalock   9/17/1923
    Frank Lewis   b. 4/25/1926
        Paul Lewis   b. 7/21/1953
        Wanda Mae   b. 12/8/1954
    Maebelle Rose   b. 12/26/1927
    David Carl   b. 8/1/1932

Mabel Naomi Titchenal   b. 10/3/1903
Married Edgar Orren Werner   7/18/1928
    Harold Lewis Werner   b. 3/19/1929
        Seya Lee   b. 11/30/62
        Liesl Kay   b. 9/3/69
    Sybil Werner   b. 4/03/1931

Acknowledgements

In December of 2010 Edna Siniff, my publisher, told me that a new division of their CMP Publishing Group was being formed. It would be called ElderBerry Books. Its purpose was to publish historical documents so these documents could be preserved.

I would not have considered attempting this book without the encouragement of Edna Siniff. She spent hours of her own time bringing these pages to print. I can not adequately express my appreciation for this much needed guidance and help.

This book would not be possible without the many members of the Johnson and Titchenal families that have kept these historical treasures. First I thank Cora Johnson Titchenal and Lewis Titchenal for writing the diaries and preserving them for us, their descendants, through their children, Bessie, Ray, Charlie and Mabel.

This family history has been passed down to us by our Grandpa Ray, my mother, Margaret Titchenal Hansen, her sister Bernice Titchenal Alley Esarey and their brothers, Richard, Glen, Gerald and Bob. Ray and his wife Eunice and Ray's older sister, Bessie Titchenal Lawrence, shared a love of history saving newspaper articles, letters and notes from speeches, sometimes written on the back of a letter, for us to have a record of their adventures and achievements.

Jay, Bernice, Eula, Margaret, Glen children of Ray Titchenal

Ray Titchenal wrote about his experiences in his book, "The Cowboy Packer" which was illustrated by Ray's grandson, Randy

Titchenal. Bessie's daughter, Lois, and her husband Chet Jacobson wrote the book "The Tree of Me and Thee." Their book included Cora's letter which she titled "To My Descendents." Their daughter, Gilla Bachellerie, has preserved letters and diaries that Cora and Bessie had kept. Gilla provided the letters dated December 11, 1885, July 11, 1886, May 22, 1887 and undated letters. After Gilla's death her husband, Bob continued to support this project that was so dear to her heart.

Several of the documents and photographs included in this book are on file with the Washington State Historical Society in Olympia. They were provided by our family in conjunction with the state's celebration of the role pioneer women played in the development of our state and to celebrate women gaining the right to vote.

My cousins, Teresa Titchenal Heaney and Christina Titchenal, contributed the photos, diaries, letters and documents their father, Glen Titchenal had in his possession. We appreciate the writings Glen left us about his memories of family life. Teresa compiled information into a book document that was used as reference material for this book.

Ray Titchenal with his grandchildren, Lewis, John, Teresa, Christina and son Glen. The dog is Tippy. Photo taken at the Chumstick Ranch. Circa 1953

Carla Johnson Smith did extensive research in recording the Johnson history and made the drawing of the family tree. That history, including the route James and Alice Hays traveled from Bates County, Missouri to Washington Territory was from "The Hays Family." It was dictated by James Hays who was a Confederate Army veteran. We thank Carla for the work she did and shared with us. She provided many of the photographs included in this book.

Joann Dennis, Carla Johnson Smith's sister, contributed photos of the Johnson family and the newspaper clipping of Phebe Titchenal's homestead cabin. Valuable Johnson history included in this book was provided by Colleen Van Beek.

Back: Carla Johnson Smith, Terry Arlene Johnson Zimmerman,
Dick Johnson, James Leon Johnson, Joann Johnson Dennis.
Seated: Richard Arnold Johnson, Isabel Woodward Johnson.

The Native Daughter of Washington Territory Pioneers' book "Pioneer Dreams… Histories of Washington Territorial Pioneers" was compiled by L. Darlene Spargo and Judy Artley Sandbloom. Our family members contributed to the information in that book, including Bessie Titchenal Lawrence, who was a charter member of the group in 1937. My mother, Margaret Titchenal Hansen wrote her history in a prior publication of the group and is included in their current book. Several of the letters and histories that are reproduced here with their blessings.

Richard Titchenal and his wife Gladys were instrumental in caring for the diaries and getting them to us to use for this publication. This book is a cooperative effort and could not have been written without the many people who preserved the diaries and letters.

Back row: Bob, Glen, Richard, Ray and Gerald Titchenal
Front row: Bernice Esarey, Eunice Titchenal, Margaret Hansen

"A History of Central Washington," published in 1929, includes information contributed by Mary Moore Titchenal, mother of Lewis Titchenal, and his wife, Cora Johnson Titchenal. That book also gives information of the no longer existing town of Okanogan. This town was established near the present day Douglas but disappeared due to lack of water. Okanogan is the location of the post office where Cora and Lewis picked up their mail. It was not the site of present day Okanogan, Washington.

We had seven family photographs published in the Wenatchee World's book, "Wenatchee Valley, Images of North Central Washington Volume II." Several of those photos are included in this book. A special thanks to Wenatchee Daily World, Cashmere Valley Record, Restitution Herald and the Waterville Empire Express for permission to use the newspaper articles included in this book.

We thank Joann Roe for permission to publish the excerpt from her book, "Stevens Pass" informing us that Lewis Titchenal was the first to suggest the old rail road bed over Stevens Pass be turned into a farm to market highway creating the Stevens Pass highway as we know it today.

Photos, books and copies of documents were shared with the Waterville and Fairfield Museums. The Wenatchee Museum and Genealogical Society aided in our research.

Transcribing the diaries was more difficult then I had anticipated. The process covered seven years. The transcript of Cora's 1887 diary was completed in 2003. I shared early transcripts with teachers and took copies to the North Central Education Service District 171 office in Wenatchee.

The diaries, letters and other documents contained in this book are not only for our family members, but for all who share our interest in history.

I could not have compiled this book of diaries and supporting documents without the help and encouragement of my daughters, Maggie Zachow Wetherbee, Kimey Zachow Skjelde and Cari Zachow. I dedicate this book to them.

Final Thoughts

The story of Cora and Lewis and their shared journey through life was remarkable in many ways. Each traveled with their families, at different times, from their home in Missouri across the plains in covered wagons to the barely settled American West.

Cora and the other women spent hours canning vegetables and fruits they had grown. Each year they planted the seeds they had saved and exchanged their seedlings with other settlers. They had to produce and process their food in order to survive the long winter months. The food had to last through the next harvest season.

When a bridge, road or irrigation ditch needed to be built, the men donated their time to get the job done. They looked for solutions to the problems they faced. When a shorter route needed to be found to get their produce to western Washington markets they convinced state officials that it was possible to build a road over Stevens Pass.

Cora was always sewing, repairing and remaking clothing. Cora and Lewis tended their cattle, horses, hogs, and chickens. They milked the cow, made butter, gathered eggs, and butchered the hogs. They salted and smoked the meat to preserve it for winter use. Yet they found time to study the Bible, attend church services regularly and went often to family gatherings. Letter writing was hugely important to them. Writing letters helped them stay connected with family and friends. Cora and Lewis's descendants have over one hundred twenty-five letters that have been preserved. These give today's generation a glimpse into their ancestors daily lives.

When I visited the area where the Titchenal homestead had been at

Badger Mountain, I tried to visualize what it was like for my ancestors the winter the snow was so deep the fence posts could not be seen. This was the winter they took the straw out of their mattresses to feed their horses and cattle. In an effort to keep them alive they cut down the birch trees to feed the limbs to the starving animals. Most of their animals died that winter.

Tragedy visited Cora and Lewis on several occasions. First, when their daughter Virginia died five days after her birth, April 14, 1891. Later, after the family re-settled in Mission, their oldest son Ray lost his wife, Vera, my grandmother. Vera died May 2, 1917, six weeks after the birth of twins, Jay and Pearl. Jay survived. Pearl did not. Jay was so small that Vera's mother, Ella Alexander, wrapped him in a flannel blanket and placed him in a shoe box. The warming oven of the wood cook stove served as his incubator. Jay lived with his grandma Ella. His two-year-old sister, Bernice, went to live with Effie, Vera's sister. Four-year-old Margaret went to live with Cora and Lewis. Those were sad times for everyone.

Three years later, Hazel, their son Charlie's wife, died after the birth of their third child. Again, Cora and Lewis took a grandchild into their home. Charlie's four-year-old son, Ralph, lived with Cora and Lewis after Hazel's death.

On January 15, 1932, their youngest child, Mabel succumbed to Tuberculosis as did her baby daughter Sybil. Sybil passed away at the age of eight months, December 30, 1931. Mabel's son Harold, almost three years old at the time, also lived with Cora and Lewis for several years following his mother's death.

Their granddaughter, Eula Betty Titchenal, daughter of Ray and Eunice, passed away December 21, 1928, after contracting spinal meningitis.

Through all of their tragic loss, Cora and Lewis remained loving grandparents caring for their grandchildren. They turned those difficult years of loss into years of love, compassion and encouragement.

Through their example of unconditional love, they created a rich legacy that lives on in our family today.

CPSIA information can be obtained at www.ICGtesting.com
Printed in the USA
BVOW020557220312

285765BV00001B/68/P